How to Build High-Perfo

Chevy LS1/LS6 V-8s

Modifying and Tuning Gen III Engines
for GM Cars & Pickups

WILL HANDZEL

CarTech
Auto Books & Manuals

Edited By: Travis Thompson

Layout By: Joshua Limbaugh

ISBN 1-884089-84-4

Order No. SA86

Printed in China

CarTech®, Inc.,
39966 Grand Avenue
North Branch, MN 55056
Telephone (651) 277-1200 • (800) 551-4754 • Fax: (651) 277-1203
www.cartechbooks.com

OVERSEAS DISTRIBUTION BY:

Brooklands Books Ltd.
P.O. Box 146, Cobham, Surrey, KT11 1LG, England
Telephone 01932 865051 • Fax 01932 868803
www.brooklands-books.com

Brooklands Books Aus.
3/37-39 Green Street, Banksmeadow, NSW 2109, Australia
Telephone 2 9695 7055 • Fax 2 9695 7355

Front Cover: *A variant of the Gen III LS V-8 powers every vehicle you see here and more. This humble pushrod engine has proven itself as a formidable powerplant in multiple production vehicles, and now you're going to learn everything you need to know to add even more power.*

Title Page: *The Gen III V-8 is a work of art. This is clear when you think about of how much it is capable of relative to its straightforward design.*

Back Cover, Upper Left: *The best way to install the hollow cam the final third of the way is with a long 3/8-inch-drive extension slid up inside the cam. This provides leverage as the cam is negotiated past the last few cam journals in the block. Up until that point, the cam can be installed by hand, as shown.*

Back Cover, Upper Right: *Set the powertrain down onto the support, remove the four 21-mm nuts in front and rear (8 total) to free the powertrain from the frame, and slowly bump the body up to separate the two systems. Watch for leftover stuff like ground wires, brake lines, wiring, etc! As you can see, the number of components lowered out of the 'Vette body is really impressive. Basically, if you plan on doing intensive work on the engine, this is the best way to get to it.*

Back Cover, Lower: *This engine was originally for the Motorola Cup series. Notice the polished aluminum dry-sump oil tank mounted up against the firewall. This is how the dry sump systems got their name — the stored oil sits in this tank before being pumped through the engine and immediately sucked out.*

TABLE OF CONTENTS

FOREWORD

Editor's note: Ed Koerner is a central figure in the Gen III engine's development – he was the original Gen III V8 Chief Engineer and is currently Vice President of GM Powertrain Engineering.

The creation of the Gen III V8 was a pivotal time for GM, so reading about the experiences of the development team in Chapter 1 of this book brings back a lot of great memories. While the work to create the Gen III V8 was grueling and the timeline incredibly short, the GM Powertrain team and all of our suppliers exceeded every goal set in front of them. The engine represents what GM is capable of and I'm proud to have contributed to its success. I give my heartfelt salute to the people of GM Powertrain who did an outstanding job executing the Gen III V8 and also to GM senior management who provided the opportunity, resources and trust for all the individuals involved to be successful.

While I haven't yet built any hot rod versions of the Gen III V8, after reading this book I look forward to building one with my son. From what I know we're doing here at GM with engines that will come out in the future, based on what we learned with the Gen III V8 program, I know the Gen III V8 has plenty of potential in it.

Many are calling the Gen III V8 "the next Chevy small block V8." If that is the case, then all I can say is it is an honor to have added to the legacy of the small block Chevy V8 engine.

–Ed Koerner

Here it is, the Gen III V-8 design. This 5.7-liter version comes from a 1998 Corvette.

DEDICATION

This book is dedicated to my wife Lori and our son, Jack.

PREFACE

Writing this book started as a way to satisfy my desire to create a shop-staple-quality enthusiasts book, but quickly became a passionate search for every last drop of information to show everyone how to hot rod the GM Gen III V-8.

Interestingly, one of the unexpected benefits of doing this book has been how it got me introduced to the many talented, driven GM employees that have and are building the legacies all GM automotive enthusiasts will be talking about for years to come. What I've found is that the Gen III LS1 V-8, and its many variants, is a fantastic production and hot rod engine, and I'm glad to have been able to learn the intricate details of its creation from the people that designed it and continue to refine it.

I hope you enjoy reading and using the information in this book as much as I did learning it and documenting it for you.

Thanks,
Will

ACKNOWLEDGEMENTS

While there are a lot of people to thank for their help on this book, I couldn't have completed it without the support and understanding of my wife, Lori. The book is as great as it is because she supported me as night after night I was doing the research, photography, and typing that it takes to create a book of this caliber. I also would like to thank my father, Bill Handzel. His presence has pushed me to continually find new ways to succeed in life. Thanks, Dad.

To all the people at General Motors, from the Powertrain, Communications, Marketing, Performance, and Racing teams, thank you. Most notably, though, I need to thank Powertrain's Ed Koerner and Sam Winegarden for their contacts and support. Also, I'd like to thank Mark Reuss at the GM Performance Division for his support. GM Historian Ron Bluhm came through with incredible access to GM materials to help make sure those folks that did the work get the credit for it. Thanks go out also to the dedicated team at GM Performance Parts. To the many others that I have not named, you know who you are, and thank you.

The team at Wheel to Wheel Powertrain was also an immense help: thanks to Kurt, Dave, Kelly, Jim, Greg, John, Eric, Brian, Bill, Craig, Jason, Denny, and Jory. Thanks guys for all your help.

Thanks to all the folks that proofread the text, including Hib Halverson and my Mom, Patricia Reis.

Also, thanks go out to everyone at SLP, Magnuson, Comp Cams, LS1-Edit, and Steve Cole at TTS (The Turbo Shop).

This book was definitely a team effort by my family, friends, and business associates — so to all of you, thanks.

AUTHOR'S BIO

To be sure, this is a great time to be me. I grew up an automotive enthusiast in Chicago, with parents that are not car enthusiasts, dreaming of working in the car business. Now I'm having a great time doing what I always dreamed about.

A little history: I earned a Mechanical Engineering degree from the University of Illinois at Champaign/Urbana, then went to work on a small SCCA racing team. A little while after that, I got a job as the Technical Editor for the race car and tech cult-classic *Circle Track* magazine in the late 1980s. I then worked full-time in the magazine business for about 10 years, writing tech for *Circle Track*, *Rod & Custom*, *Hot Rod*, and *Motor Trend's Truck Trend* magazine.

I decided it was time for another challenge, and in 2000 I started as a Design Release Engineer with General Motors in the Structures and Closures area — that's bodies and doors for the non-industry folks. For the next few years, I worked through the Engineering ranks up to Lead Designing Engineer and then in 2003 I got the chance to become the Program Manager at the GM Performance Parts division to help them grow their business.

To say I'm enjoying the opportunities I've had and continue to have at GM would be a complete understatement.

INTRODUCTION

COMPLEXITY VS. SIMPLICITY

To understand how the General Motors (GM) Gen III small-block V-8 engine ever came to be built around the ancient cam-in-block, pushrod architecture, one only need to flashback to 1993.

It's the early 1990s and the entire automotive world is caught up in the idea that the future of gasoline-fueled, internal-combustion engines can be found in the dual overhead camshaft (DOHC) engine design. An automobile company designing and building a new cam-in-block, pushrod engine in the new millennium was thought by most of the automotive business to be like selling a Corvette with a tractor engine!

As a result, before anyone knew there would be a third-generation pushrod-based Chevy small-block V-8, a DOHC vs. pushrod battle of epic proportion raged within the GM executive ranks. Lengthy debate went on between executives and engineers about whether to design and build a DOHC V-8 family or build the next generation of the small-block Chevy cam-in-block pushrod engine family. Luckily for everyone who ever enjoyed the simplicity, durability, quality, and power production of the early versions of the small-block Chevy, the Gen III pushrod V-8 was given the green light. But how this engine came to be is as much a story as the engine itself.

THE CONTENTS

As you would expect, attaining maximum performance from a Gen III LS1 V-8 engine is thoroughly detailed in this book. But the story that sets the stage for all of those power discussions is the complete development history of the Gen III V-8 — including the many people that made this engine happen. Luckily for you, Chapter 1 details the travails the engineering team overcame and provides an insider's look at never before seen prototype sketches, engines, and more. Key decision points in the creation of the Gen III V-8 are also discussed.

In Chapter 2, I'll discuss the Gen III V-8 architecture and usage with support from photos and lengthy descriptions. You'll learn of the cornucopia of technology hidden in this seemingly simple design. There are many interesting details about things like the engine block and the high-flowing nylon intake manifold.

Chapter 3 will show you the best production engine components for performance applications. There are plenty of photos for you to visually identify these components in the future, along with some suggestions for combinations.

Chapter 4 will detail everything you need to know to remove and reinstall a Gen III LS1 V-8 from its production vehicle. To some of you this might sound entirely too basic to demand a chapter. But those that have tried to take

---

Is it an LS1?
A Gen III V-8? What?

The Gen III V-8 architecture was introduced to the public as the regular production order (RPO) LS1 engine in 1997. Because of this, the industry has ended up calling every variation of the Gen III V-8 an LS1, which is slightly incorrect.

Internally, GM calls this engine architecture the Gen III V-8 — so that's what we're going

to call it throughout the book. As you've probably noticed, the book also references LS1s; that's because everyone in the business knows these engines as LS1s!

Whatever you call them, they make great hot-rod engines and you're going to be ready to jump into building one after reading this book.

---

one of these engines out of a C5 Corvette know the frustration that comes from destroying perfectly good components because the process wasn't clear. This chapter tells you what tools you'll need, shows you the step-by-step process that the top shops are following, and warns of the many common pitfalls.

POWER PACKAGES

The next five chapters are dedicated to documenting what parts the pros are recommending for excellent performance, detailing little-known steps to get everything to fit properly, pointing out common pitfalls to avoid, and explaining some proven tuning tips. The goal of these chapters is to give you enough detailed information so you can build the GM Gen III V-8 engine you desire with a minimum of outside help.

To that end, the fun starts in Chapter 5, where aftermarket bolt-on components are installed on production Gen III engines and tested for performance on a dynamometer. You'll get to see some basic installation tips and learn what kind of performance improvement to expect.

The true potential of the Gen III V-8 starts to reveal itself in Chapter 6. That's where the top end of an LS1 engine is swapped for CNC-ported cylinder heads, a performance camshaft, an LS6 intake, and some other pieces, to bump the power output by 40%! That's with no changes at all to the stock short block.

Then in Chapter 7, the buildup of a 500+ hp, naturally aspirated Gen III V-8 is fully documented for you to recreate. This is not your normal buildup coverage. Here, you'll get to see every nut, bolt, and torque sequence as it happens, so you can build a stormin' engine just like this.

Chapter 8 covers the buildup of a few truck engines, which GM calls their Vortec engines, for the truck and SUV crowd. Examples include a 400-hp LS6-headed LQ9 Escalade engine, a Magnuson supercharged LQ4-powered 6.0-liter Hummer, some 5.3-liter engines with various performance components, and a turbocharged 630-hp 6.0-liter SS truck engine, for those of you who think too much is just enough. These power numbers might sound daunting to create, but when you see how straightforward it is to build this kind of power, you'll never look to another engine for power production.

Things definitely go haywire as Chapter 9 documents the building of a 1,200-hp, C5R-based supercharged Gen III V-8 engine. The expensive and exclusive C5R block and heads were developed by GM for the Corvette racing program, but they're available from GM Performance Parts to anyone with the dough to play with them. The buildup of this engine is fully documented to show some of the custom work that can be performed to the Gen III for ultimate power production.

Finally, the electronic-control side of the Gen III V-8 is discussed in Chapter 10. The engine control is a major part of the Gen III's ability to make power and yet remain civil. In this chapter, you'll learn the basics about the production engine and aftermarket computers, how much power the production computer can handle, and how to run a Gen III with an aftermarket controller.

Throughout the text will be various sidebars talking about subjects like the production components, technology used to create these components, what the aftermarket is offering as performance parts, and recommendations to improve your Gen III's power, durability, and street manners.

A LEGACY MAKER

Beyond the numbers, the Gen III architecture is considered by practically every engine builder we have spoken with to be the finest pushrod V-8 engine ever built. The opinion of these experts is that the Gen III V-8 will overtake the previous versions of the Chevy small-block V-8 in coming years in practically every power-production usage imaginable.

So turn the page and begin the adventure into the future with the next generation of the General Motors hotrod pushrod V-8 engine.

Gen III V-8s At a Glance

Common GM Gen III V-8 Regular Production Order (RPO) Engine Codes (see Chapter 2 for more details)

Build Code	Description of Engine
LS1	5.7-liter car engine, between 345 hp/340 ft-lb, '97-present, and 385 hp/385 ft-lb, '01-present
LS6	5.7-liter car engine, 385 hp/385 ft-lb in '01, 405 hp/400 ft-lb from '02-present
LQ9	6.0-liter truck/SUV engine, 345 hp/380 ft-lb from '02-present
LQ4	6.0-liter truck/SUV engine, between 300 hp/360 ft-lb & 330 hp/370 ft-lb, from '00-present
LM7	5.3-liter truck/SUV engine, between 300 hp/360 ft-lb to 325 hp/370 ft-lb, depending on vehicle, from '99-present
LR4	4.8-liter truck/SUV engine, between 270 hp/285 ft-lb to 280 hp/290 ft-lb, depending on vehicle, from '99-present
LM4	5.3-liter mid-size SUV/SSR engine, 290hp/325 ft-lb to 300 hp/335 ft-lb

THE HISTORY OF THE GEN III LS1 V-8

There are a few acts of creation an automobile company must be great at if it plans on being successful in the car business. These actions usually include being able to:

1. Design and build visually pleasing, high quality, and durable automobile bodies/chassis.
2. Design and build powerful, reliable, and efficient powertrains.
3. Refine the components and systems noted above into a smooth riding, predictably handling machine.

General Motors has excelled at many of these actions over the years, but in the powertrain department, their track record has been truly impressive. The amount of elegantly simple, reliable, fuel efficient, and powerful engines that have propelled Generral Motors vehicles through its history is simply unmatched. Of those engines, the Chevrolet small-block V-8, of which the Gen III LS1 V-8 engines discussed in this book are a derivative, are considered the pinnacle by most car enthusiasts.

Luckily for all automotive enthusiasts, GM has used the Gen III LS1 V-8 to power numerous visually pleasing, good-handling cars and trucks. How an engine of this caliber comes to life is a story few would probably ever know.

But in the following pages you will find out how something as complex as an engine is created from a clean sheet of paper to be built in quantities in excess of 8,000 per day.

SMALL BLOCKS: GEN-I/II/III

The original version of the small block, what is now considered the Gen I (first generation), was used to power GM

The Gen III V-8 is a work of art. This is clear when you think about how much it is capable of relative to its straightforward design. This is like many great designs — they don't seem that impressive at first, but the more you look at them and work with them, the more you realize the subtle detail and capability of every aspect.

The Gen I and II V-8s powered GM vehicles for over 40 years, so they are timeless designs that are revered by the original equipment manufacturers (OEM) and aftermarket industry. It was obvious to the GM Powertrain leadership in the early 1990s that an entirely new design was needed to meet the customer, government, and company needs of the future.

vehicles, mostly Chevrolets, from 1955 to 1991 — almost 40 years. The Gen II, which came in two main versions, the LT1 and then later the LT4 (LT1 and LT4 are their regular production order (RPO) numbers), powered vehicles from 1992 to 1997. The Gen II did not live up to the Gen I legacy in many ways and was struggling to meet the emissions and weight requirements that loomed in its future. These were major reasons for it being superseded by the radically different Gen III V-8 in 1997.

The small-block Gen III LS1 V-8 is the son the Gen I didn't have. It is the most powerful, efficient, durable, and yet physically simple gasoline internal combustion V-8 engine ever built for production vehicles. Without a doubt, by creating and selling the Gen III LS1 V-8, GM pulled the 50-year legacy of small-block V-8s from the ashes and created an entirely new future for this beloved engine family.

THUMBS-UP FOR THE GEN III

On a warm, sunny day in May 1992, a blind comparison test was performed by General Motors executives on a massive pavement area called Black Lake, deep within the secretive GM Milford Proving Grounds outside of Detroit, Michigan. The conclusions drawn from this test would change the course of history for General Motors Powertrain, its customers, and the automobile industry.

At the time, the automotive business was ferociously arguing the merits of building complex, seemingly high-tech dual overhead cam (DOHC) engines, as opposed to simple, seemingly low-tech pushrod engines. This hands-on comparison by the execs was to put the debate to a seat-of-the-pants test and allow the leaders of GM to decide the course for the future of GM Powertrain.

The executive leadership of GM would drive pairs of similar-appearing

Small-Block Legacy Notes

Gen I – The Chevrolet Small-Block V-8
- Originally designed to run with a carburetor and points distributor
- Production started in '55 for Chevy, the last GM division to get a V-8
- Built essentially unchanged for almost 40 years
- Ed Cole considered the father of the Chevy V-8
- Production continued for trucks during Gen II V-8 production
- But took on Gen Ie moniker – the "e" stood for an emissions redesign on the inlet, single-piece rear crank seal, and other slight revisions

Gen II – A Modified Small Block
- Maintained original Chevy V-8 design but added some new technical aspects
- Incorporated reverse cooling system and high-swirl cylinder head ports
- Utilized cursed ABITS ignition system

- driven off spud on water pump shaft
- No one person considered the father

Gen III – The Complete Redesign, Redefining the Small Block
- Clean sheet of paper for an engine that still honors the Gen-I legacy
- Tom Stephens and Ed Koerner are considered the fathers of the Gen III V-8
- Requirements included: more power, higher efficiency, lower emissions, improved NVH, simpler design, and higher quality rankings than any previous small-block V-8
- Introduced in the Corvette in 1997 as RPO LS1, then the Camaro and Firebird in 1998
- Since '99, it has powered various versions of mid- and full-size trucks and SUVs throughout the GM portfolio under various RPO monikers

The Gen III V-8 engine was voted Wards' Engine of the Year in 1997 and Ed Koerner (right) accepted on behalf of the entire Gen III V-8 team. That a "new" pushrod engine won this award was almost unbelievable to the design team.

vehicles and compare how each vehicle felt — not knowing what type of engine was powering the vehicles. Of most interest to readers of this book were two black Corvettes parked at the end of the lineup. One 'Vette was fitted with a 330-hp early version of the LT4 Gen II V-8 pushrod engine. The other was equipped with the ZR1-spec, Lotus-designed, all-aluminum, DOHC LT5 engine. Both vehicles were equipped with automatic transmissions. Both were fully integrated for their specific

powerplants to give a real-world experience to the executives.

The results surprised even the most ardent supporters of the pushrod architecture. The executives couldn't get over how one of the Corvettes pulled from the moment they pressed on the throttle — the surge, the thrust, the torque.

In contrast, they commented on how the engine in the other 'Vette seemed to take a moment to "wind up" before pushing them back in the seat. This vehicle required more precision and planning when driving fast to keep the engine up in the RPM band where the power was.

As the day went on, executive after executive came to the same conclusion. After all had tested the vehicles, the hoods were raised. To anyone who has driven or ridden in a vehicle powered by a 300+ hp small-block Chevy V-8, it comes as no surprise that the Corvette the executives liked was powered by the Gen II pushrod V-8.

From then on, the course for GM's V-8 powertrain was set. The world's finest pushrod V-8 would be created to power the most profitable vehicle's in the General Motors fleet. This was the birth of the Gen III small-block V-8.

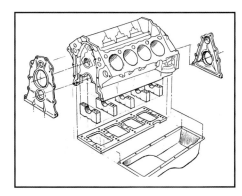

Back in late 1991 and early 1992, some early drawings were created for what the Gen III V-8 might look like once finished. This early drawing depicted how the front and rear engine covers would eliminate the need for the Gen I/II V-8 engine screw-in and press-in plugs. The final Gen III V-8 design looks very similar to this.

THE GEN III LS1 V-8 BEGINS

The initial driving force behind what would become the Gen III V-8 engine was Tom Stephens, then Executive Director of GM Powertrain. In late 1991, Stephens asked a few of his trusted engineers in the Advanced Engineering area of the GM Powertrain building off Joslyn Avenue in Pontiac, Michigan, to quietly work up the basic structure of a completely redesigned multi-use pushrod V-8. Two of those asked to do that initial work, Alan Hayman and Jim Mazzola, discuss their experiences later in this chapter.

Like much of the GM leadership, Stephens knew the Flint small-block V-8 engine plant and the tooling inside, where the Gen I and II V-8 had been produced for over 43 years, was well beyond its lifecycle. Since all new tooling needed to be created anyway, Stephens decided to roll the dice. He intended to propose to the GM brass that an entirely new small-block V-8 be built in entirely new plants with entirely new tooling. The key to his pitch to the GM leadership was that he would not exceed the estimated $1.2 billion set aside to revamp the Gen II V-8. On top of that, he would commit that the completely new Gen III V-8 would also exceed the goals set for the revamp of the Gen II V-8.

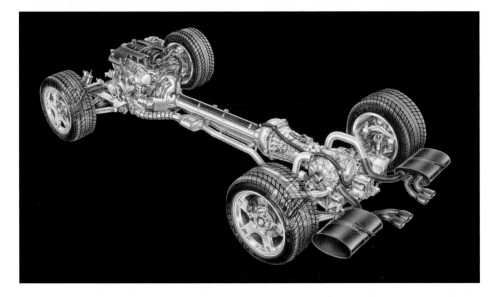

The Gen III V-8 has exceeded all expectations both inside GM and in the hot rod community. Probably the most exciting aspect of the Gen III V-8 is that the capability of this engine architecture is still being discovered both in the Corvette chassis (shown) and in other GM vehicles it powers. Look for amazing power production and durability from this engine architecture in the years to come as GM and the aftermarket create more variations.

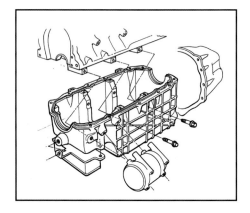

This other early drawing shows how the oil pan would be a cast-aluminum structural component to add stiffness to the engine/transmission combination. This helps the vehicle engineers to minimize low-frequency vehicle vibrations. Also, the Gen III block, heads, and oil pan were to incorporate many of the bosses required to mount the accessory components. You can see this here in the oil-pan-mounted air-conditioning compressor. The cutaway for the A/C compressor didn't make the cut, but the compressor does mount directly to the block/oil pan.

With this proposal, Stephens and his team had to produce an engine with impeccable credentials. Those credentials included producing a small-block V-8 engine that would:

- be smaller, lighter, and easier to mass produce than the current small-block V-8.
- produce more horsepower and torque per cubic inch than previous small-block V-8s (at least 1 hp/1 ft-lb of torque per cubic inch on LS1).
- have increased fuel mileage and produce reduced emissions.
- achieve higher quality and durability ratings than previous GM V-8 engines.
- be capable of being built in multiple displacements and cylinder quantities.
- be capable of being used in a rear- or front-wheel drive vehicle packages.
- and have industry-leading noise, vibration, and harshness (NVH) numbers.

Stephens used many of the original pushrod V-8 ideas proposed by the Advanced Engineering Group in his pitch to get the program okayed. Proposing to show improvement on an engine doesn't sound like such a big promise, but remember, Stephens was betting to improve on the small-block Chevy — an international icon in performance V-8s!

TEAM OWNER AND HEAD COACH

The Gen III V-8 program originally began with the Gen II Chief Engineer, Anil Kulkarni, running the Gen III program for Stephens. Kulkarni had strong opinions about many aspects of the Gen III project that differed from Stephens's vision — which lead to him moving on to other responsibilities early in the project.

Stephens then brought in Ed Koerner, a GM Powertrain small-block V-8 leadership veteran and former National Hot Rod Association (NHRA) record holder in drag racing, to run the program. Koerner, who had been the Chief Engineer for all the existing small-block V-8 engines, was made

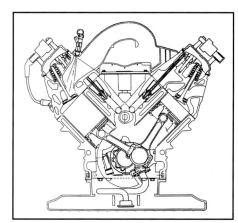

Later in this chapter, you will see that the original LS1 vehicle integration team had a hell of a time getting the oiling system to handle continuous side loads. It's easy to see why — the crankshaft-to-oil-pan floor clearance. Can you say tight!? Probably more amazing is the fact that the GM Powertrain engineers figured out how to control the oil well enough with a short-sump oil pan and wet-sump oiling system to keep things pressurized under all driving conditions.

This is one of the first truck Vortec Gen III V-8s ever built. Notice the word "Beta" on the valve cover. This means the components on this engine were built on short-run, prototype GM Powertrain beta tooling to test the initial design of the engine. Beta component testing is the first running test for any engine design and is performed to avoid basic architecture shortcomings before initiating production-type gamma tooling. This tooling is used to build the 50 or more development engines needed to do the dyno and vehicle testing to fully validate an engine's architecture.

the Chief Engineer on the Gen III LS1 V-8 development project.

Many of the initial team members interviewed for this chapter referred to Stephens and Koerner in pro football terms — Stephens was like the team owner, running interference on a corporate level, and Koerner played the role of the trusted and empowered head coach, running the plays on the field. Koerner was responsible for creating the production vision for the engine and assembling the all-star design team. The people Koerner chose to create the Gen III and the direction he provided throughout their journey are major reasons why the Gen III is the incredible V-8 engine it is.

Clearly, a major factor in the Gen III V-8's success was the trust between Stephens and Koerner, which allowed each to do what was needed to produce a quality product.

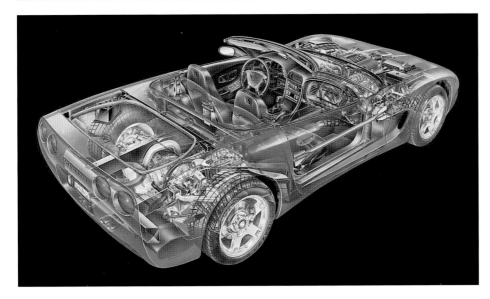

The dramatically new C5 '97 Corvette, with its new hydro-formed frame rails, rear-mounted transmission, improved single length arm (SLA) independent suspension, Gen III V-8 LS1 engine, and redesigned body really wowed the crowds during its intro. The looks and performance of the C5 set the LS1 Gen III V-8 engine in the minds and hearts of auto enthusiasts everywhere.

The dramatic differences between the Gen I/II (top of each photo) and the Gen III head design (bottom of each photo) are easily seen in these photos. Simply put, the Gen III cylinder head is superior in every way to the Gen I/II head — port flow, chamber charge motion, packaging, temperature management, weight, oil control, and valvetrain stability.

COACHING CLARITY

Koerner, who is now the Executive Vice President of GM Powertrain Engineering, is a gearhead who counts many successful racers and performance-aftermarket engine-parts-builders as friends from his days in the NHRA. His office, adorned with exploded view images of the Gen III and performance vehicles, tells anyone who enters that this is a man passionate about GM performance.

In person, Koerner, who is quick with an unassuming smile, can rattle off the vision for the Gen III V-8 as though he just woke up in the middle of the night with it.

"We wanted something of simple elegance. An engine that incorporated refined race technology. The block needed to be cast of either aluminum or iron, have six-bolt mains and have head bolts that pulled from the bottom of the block. It needed to be set up for an internally balanced crank, have a raised cam for crank counterweight clearance, and use bigger cam bearings than the Gen I and II. The bore spacing and external configuration also needed to take into account the fact that this engine was intended to be used in rear-wheel and front-wheel-drive applications.

"The heads needed to have replicated ports and a rolled valve angle (from the Gen I/II's 23 degrees to 15 degrees) to optimize injection and combustion chamber motion because of our power and emission requirements. The valvetrain would have an in-line geometry, roller rockers and roller followers, a gerotor oil pump driven off the nose of the crank to eliminate the old camshaft-driven oil pump drive, and other improvements in an effort to reduce friction and flex wherever possible. Oil control would limit any wasted pumping losses.

"For manufacturing simplicity, we'd eliminate the plugs at the back of the block by adding a rear cover and have a plastic, integrated intake manifold built using a lost core process to create smooth internal transitions for maximum airflow. The engine would have an electronic throttle control (which appeared on the '97 Corvette) to provide power management.

"Oh, and the same basic architecture had to satisfy the needs of everything from the Corvette to all the full-size trucks — which meant multiple

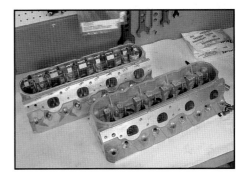

Famed GM cylinder head designer, Ron Sperry, developed the original Gen III V-8 heads (foreground). Ken Sperry's team developed the ports and combustion chamber. The Sperrys have been called on for input into just about any important production or racing GM port and chamber design over at leat the last 20 years – like the C5R Gen III racing head in the background. For the Gen III, they used every capability GM has: supercomputer flow modeling, prototype component construction, hydra single-cylinder test engines, flow benches, and dynamometers.

cubic-inch sizes which ended up being 4.8, 5.3, 5.7 and 6.0 liters and various power production levels."

This excerpt of Koerner's recollection came with no prepared notes or moment of reflection. It just seemed to pour out of him, which shows how clear his vision for the Gen III was and still is — some 10 years after he began the project.

THE DREAM TEAM

A vision without having some great players is merely a dream, and Stephens and Koerner understood that. The initial team of seven engineers, which Koerner called, "The Super Six," included Ron Sperry, Bill Compton, Brian Kaminski, Jon Lewis, Stan Turek, Don Weiderhold, and half-timer Dave Wandel. As GM cylinder head guru Sperry commented later, "Okay, that's 6.5, but we were considered six full-timers."

The team continued to grow in size until the launch of the engine in 1996, when there were well over 100 engineers and support staff. Many of the initial

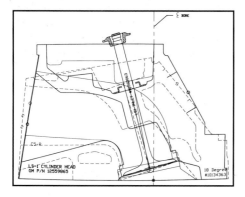

This cross section comparison of the production GM LS1, racing-only C5R, and 18-degree cylinder heads gives an idea of the advanced nature of the Gen III LS1 head design. Notice the 15-degree Gen III valve angle on the LS1 head vs. the 18-degree valve angle of the GM Racing NASCAR SB2 head and the 12-degree valve angle of the C5R Corvette racing head. Also, you can see the dramatic raised-port shape and valvetrain mount on the C5R head, the small chamber on the C5R and 18-degree head vs. the LS1 head. (Special thanks to Katech Engineering for this illustration)

team members assembled to create the Gen III V-8 have dedicated their lives to being the best in their specialized fields. They're a who's-who list you've probably never heard of, coming from the Research, Motorsports, and Production Development areas within GM. Each one of them can take immense pride in the fact they started the development of an incredible engine.

Koerner adds, "From the beginning, we had people from every corner of GM in heated debates over how to do this or that. A great example is the simple solution the team created to locate the machining equipment on the raw engine block castings. Instead of using external reference points, the machining equipment actually reaches

One of the key aspects of the Gen III V-8 is that the head bolts pull from the bottom of the engine block. By using extra long bolts that thread into blind tapped holes in the webs of the crank mains, the strength of the block is maximized, block weight minimized, bore distortion is minimized, and the block and bolt stretch can be used to create a consistent clamping load on major components.

up inside the block to locate the cylinder cores and center on them. This way, core shift and cylinder-wall thickness issues are practically eliminated in the machining of the engine block. It was a simple solution to a complex problem that solved multiple issues. The Gen III V-8 project is loaded with situations like this that came from the team."

ANOTHER PUSHROD ENGINE?

During interviews, a few of the early Gen III V-8 team members commented that they thought they had done something wrong to end up working in the development of a new cam-in-block V-8. GM cylinder head engineer Ron Sperry summed it up, "Literally, on my previous assignment I was working with many of the greats in racing on a future racing cylinder head. My GM leadership called me up out of the blue to tell me to go to the Tech Center (GM's North American technical development campus in Warren, Michigan) to figure out how to make more power with the LT1 production V-8 engine program. The LT4 top end was the result of that work but there didn't seem to be much of a future with that architecture. I figured I'd done something wrong and my career was over. Seriously. At that time, all we were hearing was V-6 this and inline 4-cylinder that. As far as the rank and file engineers were concerned, GM

The Camaro and Firebird were powered by Gen III V-8s from 1998 until they were discontinued in the 2003 model year. These vehicles have plenty of performance components available for them and can be drastically improved with very little investment of time and money.

wasn't going to build another production V-8 — and it sure as hell wasn't going to be a pushrod V-8 if they did!"

Well, Sperry soon found out GM *was* building a V-8, it would be pushrod design, and the Stephens/Koerner team was going to leverage as much knowledge and experience as they could to make this engine a winner — which was why Sperry and the rest of the team were there.

BUILDING AN ENGINE FROM SCRATCH

When building anything from a clean sheet of paper, it is interesting to understand what happened first, then second, and so on. In the case of the Gen III, it went like GM does almost all of their in-house development.

First, the Advanced Engineering side of GM Powertrain proposed an engine design of rough proportions. GM has an extensive skunk works system throughout the company that constantly creates and/or seeks out, then integrates products, processes, services, etc. to generate proposals for GM leadership to determine how, when, or if this technology will end up on GM vehicles.

In the case of the Gen III V-8, Stephens made a verbal request for an initial design because he needed to show the leadership above him something in his initial pitch. Alan Hayman and his small team of engineers in Advance Design, Powertrain — which included Jim Mazzola and Tom Langdon — did this initial work.

Hayman said, "We had little time, and there wasn't an official program underway when Stephens came and asked for an initial design. So, we looked around Advanced Engineering and saw a V-6 engine design we were working on for the V-6 Chief Engineer, Volker Harhaus, called the 'Venture V-6.' This engine was intended to replace the 4.3-liter V-6, which was similar to the Gen I/II V-8. We used many of the ideas proposed in the development of this new V-6 (which was never produced) to create the Gen III V-8 idea starter.

The intake manifold, what GM Powertrain calls the IAFM, for integrated air/fuel module, is extremely lightweight, but needed some help to keep the floor from resonating. Doug Duchardt, now the head of GM Racing, did the engineering work to come up with the three stands needed to be cast in place inside the intake — you can see one of them in this cutaway — to dampen the resonance.

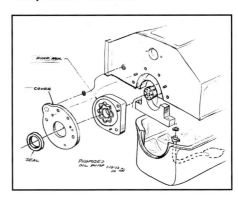

The oiling system, especially the stressed-member oil pan, was by far the most challenging aspect of getting the Gen III LS1 V-8 to work in the '97 Corvette. This drawing from early 1992 shows the idea of putting the gerotor oil pump at the front of the engine and the location of the oil passages in the block. This is very close to how the Gen III oiling system works.

The Gen III V-8 Engine Initial Team Members

Leadership:

Tom Stephens	Executive Director, GM Powertrain
Ed Koerner	Gen III V-8 Chief Engineer
John Juriga	Assistant Chief Engineer

Engineers:

Ron Sperry	overall cylinder head
Ken Sperry	intake ports and combustion chambers
Jim Hicks	camshaft and valvetrain
Stan Turek	front drive
Bill Compton	reciprocating/rotating components
Brian Kaminski	block
John Duoro	block
Alan Hayman	early engine design, cylinder head ports and chamber design
Brian Green	oil pan development
Gurdun Hobson	manufacturing design
Jim Mazzola	early engine design
Ray Shreck	crank
John Rezuski	heads and port work
Amir Haider	EGM on base engine

Important:

In gathering information for this story, it became apparent that determining exactly who was on the initial Gen III V-8 team would be practically impossible. GM does not keep complete historical data of the teams that work on various projects. Some engineers leave GM, and others are constantly changing programs based on the needs of the company. Because of this, we apologize if there are omissions (please contact the publisher if you worked on this program and feel you should be included in revisions to this portion of the book).

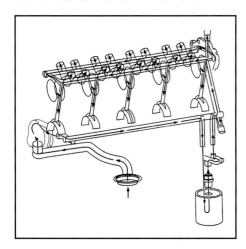

The oiling system for the Gen III V-8 pulls oil from the oil pan into the crank-driven gerotor pump at the front of the block. The oil is then sent down the main galley on the driver side to the oil filter, and then back up the back of the block to the main feed galley that runs through the lifter bodies. Oil reaches the top of the engine through the pushrods, just like the last 50 years worth of small blocks. Oil returns to the oil pan through a series of drain-back passages throughout the heads and block.

"The first design we proposed, on a project we called the Venture V-8 or VV-8 internally, was denoted as project 57B. There was actually a 57A, but the 'B' version had already been chosen over 'A', so the 'B' is what Stephens discussed with the leadership.

"The 57B design had the following:

- a V-8 with two banks of four cylinders at a 90-degree angle to each other
- 4.40-inch (111.76-mm) bore centers (the same as the then-current small block)
- 4 bolts per cylinder bore, head, and block design
- a raised cam to achieve a 146.08-mm crank-to-cam centerline distance, which allowed the use of a larger diameter camshaft than the Gen I and either a 3/8-inch or 8-mm link timing chain
- 6.2-liter diesel cam bearings, which allowed a 19-mm cam base circle
- a deep skirt engine block to

accommodate cross-bolted mains that would add structural rigidity while improving noise, vibration, and harshness (NVH) control and stiffness
- investment cast valvetrain rockers
- the valvetrain "protected" (which means it was designed to handle up to a certain number) for 14-mm lift, even though initial versions would not have anything near that much valve lift
- a cylinder head and block with cast-in oil drain holes
- a large valvespring package in the cylinder head"

The 57A design was similar to the 'B' design in all respects except it was penciled with 5 head bolts per cylinder — which is the design the Gen I/II small-block V-8s were built with. Much consideration and computer modeling was performed by a team run by Engineering's Roy Midgely. Dan Hancock, the Director of Advanced Powertrain, at the time was behind the 4-bolts per cylinder 57B design. The design team

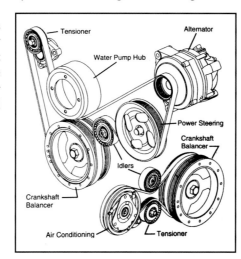

The development of the front drive was considered in every facet of the engine. This contributed to most of the accessories being nearly direct-mounted and reduced the amount of noise the front drive created. GM Powertrain's Stan Turek headed up this component set. One of the neat features the team discovered was that by giving the A/C compressor its own belt, they could reduce the noise by a substantial 7 decibels.

The LS1 Beta engines showed that the engine would require some help to improve its bay-to-bay crankcase breathing. This was expected, but the "windows" that needed to be added were more substantial than expected. The early LS1s have a machined hole through all the main webs. Later, cast-in ports in the main webs (shown), introduced first on the LS6 and then on all Gen III engines, insure there was sufficient area for the oil vapor to move around in the bottom of the engine at high RPM.

evaluated this aspect from many angles and presented them to Stephens who eventually made the executive decision that the 4-bolts per cylinder design was the right choice for the engine.

Jim Mazzola, of GM Powertrain Advanced Engineering, remarked, "Looking back, those were pretty exciting times. From the initial design to the difficult refinement stages, we felt like we were building GM's future. Our bread and butter. The entire team felt very strongly about raising the bar on pushrod engines. This feeling is unusual in the Advanced Engineering group as we work very much in the background of engine development, so it was very special."

MAKING IT HAPPEN

The team was led on the ground by Gen III Base Engine Manager, John Juriga, who worked 19 years in the

Max Lift

An interesting note is that while the Advanced Engineering-proposed valve lift protection was 14 mm, the production team felt 13 mm of lift was suitable. Because of this, the rockers were shortened 1 mm and the valvesprings were designed smaller than the original proposal.

From the beginning, the Advanced Engineering team saw the Gen III V-8 as having high-RPM, high-power output capabilities that the increased lift would provide, but the leadership on the production side didn't feel as strongly about this possibility. To their credit, the production side of Power-train finally saw the light after the Gen III was out a few years, and the higher lift found its way into the Gen III V-8 late in the production run as the power potential continued to show itself. To do it, however, Engineer Jim Hicks had to reduce the base circle of the cam lobes to get enough lift and lengthen the valves (on the '02 LS6).

Look for even more flow and camshaft development results in the Gen IV version of the GM small-block V-8 program, as increasing the lift has been very fruitful in producing power.

small-block V-8 program. Juriga adds, "I ran the Gen III V-8 program initially for Anil Kulkarni, and then Ed Koerner, in the creation of things like the block, heads, crank, rods — essentially everything short of the fuel system, catalytic converters, and electronic controls. We were told from the beginning by the GM leadership that the initial analysis of the research pointed to a pushrod engine, but there was a question as to power production. From the beginning, no one in the trenches on the team questioned whether power production would be an issue if we got the ports and valvetrain right."

THE FIRST LINE — INJECTOR ANGLE

So, the basic structure of the Gen III V-8 was suggested by Advanced Engineering, but the engine design process was just getting started towards a final design. Most importantly, the final creation of the most important component was yet to come — the cylinder head. The responsibility for this would fall on Ron Sperry. Ron's brother, Ken Sperry, has been a leader in port airflow development at GM for decades and was brought in to lead the team creating the port and combustion chambers for brother Ron's Gen III V8 head. Other airflow team-members included Advanced Engineering's Alan Hayman, valvetrain wizard Jim Hicks, and some computer-based engine analysis techs (the project started with Chuck McGuire and ended with Jerry Clark doing this).

The ultra-thin, centrifugally cast, iron cylinder liners have serrated backsides (arrow) that lock them in place during the casting process. To achieve tight enough tolerances for this to work, GM Power-train engineers created advanced semi-permanent casting-core technology. Standard core shift, which is the movement of the molds during the molten metal pouring, would have otherwise made this setup impossible.

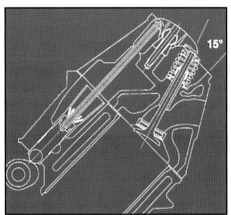

One of Chief Engineer Koerner's hard-and-fast requests was for an in-line val-vetrain. This meant there would be no side angularity in the pushrod or offset rockers to get the pushrods out of the way of the intake port. While offset valve-train components are seen all the time on hot-rod engines, remember, GM needs to build engines that last over 100,000 miles with no problems.

The angle between the fuel injectors and valves was the first line locked in during the creation of the Gen III V-8. Since fuel-injector technology in 1991 wasn't what it is today, the team started with the best injectors available and built the engine around them. This was done to maximize efficiency and power production while minimizing emissions.

Intake Manifold Development

While Ron Sperry started the intake development, it quickly became too big of a job to do both the intake and cylinder head development. A young engineer named Doug Duchardt was brought over from the Milford Proving Grounds to work with Sperry. Duchardt recounts the experience: "I joined the team in late '94 to finish the intake manifold development. They didn't call it an intake, though. It was called an IAFM — integrated air/fuel module — because the intake shows up at the plant fully loaded with the fuel injectors, lines, and other pieces needed to run the engine. The basics of the intake were determined, but there was a lot to do as far as figuring out how to manufacture it and integrating components like the fuel rail, throttle body, manifold air pressure (MAP) sensor, and other components to it."

How the IAFM is created is a story in itself. Duchardt explained, "The Gen III intake is built as one piece. To do this, a mold is used with a tin bismuth core that creates the inside shape of the intake. The core weighs about 200 pounds and is melted out after the molded part has solidified. With its 3-mm thick walls, the intake is made of about eight pounds of injected nylon. The tin core is melted out by dipping the intake in a series of hot baths of liquid. The brass anchors used to mount the various components are then heat staked into the nylon."

If you look inside an LS engine intake and see the three pillars in it, those were added by Duchardt to eliminate a resonance problem with the flat floor of the intake. These pillars do not affect performance.

An interesting note is where Duchardt has gone within GM. He is now the Director of GM Racing, replacing the recently retired Herb Fishel, overseeing all of GM's racing programs.

Ken Sperry summed up this part of the project, "the members of the team had all worked together either on the Gen II V8 development or other projects, so there was immense knowledge and talent in each member and we respected each other. The team members were very comfortable speaking their minds—which can be good and bad. But that debate was usually towards making the product better, which I think is a major reason it is so good."

One of those initial starting points was fuel injector placement. Koerner starts us on this point, "At the time, fuel-injector technology wasn't nearly what it is today. The choices were very narrow and the team knew getting this right would be critical to achieving the power, emissions, driveability, and other requirements set for this engine. Because of this, the fuel-injector location in relation to the valve angle placement was the first line set in the creation of the cylinder head and intake manifold."

Ron Sperry's take on this issue concurs, "The first step in building the top end of the Gen III V-8 was to locate the angle of the fuel injector to the valve angle. So the team focused on getting the fuel injector fuel cone (the spray) to hit the back of the intake valve on the far side of the valve. This did result in some airflow compromises, but nothing drastic. Later on, fuel-injector advancements allowed improvement in avoiding port wall wetting, which made the injector location less critical, so we'd do things a little differently now, but for that time, it was the best choice."

The next step was to develop the intake and exhaust ports. Koerner had success with replicated ports in past applications and wanted them on the Gen III V-8. He also wanted the valve-train to be in line, which was a constraint to port location. Add in the problem of the four head bolts getting in the way and it's easy to see there was little room for the intake ports. Both

Sperrys chuckle, "People wonder where the 'cathedral' intake port (tall and narrow) design came from. Hell, there wasn't really any room between the head bolts and the in-line pushrods for a traditional port we just kept squeezing the port narrower and taller until we got the flow 'right' — the cathedral port got us the port volume in the small space available to us. It was as simple as that."

Regarding the efficiency of the intake port, Ken Sperry adds, "The intake port was so good, we actually had to slow the airspeed down. We found that an airspeed of more than 350 feet/second could easily be achieved, but this would not allow the air to 'turn' at the short side radius just before the valve seat—it would just skip past and all the air would go through the backside of the intake. This effectively reduced the swept area of the intake valve and hurt flow and power production." So to correct this, "the short side radius and back of the bowl shape resulted from intense computer modeling and physical testing to get the air to turn, use all the valve to get the air in the combustion chamber and induce swirl without a lot of bandaids that ultimately cost you in total airflow."

When they had the intake port roughly determined, the Sperry brothers' team quickly came up with a very efficient exhaust port and went to work creating a port/combustion chamber combo that netted excellent flow characteristics. Their experience really shows here. Comments Ron, "High raw flow numbers are not worth a damn unless everything is working to maximize complete combustion. The desired result is to achieve a high yield combustion pressure pushing the piston down. This is what creates power and also results in excellent emissions numbers.

"We worked with what we call the Hurricane and Tornado-style combustion swirl effects when developing the port/chamber combo for the Gen III. The hurricane swirl has a wide diameter while the tornado has a very tight swirl. To put this in specific numbers, the

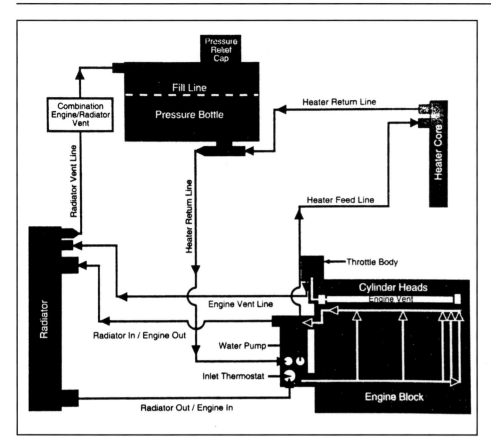

The cooling system for the Gen III V-8 is different from previous small blocks in that the thermostat is on the inlet side of the engine. The coolant circulates through the engine and heater core until the engine is up to temperature — bringing the engine up to temp and providing heat to the interior in only a short amount of time. The steam vents in the top of the engine help to get the steam pockets out of the engine that cause localized hot spots that lead to detonation and pre-ignition.

Gen III V-8 early proto designs were run on the hydra. These engines were used to evaluate coefficient of variation (COV), indicated mean effective pressure (IMEP), swirl, and other parameters. Using the hydra, Hayman, Jim Hicks, Rick Frank, and others worked with the Sperry's to lock down the valve angle, coolant flow, valve cover rail location, and other aspects.

DYNO DEVELOPMENT

As with any development project, there would be failures and successes with the Gen III V-8 development. While the engines showed impressive power output in the first dyno runs, certain deficiencies were discovered.

The Gen III V-8 deep skirt engine block design provides impressive rigidi-

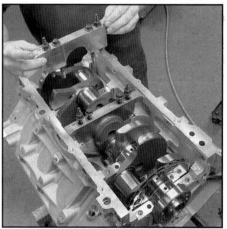

The factory powdered-metal main bearing caps are held in the block with six fasteners for maximum strength and rigidity. The deep skirt design hinders crankcase bay-to-bay breathing, so the main caps do not extend all the way to the side wall of the block below the bolt bosses, which leaves room for the main webs to have windows that improve airflow.

The deep-skirt block design has impressive strength and rigidity, which is important for the aluminum-block versions of the Gen III. This design aspect produces an unusually strong iron block that is capable of much more power than the production engine makes. All the main caps are held in place with four vertical 10-mm-diameter bolts and two 8-mm-diameter bolts.

hurricane swirl would result in 1 complete swirl per fuel injection cycle, while the tornado swirl would result in 1.2 or more swirls per fuel injection cycle. To give you an idea how valuable this is, we gained 8 hp by achieving 2 swirls per fuel application."

As a note, Ron Sperry made a point to clarify that the Gen III V-8 engine is not considered a "fast-burn" engine. He explains, "The fast-burn intake port was designed before we had really powerful computer modeling of the intake flow. Before the Gen III head was created, we did most of our testing on physical models and the data seemed to show us that shooting the air/fuel mixture vertically into the combustion chamber with as much force as possible would net power. Luckily, we were able to use advanced computer modeling in the design of the Gen III head and saw

that in actuality the gain was negated by the air/fuel charge actually pushing against the piston coming up in the bore — eating power! So while the fast-burn port/chamber design did produce a power gain, the Gen III V-8 port produces more power with the use of an improved 'swirl'."

SINGLE-CYLINDER TESTING

The initial physical testing was done on a single-cylinder test engine, called a hydra engine, in the Advanced Engineering area of GM Powertrain. This engine is no more than a low-RPM test bed (they usually operate at less than 3,500 rpm) that can have different cranks, connecting rods, pistons, and cylinder heads easily installed. These test engines were widely used before today's computer capability, and the

ty and reduces the noise coming from the engine, but on the initial engines, the crankcase bay-to-bay breathing was not sufficient. At 1,200 rpm, having the two front cylinders rising while the two rears were falling forced oil into the front cover. To fix this, the area under the intake was opened up to allow bay-to-bay breathing capability and small 'scoop' ports were cast into the block on the side of the main caps (an idea patented by Advanced Engineering's Jim Mazzola and Terry Black). This eliminated the initial idea of putting the alternator and starter in the area between the intake and lifter bay.

Later on in the development, it was discovered that at high RPM, the pistons moving up and down in the bores pushed oil vapor and air in all the wrong places in the crankcase. The deep skirt and main caps were sealing off each pair of cylinders, limiting where this pressurized oil vapor could go. On at least one of the prototype engines, the subsequent buildup of pressure blew the rear section of the block off. The short-term solution to this issue was to machine holes through all the main cap webs and the long-term solution was cast-in bay-to-bay breathing "windows" in the webs. Additional windows were developed for the LS6 high-RPM, high-horsepower engine package.

Also, from the beginning, the Gen III V-8 was designed to produce overall net power. This meant common parasitic power losses, like friction and pumping losses, were to be minimized from the beginning. One interesting byproduct of the lowered power losses was poor idle quality. It was discovered idle quality is usually improved by some frictional losses. On the Gen III, with its roller lifters, roller rockers, and low tension piston rings, the only friction at idle is really the piston moving up and down in the bore and the rocker arms wiping across the valvestem. To improve idle quality, the development engineers "built-in" a load on the engine when needed.

IN THE VEHICLE

One of the more interesting challenges involved the oil pan and oiling sys-

Timeline of Gen III V-8 Creation

Late '91	Stephens asks GM Powertrain's Advanced Engineering to quietly "pencil up" an initial Gen III V-8 design, buying pizzas for the team to offset the extra work needed
May '92	A "blind test" of engine designs by GM executives occurs at "Black Lake" inside GM Milford Proving Grounds. Pushrod — development green-lighted
Late '93	First dyno testing begins with prototype "beta" Gen III V-8 engines
Mid '94	Gen III estimated at 10 percent of design requirements (called Concept Approval in GM development process)
Early '95	Chief Engineer Koerner gives presentation to Chairman Jack Smith and other GM execs regarding progress of Gen III V-8 program, receives round of applause for progress and design potential (this response is not normal for these presentations)
Late '95	Gen III V-8 development nearing completion in vehicles and on the dyno
Mid '96	LS1 version of Gen III V-8 unveiled to media
Mid/Late '96	Production of LS1 Gen III V-8 begins at Romulus, Michigan assembly plant

tem. Since the LS1 sits very low in the Corvette, the oil pan is extremely shallow. Hayman details the scene, "The deep skirted engine block is a winner with regard to strength, rigidity, and NVH, but combine that with a shallow pan and it becomes difficult to get the oil away from the crank and out of the bottom of the engine. The tight confines of

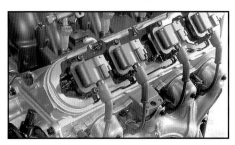

The ignition system is another one of those component sets that looks deceivingly simple. The four coil-near-plug setups on each valve cover are wired to the powertrain control module and fire based on readings from the crank and cam sensors.

the engine block walls increase the chances of the crank "roping" a lot of oil on it, which results in a parasitic loss of power. Also, the spinning crank whips the oil all over the engine instead of leaving it in the oil pan. To visualize this, imagine pouring oil on a fan pointed upwards. Obviously, the oil would end up everywhere except on the fan."

This problem really showed itself in the early validation testing stage of continuous high lateral loading. Some of the early LS1 test engines would struggle to get constant oil flow, so there were many, many tuning changes made to the design of the oil pan to minimize this issue. A special team consisting of Brian Green, Tommy Morrison, Nick Cole, George Fultz, Dave Klaasen, Tom Bierbauer, Jim Minneker, and others thrashed long and hard to get this issue under control. Fultz would eventually help GM design a special dyno cell to duplicate the many challenging scenarios the LS1 engine team encountered in vehicles. This will allow the testing of

The Vortec V-8 engines in all GM full-size trucks and SUVs have identical architecture to the engines in the Corvette, Camaro, and Firebird. The GM Vortec engines have different displacements, cast-iron blocks, some wider sealing surfaces, and a different intake than the LS1 and LS6, but the same performance parts will easily bolt on and make power.

future engines to occur much earlier in the development process than it did in the Gen III V-8 development.

PASSING THE TORCH

In late 1997, with the LS1 launch successful, Koerner was given a new leadership position inside GM Truck. Sam Winegarden, a GM leadership veteran of the 3800 V-6 and Northstar V-8 engine programs, was given the Chief Engineer job for the Gen III V-8. "From the beginning, I knew this program was big. It was obvious this team was working on an American icon, and they held the job in that context," said Winegarden.

From the beginning, Winegarden had some big projects to launch and run smoothly in the spotlight. Some of them would include leading the Gen III V-8 team through the truck engine launch, the introduction of the LS6 385- and 405-hp engines, and the LQ9 345-hp Escalade truck engine. The truck engine requirements took the daily production from approximately 2,000 engines per day to over 8,000 engines per day. Winegarden commented, "I'm very proud of how the engineering and manufacturing team handled that. The Romulus, Michi-gan, engine assembly plant broke the existing Powertrain record for 'launch speed acceleration' — a measure of the production facility going from startup to maximum production levels. Then, six months later, the St. Catherines, Ontario, Canada, engine assembly plant took some of the lessons learned from the Romulus launch and beat the Romulus record in the same category. Now, both plants are usually number 1 or number 2 in the Harbour Report on plant efficiency and both are beating the competition in Quality ratings of problems per hundred, or pph."

Considering the complexity of building engines in a large scale manufacturing facility, these achievements are incredible.

THE LS6 STORY

Winegarden likes the LS6 story because he believes it really showcased the ability of the Gen III V-8 team to raise the bar. "Dave Hill, the 'Vette Chief, came looking for some help on a mid-cycle program to create some excitement for the Corvette brand. A team led by Dave Klausen that included Ron and Ken Sperry, Jim Hicks, John Rydzewski, and Tony Roma had already been playing around with cylinder-head modifications, camshafts, and other components in the test cell and thought they had a package for Hill. Frank Hanenburger did some of the Z06 intake manifold development (he's the son of recently retired Holden CEO Peter Hanenberger) and Chuck White was the designer that did the tube (computer math modeling) work. John Juriga oversaw the program and we made it happen in a very short timeframe with a minimum investment on GM's part. I'd say it's been a huge success," said Winegarden. This would obviously be a huge understatement.

To think the LS6 came from the trenches of the GM organization leads one to wonder what other cool, amazing power parts lurk down there!

What Was the Gen III V-8 Built to Propel?

The North American division of General Motors has survived and thrived on their Chevrolet and GMC truck and SUV sales for years. For this reason, it comes as no surprise that the Gen III V-8 program was initiated when GM wanted a new engine family to bring these vehicles to world-class quality and capability. To walk before they ran, GM chose to have the relatively small production run of the Corvette be the first platform to feature the Gen III.

Doing this accomplished two goals. First, GM could burnish the image of both the Corvette and the Gen III LS1 V-8 by introducing the engine in America's sports car. Second, with about 40,000 vehicles built per year, development and manufacturing would have a chance to gain confidence before stepping off into the 1 million plus vehicle-per-year demands of the truck and SUV market.

The advantage to automotive enthusiasts everywhere is that the cool Corvette parts will bolt onto the Vortec line of Gen III V-8 truck engines to produce durable power at a reasonable cost.

The 405-hp LS6 Z06 Corvette engine is really only the beginning of the potential the Gen III V-8 architecture has shown with its "simple pushrod design." Considering that this engine exceeded all expectations at its introduction, has a design that honors the legacy of the small-block Chevy engine, and will be the engine design hot-rodders talk about for years to come, it's a great win for the GM Powertrain engineering team.

THE LQ9

Winegarden continued, "Once the LS6 program was up and running, various members of the V-8 team started to look around at other possibilities. Tim Cyrus was the Assistant Chief Engineer for the truck engines, and when he saw the LS6 castings, he started pushing for a 6.0-liter performance package. A few of his dyno team members and he did the work to create a head, and Cadillac decided to use it to further distinguish their Escalade in the full-size SUV portfolio.

"The LQ4/LQ9 aluminum head ended up having LS6 ports but slightly larger combustion chambers (72 cc vs. the LS6 64 cc) to accommodate the desired compression ratio of the 6.0-liter engines. It was neat because without a lot of work, we had the 345 hp and 380 ft-lb of torque LQ9 engine that the Cadillac folks were thrilled with."

THE FUTURE

Winegarden is especially excited about the future for the small-block program, "We released a few versions of the Gen IV V-8 engine in 2005. The Gen IV V-8 takes everything we learned from the Gen III and builds on it. I think if automotive enthusiasts liked the Gen III, they are going to love the Gen IV. It makes lots of power, yet remains simple. We have made gains in the cylinder head, intake manifold, and oiling system, among other areas. It will have displacement on demand (DOD) on some models that allows us to attain greater miles per gallon (mpg) than a similarly sized displacement engine that doesn't have DOD by deactivating cylinders when you don't need them as you drive down the road. And you're going to see some new displacements and combinations in years to come that will bring even more excitement to this line of engines."

And that is what most hot-rodders ask GM to do — keep making their products better but don't abandon the past. Look for the Gen III V-8 to continue to grow in interest. This will happen because the leadership of GM charted a course for the hard-working and dedicated employees and suppliers of GM Powertrain to follow while creating a great engine architecture. Now, the automotive aftermarket companies are stepping up with performance equipment to compliment the most impressive hot rod engine ever built. Look for great things with the Gen III LS1 V-8 engine architecture as time goes on.

Summary of the Many
Gen I/II/III Similarities and Differences

Similarities

- Gen III has the same 4.400-inch bore spacing as Gen I and II — a nod to its past
- 90-degree angle spacing of cylinder banks
- Two overhead valves per cylinder
- Valvetrain oiled through pushrod

- Connecting rod crank pin diameter of 2.100 inch
- Lifter diameter of 0.842 inch
- Single piece rear crank seal (like on later versions of Gen I/II)
- Starter located on lower passenger side of block
- Oil filter located on lower driver side of block

Differences	Gen III	Gen I and II
Block length	519.0 mm (LS1)	553.2 mm (LT1)
Block width	460.0 mm (LS1)	434.6 mm (LT1)
Block deck height	9.240 inch	9.025 inch
Firing order	1-8-7-2-6-5-4-3	1-8-4-3-6-5-7-2
Cylinder bank offset	0.9488 inch	0.8800 inch
Block design/main cap mounting	Deep skirt engine block with 4 vertical and 2 side fasteners in the main caps	Mostly 2-bolt mains, some vertical or splayed with 4 bolts. No provision for side bolting into block
Distributor drive	No distributor capability	Distributor drive at rear of cam
Rotation sensors	Engine block mounted crank and cam location sensors	No direct electronic crank and cam sensors
Weight	430 lbs for a complete LS1 (add approx 65 lbs for iron truck block)	531 lbs for most complete Gen I/IIs
Connecting rod	6.098 inches long On-center beam connecting rod	5.700 inches long Offset connecting rod 0.060 inch in piston
Piston pin diameter	0.940 inch	0.927 inch
Crank thrust bearing location	No. 3 (center) main bearing	Rear main
Cylinder head ports	Replicated (all are the same)	Mirrored (pairs of intake and center exhaust ports are mirror images of each other for packaging)
Crank flange location	0.040 inch closer to bellhousing mount on block than Gen I/II	
Thermostat location	Intake side of water pump	Exit side of engine
Intake inlet temperature control	No coolant or hot oil touches intake	Water passes through and oil hits bottom of intake
Intake Construction	Intake made of nylon	Intake made of cast iron or aluminum

THE GEN III LS1 V-8 ENGINE BASICS

The General Motors (GM) Gen III LS1 V-8 is one of the many successful engines to come out of GM Powertrain since it was formed to be the global powertrain provider for GM. As this book goes to print, about 8,000 Gen III small-block V-8 engines are built *each day*, in multiple cubic inch and power combinations, in multiple plants all over North America. These engines are the production powerplants for everything from Chevrolet Corvette sports cars and Australian Holdens (the Pontiac GTO in the States), to GMC Yukon SUVs and any of the V-8-powered Chevrolet and GMC pickup trucks. They're also sold as crate engines by GM Performance Parts and marinized versions are sold by GM Powertrain.

A variant of the Gen III V-8 powers every vehicle you see here and more. This humble pushrod engine has proven itself as a formidable powerplant in multiple production vehicles, and now you're going to learn everything you need to know to add even more power.

GEN III LS1 V-8 USAGES

The Gen III V-8 is built in four displacement sizes, with three initially using a cast iron engine block and one using an aluminum block. The most well known Gen III V-8 is the 5.7-liter all aluminum engine — known by its three-digit alphanumeric regular production order (RPO) engine code: LS1 (all GM engines are denoted by an RPO code). The LS1 was the first version of the Gen III V-8 architecture to hit the streets in the 1997 Chevrolet Corvette and then soon after in the Camaro and Firebird. It

made such an impression that the majority of automobile enthusiasts call all the Gen III V-8 engines an LS1, whether it is a Vortec LQ9 in an Escalade or a LS6 in a Z06 Corvette.

The 6.0-liter cast-iron block, aluminum-head, Vortec-branded LQ4 and LQ9 truck engines will also be covered extensively in this book, as automotive enthusiasts usually lean toward engines with bigger displacements. The LS1 and LS6 are the performance engines from GM, and the LQ4 and LQ9 are the biggest displacement production Gen III V-8s available, so it is easy to understand

why this book would focus on them.

There will also be some discussion of the two other Gen III V-8 variants, the 4.8-liter LR4 and 5.3-liter LM7 cast-iron block, aluminum-head engines. These are very common in trucks and SUVs. The 4.8- and 5.3-liter engines use common architecture to the LS1 and LQ Gen III V-8 engines, so the information presented on the 5.7- and 6.0-liter Gen III components and modifications can be applied to them. They won't be discussed as much as the 5.7- and 6.0-liter Gen IIIs because these smaller engines won't make the same amount of power

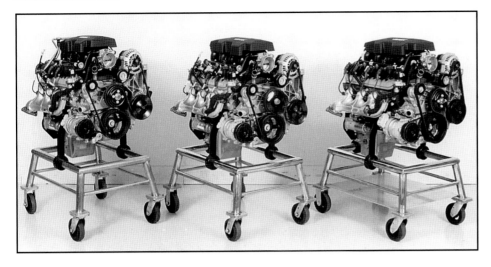

The original 6.0-liter Vortec LQ4 (right) originally came with iron heads and an iron block. After 2001, all Vortec 300- and 345-hp 6.0-liter LQ4 and LQ9 engines switched to aluminum heads. The LQ Gen III engines have a strong following for their strength and ability to handle considerably more power than they made in stock form. The 4.8- (left) and 5.3-liter (middle) Gen III V-8 engines provide solid power, but most hot-rodders go for the 6.0-liter because of the "when in doubt, punch it out" rule of thumb. More cubes mean more power.

for the investment of time, effort, and money due to their smaller displacements. But many of the upgrades performed here will work on the 4.8- and 5.3-liter engines, so if that's what you've got to work with, they will respond to improvements. In fact the 5.3 cast-iron block can be bored out to a 5.7-liter bore size – all the more reason to discuss 5.7-liter performance packages.

As you'll see, later chapters in this book have specific engine buildups on 5.3-, 5.7-, and 6.0-liter engines to give you "recipes" for making certain levels of power. Also, there is a racing-only aluminum engine block available from GM Performance Parts, called the C5R, which will be used as the foundation for a 1,000+ hp engine later in the book.

THE DETAILS TO MAKE HORSEPOWER

This chapter will give you the technical information regarding the basic materials, manufacturing processes, and assembly methods used by GM to create the Gen III V-8. There is a plethora of details and minutia we could bury

Gen III V-8 Complete Engine Specs and Part Numbers

RPO Code	Cubic Inches	Liters	Comp. Ratio	Part # (complete engines)
LS1	345	5.7	10.19:1	12562189
				12562191
				12562192
LS6	345	5.7	10.46:1	12562190
LR4	293	4.8	9.47:1	12562194
				12577188
				12562198
				12562086
LM4	325	5.3	9.49:1	12579396
LM7	325	5.3	9.49:1	2562201
				12562087
L59	325	5.3	9.49:1	12565156
LQ4	364	6.0	9.41:1	12562211
				12562122
				12562123
				12568076
				12575147
				12575148
				12562090
				12562092
				12562223
				12562227
LQ9	377	6.0	10.08:1	12568077

The aluminum Gen III V-8 engine block used as the basis for the LS1 weighs 103 lbs. This impressive figure is achieved using thin-wall cast-iron liners, main webbing that takes advantage of the pull-from-the-bottom head bolts, and an oil pan that acts as a structural member to assist in block rigidity.

you with here, but instead of trying to teach you how to design an engine for mass production, the information shared in this book is focused on helping you create performance with the existing Gen III V-8 engine.

To that end, the details listed here usually have explanations on why they were done and how they impact the performance of the engine. Possibly more important, the usages of the Gen III V-8 are discussed along with how to identify the various engines and components, so you can find desirable engines and components using external and internal visual clues. You can combine this info with the info in the next chapter to decide which factory components are desirable when building a production-based performance Gen III V-8.

Gen III V-8 Engine	Bores Inches (mm)	Block Part Number	Crank Stroke Inches (mm)
LS1/LS6 (aluminum)	3.893 (99)	12569379 12560625 12561167	3.622 (92)
LM4 (01-02) (aluminum)	3.779 (96)	12566909 12583663	3.270 (83)
LR4/LM7 (98-04) (cast iron)	3.779 (96)	12551359	3.622 (92)
LQ4/LQ9 (99-04) (cast iron)	4.000 (101.6)	12551365	3.622 (92)

(All part numbers (PN) were gathered in 2003 and current PNs are subject to change at any time.)

ENGINE BLOCK

The LS1 and LS6 version of the Gen III V-8 block is created using a semi-permanent mold casting process with 319-alloy aluminum heat-treated to T5 specs. The block design is a tour-de-force of technology to maximize strength while minimizing weight and noise. The design was mainly done with the aluminum material in mind, so the iron block is much stronger than any

Gen III V-8 Component Specifications and Details

Engine Block: cast of 319-T5 aluminum (All 5.7 liter, select '03 5.3 liter, '05 6.0 liter) or cast iron (Most 4.8/5.3/6.0-liter)

Crankshaft: cast nodular iron, internally balanced, rolled fillet journals for strength, integral two-piece 24x crankshaft position sensing ring installed near rear of crankshaft
  • Revised firing order from previous GM small block V-8s
  • Drilled main journals for lower end breathing and reduced weight

Oil Pump: gerotor-style, driven off front of crankshaft

Oil Pan: cast 356-T6 aluminum wet sump, stressed member for reduced noise/vibration/harshness (NVH), incorporated oil filter boss, drain plug, oil level sensor mount, and oil pan baffle
  • Corvette-rear sump, "batwing" kick out design
  • Camaro/Firebird-rear sump design
  • Truck-rear sump design
  • Holden/GTO-front sump design

Connecting Rods: reversible, cracked, hot-forged, powder-metal rods made of a steel alloy

Piston Pin: steel, 0.940-inch (24.0-mm) pin, pressed into piston

Pistons: eutectic cast aluminum, flat top with no valve reliefs. LQ9 345-hp 6.0-liter pistons coated on top and sides

Rings:
  First Ring — molybdenum-filled 9254 steel, 0.059 inch (1.5 mm) thick
  Second — cast iron, tapered face with reversed twist
  Oil Control — expander with support rails

Cylinder Heads: Semi-permanent mold and sand-cast 356-T6 aluminum (except on some '99 and '00 LR4 and LQ4 cast-iron heads)

Valves: 2.00/1.55 inch intake/exhausts

Valvesprings: "beehive" shape wound from 4.6-mm diameter chromium silicate (Cr-Si) ovate (oval shaped) wire

Retainers: steel

Locks: 10-degree design, steel

Camshaft: ground from a gun-drilled (17-mm hole) 5150 steel billet, spins in large cam bearings

Lifters: roller-type, hydraulic, nested in plastic carriers of four each

Rockers: investment-cast steel, needle roller bearing pivot mounted to investment-cast aluminum rocker-arm stand

Pushrods: steel, 0.320 inch (8 mm), 0.075-inch wall thickness

Cylinder Head Gaskets: sandwich design of graphite layers over a steel core

Ignition: coil-near-plug design, one coil per cylinder

Fuel Injection: sequential port injection

Exhaust Manifolds: cast iron, catalytic converters mounted to manifold outlet (except for '97-'98 LS1 dual wall, welded manifolds)

Water Pump: aluminum housing, integral thermostat housing

previous GM production iron block. The Gen III team knew a strong block would be needed to maintain round bores for maximized fuel economy and performance while minimizing durability issues and emissions, so that's what they built. To do all that, the head bolts pull from the main webs, the crank main caps are cross-bolted on the deep skirt block, and the design was fully evaluated with finite element analysis (FEA) computer modeling to add ribbing in areas that required increased rigidity.

Bore centers are at the traditional small-block Chevy 4.40 inches (111.76 mm), but the cylinders themselves are the story. On the aluminum LS1 and LS6 engine blocks, each bore is actually a thin, centrifugally cast iron liner with a serrated outside diameter. The liners are cast in a centrifuge to maximize the density of the iron, and then cast in place with the block. The thin liners limit how much the 3.898-inch (99-mm) inside-diameter cylinder bores can be machined out — GM recommends the '97 to '98 LS1 blocks be honed only 0.004 inch and '99 and later blocks can only be machined 0.010 inches. The serrated outside diameter surface helps to lock the liner in place in the block and dissipate heat through the increased surface area. The fact that GM figured out how to hold these liners to such tight tolerances during the casting process is an impressive engineering feat.

The main caps fit between two vertical steps in the block to create a "swedge fit" between the cap and engine block to lock the cap in place, instead of using dowel pins to locate and lock the main caps in place. Six fasteners lock each main cap in place to provide impressive rigidity.

Engine Block Details	Part Numbers
Block – Casting Number:	(this it the number that will be cast into the block)
LS1	12559378, 12560626
LS6	12561168 (some '01/02 LS1s used this block; all 03-04 LS1s used this block)
Block – Machined Number:	
LS1	12559379, 12560625
LS6	12561167
Block – Assembly:	
LS1	12559377, 12560624,
LS6	122561166 (some '01/02 LS1s used this block; all 03-04 LS1s used this block)
Main Bearing Caps:	
Front & Rear	12561647
Middle Caps	12561646
Main Cap Center Bolts (10):	12560272
Main Cap Stud Bolts (10):	12560273
Main Bearings – Top/Bottom:	12561328/12561329
Thrust Bearing – Top/Bottom:	12561330/12561331
Cam Bearings, 1&5/2&4/3:	12558537/38/39 up to '03
	12574413/14/12558539 in '04 ('04 bearing has larger outside diameter with thicker shell—increases bore size in block)
Main Cap Cross Bolts:	12556127
Side Drain Bolts:	12560196
Coolant System Plugs:	12561663
Valley Cover Plate:	
LS1	12561106
LS6	12568002

ENGINE BLOCK DETAILS

Block Type:	Cam-in-block, non-Siamese bore (means there are water passages between bores), deep skirt
Material:	319-T5 aluminum
Weight:	Alum. = 107 lbs (48.85 kg), the iron block weighs about 65 lbs more
Length:	20.43 inches (519 mm)
Width:	18.11 inches (460 mm)
Bore:	3.893 inches (99 mm)
Cylinder Bank Offset:	0.949 in (24.10 mm)
Deck Height:	9.240 inches (234.7 mm)
Bank angle:	45 degrees
Main bearing housing bore diameter:	2.751 inches (69.875 mm)
Camshaft bearing block bore diameter:	
'97-'03	Stepped 0.25 mm from No. 3 bearing bore to 2 and 4, and the another 0.25 mm to 1 and 5
1 and 5	2.3276 – 2.3295 inch (59.12 – 59.17 mm)
2 and 4	2.3177 – 2.3197 inch (58.87 – 58.92 mm)
3	2.3079 – 2.3098 inch (58.62 – 58.67 mm)
'04	Stepped 0.50 mm from No. 3 bearing bore to 2 and 4, and the another 0.50 mm to 1 and 5
1 and 5	2.3472 – 2.3492 inch (59.62 – 59.67 mm)
2 and 4	2.3276 – 2.3295 inch (59.12 – 59.17 mm)
3	2.3079 – 2.3098 inch (58.62 – 58.67 mm)
Forward bank of cylinders:	Driver side
Rotation of crankshaft:	(looking from front) Clockwise
Interesting features:	
•	Cylinder head & bearing main cap threads rolled, all others cut
•	Crank thrust wall at No 3 (center main)
•	Crank centerline used to locate cylinder and cam bores along with cam and crank sensor bores during initial machining process
•	LS6 block has enlarged as-cast breathing ports in main webs to handle sustained high-RPM usage with minimal crankcase oil vapor and pumping problems

The iron engine blocks don't have cylinder inserts. Because of this, the 4.8- and 5.3-liter iron blocks can be bored out to 99 mm (from the 96 mm original bore) to build an iron version of the 5.7-liter engine (the 4.8-liter engine adds the 3.662-inch stroke crank to attain 5.7 liters of displacement). The 6-liter engine block's 4.000-inch (101.6-mm) cylinder bores are nearly the max for wall thickness, so it isn't recommended to bore these out for more cubic inches.

CYLINDER HEAD DETAILS

Valve Angle: 15 degrees (vs. 23 of previous Chevy Small Block)
Valve Seat Machined Angles: 30, 45, and 60 degrees to blend into chamber
Distance Between Valve Guides: 1.913 inches (48.6 mm) on all heads
Valvestem Diameter: 0.315 inch (8.001 mm)
Factory Recommended Valve-to-Guide Clearance: 0.0016 to 0.0036 inch (0.041 to 0.0914 mm)
Valve Guide Material: sintered iron (pressed in place)
Valve Guides (16/head): PN 10215342
Coolant Plugs (2/head): PN 1647542
Valve Seats: Exhaust (4/head)   PN 10215341
              Intake (4/head)   PN 12553180
Head Bolts: (Do Not Reuse These Stretch-to-Torque Fasteners!)

Description	PN	Type	Torque & Twist Specifications ft-lb (N-m) degrees twist
Long (16/eng)	12560744	M11 x 2.0-155.5	22 (30), 76 deg, 76 deg
Short (4/eng)	12560745	M11 x 2.0-101	22 (30), 76 deg, 34 deg
Short (10/eng)	12558840	M8 x 1.25-46	22 (30), no twist

Visual difference between LS1 and LS6 head: LS1 exhaust port is oval shape, LS6 exhaust port is "D" shaped

CYLINDER HEADS

The Gen III V-8 cylinder heads have replicated ports and combustion chambers similar to many aftermarket, high-performance cylinder heads offered for past small-block and big-block GM pushrod V-8s. This means all eight cylinders use the same shape ports and combustion chambers, which allowed the engineers at GM to focus on optimizing just one combo of ports and chamber shapes. Doing this made it easier to maximize power and efficiency in the overall engine while minimizing emissions.

The distance between the exhaust and intake valve guides and hence, the valves, is common for all the production Gen III V-8 cylinder heads. This was viewed as a power potential limiter by the port, chamber, and valvetrain engineers, but was done to minimize tooling investment and simplify manufacturing. Changing the valvestem centerline spacing is a big job, but it's acknowledged that putting them closer together with bigger intake valves will release more power potential.

Gen III V-8 Production Cylinder Heads

Usage	(bare casting)	(mach casting)	(assembly)	In/Ex Port Vol. (cc)	ComChmbr(cc) +gasket vol.
	GM Part #				
LS1				200/70	66.67
97-98	10215339	10215339	10215337		
	12558806	12558806	12558808		
99-01	12559853	12559854	12559856		
01-04	12564241	12559854	12559856		
	12559853	12564242			
LS6				210/75	64.45
01-04	12564243	12560800	12560802		
			12568315		
			12564824		
LR4/LM4/ LM7/L59				200/70	61.15
99-00	12559862	12559863	12559865		
01-04	12561706	12561708	12563678		
	12569862	12559863			
LQ4				210/75	71.06
99-00	12561873	12561874	12561876		
01	12562317	12562318	12562320		
02-04	12562317	12562318	12565363		
			12565364 (also rpo KL5 nat. gas head)		
LQ9					
02-04	12572317	12562318	12565363		
			12565364		

This cutaway of a Gen III engine shows how compact and busy the rotating and reciprocating-component area is. To get everything tight, GM engineers did things like have the cast crank counterweights cam-ground to clear the bottoms of the pistons. The powdered-metal rods and eutectic-aluminum pistons were chosen because they have good durability, performance, and piece cost for their size and weight.

The small chamber volumes of all the cylinder head variations provide excellent quench area to work with the flattop pistons. This helps to put all the air/fuel mixture in a tight area to maximize the combustion process and provide the maximum force pushing on the piston.

The high-output LS6 features cylinder heads with higher-flowing ports and chambers compared to the base LS1, but the heads aren't the only reason for the increased power output. A more aggressive camshaft, freer breathing airbox and mass air flow sensor (MAF), lightened valvetrain components, and various other pieces took advantage of the improved ports and more efficient combustion chamber for higher RPM and more power production throughout the powerband.

The reason this needs to be explained is so you don't bolt on a set of LS6 cylinder heads and wonder why you didn't get a huge leap in performance! Better flowing cylinder heads require all those additions and possibly a freer flowing exhaust to take advantage of the increased flow capabilities. The heads are the core part of the success with the Gen III V-8, but you'll need to enable them to make the power potential they contain.

CRANKSHAFT

The Gen III LS1 V-8 engine crank is made of nodular cast-iron but has far superior strength to what most would think of from a cast crank. This is because the Gen III crank has rolled fillets on the journals to reduce stress risers and variable-radii undercuts on the counterweights to increase the bearing surface area.

Rolled fillets are created by a roller being forced into the edge of the crank bearing edge around its circumference to compress the material into the shape of the smooth transition. This minimizes the chances of a stress riser, or crack, forming in this area by compressing the material in this area and eliminating a sharp edge where the crank transitions from a machined surface to the as-cast portion of the crank.

CRANKSHAFT DETAILS

Crank	Stroke in inches (mm)	Part Number (w/ Reluctor Ring)
LS1/LS6	3.622 (92)	12559354

Other Crank Components:

Description	Part Number
Rear Crank Plug	24502262 – installed to seal the hole in the crank, located just past the step in the crank ID to clear the thrust bearing
Crank Key	12561513
Balancer	12560115
Balancer Bolt	12557840
Flywheel Bolts	12572730

Main Journals	2.559 inches (65 mm)
Factory Recommended Main Journal Clearance	
LS1	0.0015 to 0.0019 inch
Main Journal Width	0.905 inch (22.99 mm)
Factory Recommended Crankshaft End Play	
LS1	0.0016 to 0.0079 inch (0.041 mm to 0.201 mm)
Rod Crank Journals	2.0995 inches (53.328 mm)
Factory Recommended Rod Journal Clearance	0.0019 to 0.0031 inch (0.048 mm to 0.079 mm)
Rod Crank Journal Width	1.902 inch (48.37 mm)
Rear Seal inside diameter	4.527 inch (114.99 mm)
Base Circle Diameter on flywheel bolts	3.110 inch (78.99 mm)
Torque on flywheel bolts	74 ft-lbs (100 N-m)
Firing Order	1-8-7-2-6-5-4-3

Interesting Feature:
- This cast crank is known to consistently handle over 500 hp naturally aspirated and 650 hp turbocharged in street engine usage — a very impressive amount for a cast crank.

TRUCK CRANKSHAFT PORTFOLIO

(The figures from the Crankshaft Details chart apply to these, except for the main journal clearance and crankshaft endplay)

	Stroke in inches (mm)	Part Number
LR4 (4.8-liter)	3.267 (83)	12559356
LM4/LM7 (5.3-liter)	3.662 (92)	12559357
LQ4/LQ9 (6.0-liter)	3.662 (92)	12559768

If you're looking at a Gen III V-8 with bolts around the perimeter of the valve cover, it's a 1997-98 model. The Gen III engine design was originally proposed with a center-bolt design, but the design wasn't fully validated for the 1997 launch. Since the perimeter design was well known from previous small blocks, it was implemented instead. The 1999 and later center-bolt valve covers and heads are more desirable for other features that improve their performance and durability.

One of the biggest development snafus and manufacturing challenges was the "batwing" oil pan for the Corvettes (left). The oiling issues were resolved before going to production, but the shallow pan made oil control a challenge. The first batwing pan was a single casting that was very difficult to manufacture. In 1998, a two-piece batwing pan was introduced. Both pans perform well under the most extreme conditions.

The Camaro and Firebird oil pans (middle) are called rear sump because the deep portion of the oil pan is towards the rear of the engine. Since the oil pump is at the front of the engine, a long pickup winds its way from the lowest point of the oil pan up to the pump. This pan is often used when a Gen III is installed in a past model vehicle — but often the first two inches of the pan hits the crossmember, so either the oil pan or crossmember needs to be trimmed to fit. The Camaro windage tray does not run to the front of the engine, like on the Corvette or truck pans, since the oil pan is very close to the crank at the front of the engine.

The truck oil pan (right) has a deep sump, which is good for oil capacity and power production, but it's difficult to package on cars with low hoods and low ground clearance.

CONNECTING ROD DETAILS

Details	Part Number
Connecting Rod	12568734
Rod Bearings (16)	12451342
Material: steel alloy	PR1159M

Rod Center-to-Center Distance:	6.098 inch (154.89 mm)
Rod Crank Bearing Bore Diameter:	2.225 inch (56.519 mm)
Rod Crank Bearing Width:	0.9449 inch (24 mm)
Factory Recommended Rod Crank Bearing Side Clearance:	
	0.012 to 0.015 inch (0.305 to 0.381 mm)
Rod Piston Pin Bore Diameter:	0.9436 inch (23.97 mm)
Rod Piston Pin Boss Width:	0.9449 inch (24 mm)
Factory Recommended Piston Pin Press Interference:	
	0.0008 to 0.0017 inch (0.020 to 0.043 mm)
Factory Rod Bolts:	M9 (means 9 mm) x 1.000 inch
Factory Recommended Torque:	D20 (15 ft-lbs) plus 65 degrees of twist

Interesting Features:
- The LS1 rod uses a 0.945-inch (24-mm) piston pin pressed into the little end of the rod
- The factory rod bolts are 9-mm hex-head bolts and should be replaced with aftermarket (ARP, Katech) bolts in 450+ horsepower applications
- The factory rod bolts are torqued to a relatively low 15 ft-lbs, then twisted at least 60 degrees more to provide sufficient stretch to clamp everything in place

TRUCK CONNECTING RODS

Description	Part Number
LR4	12568736
LM4/LM7/L59	12568734
LQ4/LQ9	12568734

The crank also has a 0.9645-inch (24.5-mm) hole drilled through the number 2, 3, 4, and 5 mains to reduce its overall weight 143 lbs (65 kg) and allow air and oil vapor to flow through the holes between the cylinder bays to improve bay-to-bay breathing.

CONNECTING RODS

Automotive enthusiasts have found the "cracked," powdered-metal Gen III V-8 connecting rods weigh less and handle just as much power as the famed Chevy "pink" rods. In case you're wondering, the Gen III V-8 rods are called a cracked rod because the big end cap of the rod is created through a cracking process. It goes like this — after the rod is created, a groove is machined on the inside diameter of the rod's big end where the parting line is intended. Then, a side load force is applied to the rod to split off the cap portion of the rod. When torqued in place, the two pieces mate up precisely and lock tightly together on the jagged micro-edges of the break.

The rod itself is made from powdered steel that is packed into a mold under pressure and heated to just below the melting point of the steel to get the steel to bond. A forging process is then performed, followed by shot peening, to end up with a rod of very predictable size and weight. This eliminates the

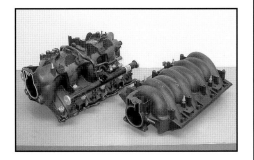

Initially, the low-profile car intake was to be the intake for all the vehicles. But the truck and SUV intake inlets ended up needing to be about 3 inches higher to clear the radiator fan. The tall truck intake flows a little less at high-RPM, high-horsepower situations than the LS intake, but it does pretty well below 5000 rpm — though it's not the prettiest thing in the world.

When in Doubt, Punch it Out

In general, adding more cubic inches is a cheap way to get more power for the same investment in parts. This is because if one is comparing engines built with the same parts, the bigger engine will have the potential to make more power. While big inchers will consume a small percentage more fuel, you need to ask one key question — If you're going to spend the money on aftermarket components and their integration into the factory system to make power, why not get the most horsepower out of them? For this reason, more cubic inches are always a safe bet for a performance engine.

The best Gen III candidates for over-bore are the 5.3-liter blocks, as they are easily bored to the 3.893 inch (5.7-liter bore size). The aluminum block Gen III V-8 engine has cast-in cylinder liners that are only about 0.100-inch thick, which limits how much you can over-bore the cylinders. There are engine shops that are completely boring out these liners and gluing oversized liners in place to increase the engine size. The GM production Gen III V-8 engine block engineers have experience with these applications and suggest caution when building an engine for extensive street duty.

Their concern is in maintaining stability in the clamping load of the cylinder head to the liners. Based on the engineers' experience, they feel getting a good seal at the head gasket is difficult with the liners glued in place on a press fit because the head bolts pull from the bottom of the block, not the deck surface. If you are absolutely convinced this process if for you, do the homework to find a machine shop that is very familiar with this process to minimize the chances of having a leaky head gasket.

Head gasket choice is critical to sealing the deck surface on a sleeved engine. Many hard-core racers use coated copper gaskets with metal O-rings set in a machined groove in the deck surface of the block. These gaskets require regular re-torquing to insure the clamping load is maintained.

A sleeved block is best suited for hard-core performance applications, where minimal usage between engine maintenance occurs. This is mainly due to the potential for seepage at the head-to-block mating point. Even in high-horsepower racing applications, glued/pressed-in liners will work because the slight seepage can be followed in the regular between-rounds maintenance.

PISTON DETAILS

Piston (bare): PN 12575663
Weight: 434 grams
GM Recommended Piston-to-Bore Clearance: 0.0007 to 0.0021 inch (0.0178 to 0.0533 mm)
GM Recommended Piston Deck Height in Operation: 0.008 inches (0.203 mm) above deck surface

Top land thickness: 0.177 inch (34 mm)

Ring Specs

	Part Numbers	Thickness inch (mm)	Rec'd Gap inch (mm)	Gap Clocking
Top:	12552018	.059 (1.500)	0.009 (0.229)	none required
Second:	12575803	0.59 (1.500)	0.017 (0.432)	none required
Oil Spacer:	12572020			
Rails (2):	12575665	.118 (3.000)	0.001 (0.025)	25 degrees from top/second gap, 25 degrees of expander to rails

Interesting fact:
- The LQ9 345-hp Escalade 6.0-liter engine comes with pistons that have a moly coating on the skirts and a heat rejection coating on the top of the piston mainly to cure piston cold-start noise. All Gen III pistons from 2003 and on have coated sides.

need for material pads at each end of the rod (like on the pink rod) and machining to get the proper sizing, balance, and lengths.

PISTONS

As with the cast crankshaft, the piston material, cast eutectic aluminum, is not usually thought of for high-performance applications because many consider them more brittle than forged aluminum pistons. However, these pistons work in this application because the engineers at GM did their homework to create a design that is light, seals the bore, and works well with the combustion chamber. As a testament to their ability, it is widely accepted that the stock pistons can handle just over 500 hp before needing to be replaced by aftermarket forged pistons.

Since the pins are pressed into these lightweight pistons, some performance engine builders do not like to remove and reinstall these pistons more than once to minimize the chances of introducing stress risers in the piston pin bores.

If you do swap aftermarket forged aluminum pistons into your Gen III, the factory knock sensors will likely need to be disabled or desensitized in the factory powertrain control module (PCM) software, as the forged pistons "sound" like combustion detonation to the knock sensors. You'll know this is true when the "Service Engine Soon," or SES, lights up during operation with the forged pistons.

VALVETRAIN

Some might write off the Gen III V-8 as crude because it is a cam-in-block, pushrod V-8; but don't be fooled. While the basis is simple, the engineers at GM spent considerable time and effort to create a system capable of high performance.

CAMSHAFT DETAILS

Camshaft journal diameter		2.1659 inch (55.14 mm)
Camshaft Lobe Base Circle Radius		
	Inch (mm)	
'97-04 LS1	0.776 (19.7)	
'01 LS6	0.760 (19.3) (reduced to create increased valve lift)	
'02 and up LS6	0.748 (19.0) (reduced more for added valve lift!)	

The '02 LS6 uses 0.6 mm longer hollow-stem valves to keep the valvetrain weight at a minimum while correcting valvetrain geometry with the reduced base circle radius cam and higher rate valvesprings. This was done to control valve motion with the 0.025 inch increased lift

Factory recommended endplay	0.003 to 0.008 inch (0.0762 to 0.203 mm)
Roller lifter diameter	0.700 inch (17.78 mm)
Valve material	
LS1/LS6 '97-'04	Stainless steel
LS6 '02 and up	Hollow valvestems — with the exhaust stems sodium filled to manage heat and the intakes hollow to reduce weight due to increased stem length (the LS6 cam has a smaller base circle for increased valve lift)
Valvestem diameter	8 mm
Valve face angles	30, 46, and 60 degrees
Rocker ratio	1.7:1

Valve Lift	Intake	Exhaust
	Inch (mm)	Inch (mm)
'97-00 LS1	0.472 (11.99)	0.479 (12.17)
'01 LS6	0.525 (13.34)	0.551 (13.33)
'02-04 LS6	0.525 (14.01)	0.547 (13.91)

The Gen III V-8 valvetrain design is common for all the Gen III engine variants. This is great for hot-rodders, because LS6 valvesprings or the '02 and later LS6 hollow-stem intake and sodium-filled exhaust valves will fit in other Gen III engines that use the same size valve.

The factory camshaft is gundrilled to reduce weight and actuates hydraulic roller lifters that allow for aggressive cam lobe shapes. The rockers are investment cast with a roller fulcrum for light weight and minimal frictional losses. The valvesprings are coiled in varying diameters with oval-shaped wire, so they look like a "beehive" and are called so. These springs eliminate the need for a damper spring inside the main spring and the ovate wire helps to improve the high-rpm valve control.

The camshaft is a large diameter as compared to previous small blocks, which improves rigidity to provide increased valvetrain stability at high engine speeds.

OILING SYSTEM

The Gen III V-8 oiling system improves on the simple yet effective design of the Gen I and II small-block V-8s. The oil pump is no longer driven by a

OILING SYSTEM DETAILS

Oil pump gear dimensions	
Diameter *inch (mm)*	Thickness *inch (mm)*
3.543 (89.99)	0.421 (10.69)

Factory pressure relief setting:	60 psi at 5,000 rpm
Oil system capacity:	5.5-6.5 quarts (depending on pan)
Recommended oil:	Mobil 1 5w-30

Oil Pan Details

Vehicle	PN	Sump Location	Volume (Quarts)
Corvette	12561828	Rear	6 to 6.5
Camaro	12558762	Rear	5 to 5.5
GTO	12561541	Front	5 to 5.5
Truck/SUV	12560383	Rear	6 to 6.5

Oil Pan Components

	Pickup PN	Windage Tray PN	Dipstick Tube PN	Dipstick PN
Corvette	21558750	12558189	12556405	12562468
Camaro	12558251	12558253	12551577	12551581
GTO	12572654	12558189	12561544	12562468
Truck/SUV	12563961	12558268	12563918	12558684

shaft connected to the distributor, like on the Gen I and II. Instead, the pump is a gerotor design that slides over the snout of the crankshaft. The pressurized oil flows out of the pump body into a main galley that runs lengthwise down the driver side of the block. At the end of the main galley, the oil flows down through a fitting on the oil pan, through the oil filter, and then up a passage in the back of the block into the lifter galley passages that oils the rest of the engine.

Oil control is very important to GM as higher oil pressure ties up horsepower in pumping losses and increases oil consumption, which can lead to higher emissions. Because of this, any performance upgrades should be accompanied by increased spring pressure on the oil bleed-off spring in the oil pump and a simple port job on the oil-pump outlet to insure maximum oil flow.

INTAKE TRACT

The Gen III LS1/LS6 V-8 intake manifold is impressive for its low height, light weight, and high flowing characteristics. The intake is made with injected nylon and has a wall thickness of 3 mm. The injector bosses are located at the end of the intake manifold ports, pointing directly at the back side of the intake valve head. The air enters the intake manifold at the front through a mass airflow (MAF) sensor and throttle body. The airboxes and connecting tubes on the Corvette, Camaro, and Firebird are located just over and in front of the radiator. This was done to maximize laminar airflow into the engine and minimize engine heat from increasing the temperature of the intake air.

The higher-flowing '01 LS6 intake was standard across both LS1 and LS6 in '01 and beyond and is highly sought after for its ability to increase power output as a simple replacement of the pre-'01 intake.

The original LS1 intake was impressive, but the 2001 and later LS6 dropped-floor intake (shown being installed) has more volume, flows better, and doesn't need an EGR valve because of an improved camshaft/controller combination. The LS6 intake design became the standard car intake in 2001 on all LS1s, too.

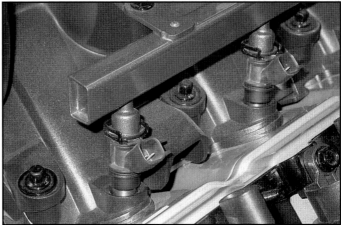

The low-profile Gen III car intake manifold takes in air from the front into an open area under ports that loop over the top of the open area and into the cylinder head intake ports. The intake and cylinder heads were designed from the beginning for a fuel-injection system. To take full advantage of the setup, the fuel injectors are located at the end of the intake manifold ports to shoot the fuel at the backside of the intake valve (shown).

INLET DETAILS

Intake Manifold	GM Part Number	
	Casting	Assembly
LS1 ('97-'01)		
F-car	12560688 (97-00)	122561855 (97-00)
(LS6 intake)	12561184 (01-04)	12568465 (01-04)
Y-car	12556333 (97-00)	12561856 (97-00)
(LS6 intake)	12561182/4 (01-04)	12561179 (01-04)
Truck (4.8/5.3/6.0 L)	25321788 (99-01)	17099289 (4.8/5.3)
	12573944 (02)	
	12574009 (03)	

	Diameter (mm)
MAF	
LS1	75
LS6	80
LQ4/LQ9	80
Throttle Body	
LS1	75
LS6	80
LQ4/LQ9	80
Airbox type	
Corvette	straight in front of intake
Camaro	straight in front of intake
Firebird	straight in front of intake
Full-size trucks, SUVs, and mid-size SUVs	passenger side of fender

Ed Koerner, Gen III Chief Engineer, said, "The Gen III needed the electronic throttle control (ETC) so cars like the 400-hp Z06 Corvette wouldn't be undriveable (due to traction control being able to minimize tire spin). I wanted something my wife, son, and anyone else could drive safely." The ETC first came on the '97 Corvette, then on the selected trucks. The F-cars and most trucks have cable-actuated throttle bodies.

The truck manifold has similar low-RPM, low-valve-lift flow capability of the LS1 intakes, but doesn't have the same flow figures at high rpm. This makes sense, as trucks are used more in the low- to mid-RPM range. The truck intake is approximately 3.11 inches taller overall than the LS1 intake and the throttle body mounting point is about 3 inches taller than the LS1. This is to clear the radiator/fan clutch/fan on the trucks.

ELECTRONIC FUEL INJECTION

The fuel-injection system on the Gen III LS1 V-8 is sequential. This means each injector opens to release fuel into the intake port just before the intake valve opens. Previous GM fuel injection systems were batch fire or bank fire. With a batch-fire system on a V-8, all the injectors open eight times for each complete firing sequence of the engine. On a bank-fire system, the injectors on each bank of the engine open four times per complete firing sequence of the engine. On a sequential fuel-injection system, each injector opens only

once per complete firing sequence. The sequential system doesn't offer a big leap in power output, but it reduces emissions while improving low-RPM driveability and fuel mileage.

The calibration to operate the sequential fuel-injection system is exponentially more complex than a batch- or bank-fire system. It uses many sensors on the engine and vehicle to make its decisions. The Gen III V-8 is equipped with very advanced crank and cam position sensors, so the PCM can quickly determine which cylinder is the next to fire to initiate the fuel injection. The crank sensor is located next to the starter on the passenger side of the engine and the camshaft sensor is located at the back of the engine above the lifter valley. The crank has a 24x reluctor wheel on it, which means it is a wheel with 24 steps on it so the computer can read where the crank is in its rotation very quickly. The cam sensor has a 2x shape into it, which allows the computer to quickly determine where the crank is in the four-stroke cycle of the number-1 cylinder and fire the

appropriate injector and spark plug to run the engine.

Simply put, GM has invested in engineering resources, along with tool-

The oiling system was changed to simplify the manufacturing and assembly process of the engine. This is a cutaway of the gerotor-style oil pump and balance pulley, which slides over the crank snout and is driven by the spinning crank. A gerotor pump has excellent qualities for a production engine: compact, simple, efficient, and durable. Note the combination crank balancer/pulley and its efficient design.

ing and piece costs to create a sequential fuel-injection system that produces impressive emissions, fuel consumption, and driveability results.

INJECTION DETAILS

LS1

Fuel injector static flow rate: 3.6 g/s
Cranking fuel pressure: 53 to 63 psi
Electronically controlled engine redline: 6,000 rpm
Fuel shutoff: 6,200 rpm

ELECTRONIC CONTROLS AND CALIBRATION

Probably the most complex system on the Gen III V-8 is the powertrain control module (PCM). So far there have been two PCMs for the Gen III. The first is called the "cast" controller, a name given for its external case. The PCM used now is called the P59 within GM, and has computing capability on par with a home computer. The reason for the increased computing power is the size and complexity of the calibrations. The Gen III V-8 calibration started as a 375-kb file that had jumped to a little over 1 Mb in size in 2003. The calibration is made up of many, many tables that cross-reference each other, so it's very complex. The reason for the cross referencing is to take advantage of the ability of the sequential fuel-injection system to alter fuel and timing many times per degree of crank rotation based on input from various sensors located on the engine.

One of the great advantages of the electronic PCM is its ability to diagnose issues through data interpretation. Late-model performance enthusiasts often talk about codes or DTCs they are experiencing. This is a reference to the on-board Diagnostic Trouble Codes (DTCs) that are issued by the PCM when it deduces a problem exists. The driver will be notified through the SES, or Service Engine Soon, light on the dashboard being illuminated, that an issue exists. To see which of the 2000 or so DTC codes is causing the SES to come on, a Tech II or other style of scan tool is plugged into the data link connector under the dashboard of the vehicle.

SAMPLE OF COMMON DIAGNOSTIC TROUBLE CODES (DTC)
(From a '98 LS1 PCM)

Code	Description
Fuel System (displayed in voltage)	
P0171	Fuel Trim System Lean, Bank 1
P0172	Fuel Trim System Rich, Bank 1
P0173	Fuel Trim System Lean, Bank 2
P0174	Fuel Trim System Rich, Bank 2
Coolant (displayed in degrees)	
P0117	Low Voltage (engine coolant is hot)
P0118	High Voltage (engine coolant is cold)
P0125	Excessive Time to Closed Loop
P1114	Intermittent Low Voltage
P1115	Intermittent High Voltage
MAF (displayed in grams/second)	
P0101	Mass Airflow System Performance
P0102	Sensor Circuit Low Frequency
P0103	Sensor Circuit High Frequency
Intake Air Temperature (IAT) Sensor (displays air temp in degrees)	
P0112	IAT Sensor Circuit Low Voltage (air is hot)
P0113	IAT Sensor Circuit High Voltage (air is cold)
P1111	IAT Sensor Circuit Intermittent High Voltage
P1112	IAT Sensor Circuit Intermittent Low Voltage
Manifold Air Pressure (MAP) sensor (displays voltage)	
P0107	MAP Sensor Circuit Low Voltage (manifold pressure is low or high vacuum)
P0108	MAP Sensor Circuit High Voltage (manifold pressure is high or low vacuum)
Throttle Position Sensor (displays voltage)	
P0121	TP Sensor Circuit Insufficient Activity
P0122	TP Sensor Circuit Low Voltage (closed throttle, ex. 0.6 at idle)
P0123	TP Sensor Circuit High Voltage (open throttle, ex. 4.0 at WOT)
P1121	TP Sensor Circuit Intermittent High Voltage
P1122	TP Sensor Circuit Intermittent Low Voltage
Knock Sensors (KS) (displays voltage)	
P0325	Internal PCM Malfunction to KS system
P0327	Front KS Circuit malfunctioning
P0332	Rear KS Circuit malfunctioning
Crank Sensor (displays pulses from sensor)	
P0300	PCM Detects a Misfire
P0335	Crankshaft Position Sensor out of range
P0336	Crankshaft Position Sensor out of range
Camshaft Sensor (displays voltage)	
P0341	Camshaft Position Sensor Circuit Performance
P0342	Camshaft Position Sensor Circuit Low Voltage
P0343	Camshaft Position Sensor Circuit High Voltage
Idle Speed (displayed in rpm)	
P0506	Idle Speed Low
P0507	Idle Speed High
Ignition (displays input signals)	
P0351	Ignition Control (what many call the coils) malfunction through one of the eight controls

To purchase service manuals with a full array of DTCs and other info, call 800-551-4123.

IGNITION

The coil-near-plug design of the Gen III V-8 ignition is often called a coil-on-plug design, but that's inaccurate. On the early prototype Gen IIIs, the coils were located on the plugs, but they didn't survive early testing schedules due to the exhaust manifold temperature. To cure this, the coils were moved to the valve covers with a shorty spark plug wire connecting them to the plug.

The PCM tells the coils when to fire the spark plug. The PCM references the 24x crank trigger and the single-phase (2x) cam location sensor located in the lifter valley to know where the crank is in its 360-degree rotation and what cylinders are on the compression stroke.

This *angle*-based system is different from most aftermarket controllers, which work in 90-degree *time* increments. The reason the angle-based system is used is because it is more accurate

The coil-near-plug ignition system is driven by the PCM reading signals from the crank and cam triggers, the knock sensors, and a few other assorted sensors to determine when to fire each coil. There are three different-appearing coils on Gen IIIs, but GM engineers tell us that's only because different suppliers build them — they are supposedly identical in their operation. Most high-performance engine builders say to use the truck coils, since they seem to work best in high-RPM, high-combustion-ratio engines.

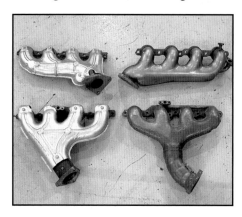

The first-year exhaust manifolds for the LS1 (right) were made of two thin-walled stampings welded together to maximize the temperature going to the catalytic converters. In 1998, GM introduced a cast-iron manifold (left) that still met the startup emissions requirements but reduced the piece cost.

External Clues: 5.7-Liter Gen III Corvette (Y-car) and Camaro/Firebird (F-car)

		F-car	Y-car
Engine Block			
	Cast aluminum	LS1	LS1
	"Windows" cast in main webs		Some '01-02, Most post-'01 LS1/LS6
Intake Manifold			
	Low-profile intake manifold with front-mounted throttle body, stepped floor w/room for steam tubes to run underneath and designed for EGR system		LS1, '97-'01
	Stepped floor w/ room for steam tubes to run underneath and not equipped for EGR in intake		LS1, '97-'01
	Dropped, flat intake floor, steam tubes don't fit and designed to accept EGR system		LS1, '01-'03
	Dropped, flat intake floor, steam tubes don't fit and not equipped to handle EGR		LS6, '01-'04
Throttle Body			
	Cable actuated	'98-'03	
	Electronically-actuated		'97-'04
Valve-cover hold-down bolt location			
	Located on perimeter of cover		'97-'98
	Centered on valve cover	'98-'03	'98-'04
Oil Pan			
	"Batwing" sump design		
	One piece		'97
	Two piece		'98-'04
	Rear-sump design	'98-'03	
Exhaust Manifolds			
	Double wall, welded stamped sheetmetal, center/rear dump	'98	'97-98
	Rear dump, cast iron		'99-03
	Swept back, cast iron	'99-03	
Crankshaft Pulley			
	Centered Over Hub	'98-'03	'97-'04

than the time system, which makes it possible to reduce the emissions and increase driveability.

As a tip, the truck coils have slightly larger heat sinks, so many Gen III enthusiasts believe they are often chosen for high-horsepower, high-heat applications.

IGNITION DETAILS

Coil Energy Storage: 60 mJ
(almost double the LT4 ignition)
Spark plug wire length: 219 mm
Spark Plug: AC 41-931
Spark Plug Gap: 1.5 mm

EXHAUST

The exhaust manifolds on the early Gen IIIs were pretty high-tech to get the catalytic converters up to temperature very quickly to minimize startup emissions. The '97 to '00 car-based Gen III LS1 V-8 engines used fabricated exhaust manifolds that were made of 0.8-mm-thick 309 stainless steel inside a 1.8-mm 409 stainless steel wall, with a 3-mm air gap between the two walls. This obviously expensive exhaust manifold was replaced with a conventional cast iron manifold in the 2001 model year vehicles once the engine management was improved enough at startup to keep the emissions in line.

Beyond the manifolds, the factory exhaust systems all have O2 sensors before and after the catalytic converters. The onboard diagnostics (OBD-II) software in the PCM is always comparing the inputs from the O2 sensors, expecting to see improved emissions on the downstream sensor. This way, when the converter starts to loose its effectiveness, the SES light comes on. This light will also come on if the catalytic converter is removed.

An interesting point to note is the placement of the O2 sensors. Almost always, the sensors will be pointing down into the tube to minimize the chances of moisture collecting on the sensor. Also, a standard of O2 placement on tube headers is to have it 8 inches down from the merge-point of the

primaries into the collector — when you have 2-inch primaries.

There are four oxygen sensors in the exhaust system, while there are only two catalytic converters. The exhaust tubes are stainless steel for the Corvette/Camaro/Firebird from 1997 to 2003, except for the Z06 exhaust, which is made of titanium for lighter weight.

All Gen III engines use an integral harmonic balancer/pulley assembly to save weight and simplify the front drive system. The 'Vette balancer/pulley has a hub that looks centered over the pulley to save space in front of the engine, though it's actually offset by 0.600 inch. The Camaro/Firebird balancer/pulley has a one-inch drop in it. The truck unit has a considerable amount of drop, approximately 2.25 inches, in the hub as it has space to spare. The balancer/pulley is just pressed onto the crank hub — there is no key locking it in place on the crank.

FRONT ACCESSORY DRIVE

The Corvette and Camaro/Firebird front accessory drives are mostly common, while the truck Gen III V-8 engines use multiple front drives. The difference is the placement of the A/C compressor, power-steering pump, and alternator.

The F- and Y-body car systems use a single belt to run everything but the A/C compressor, which runs on its own belt to minimize NVH.

The LS1 F-car front drive will work in most hot-rod applications. Here are the part numbers to assemble a complete front engine accessory drive (FEAD).

FEAD INFO

Part No.	Description
Alternator	
10464402	Alternator
11515767	Bolt
12556915	Brace
11509666	Bolt
12564401	Pulley
11516366	Bolt
12563327	Bolt
11516360	Bracket
A/C Compressor Mount	
11515771	Bolt
11515771	Bolt (4 required)
12556677	Bolt (2 required)
1137028	Bracket
A/C Compressor Drive	
11098341	A/C Compressor
12557335	Bolt (2 required)
12569529	Idler Pulley
12560345	Belt
26040467	Tensioner
Power Steering Pump	
26068934	Cap, Power Steering Pump
12569527	Reservoir
12559885	Belt
14078895	Pulley
14058896	Bolt (2 required)
12555693	Brace
11515757	Bolt (2 required)
26068936	Pump
12557331	Bracket
11515767	Bolt (3 required)
Pulley Tensioner	
12560345	Tensioner
11516356	Bolt (2 required)

The LS Gen IIIs

The LS Gen III V-8 weighs 430 lbs fully dressed and is actually a little more compact than the exterior dimensions of the first-generation small-block Chevy.

5.7-Liter LS1/LS6

Eng. Codes	Years /Vehicles	Factory Power
LS1	97-02 Camaro	345 hp/350 ft-lbs
	97 Corvette	345 hp/350 ft-lbs
	98-present Corvette	350 hp/375 ft-lbs
LS6	01 Z06 Corvette	385 hp/385 ft-lbs
	02-04 Z06 Corvette	405 hp/400 ft-lbs
	04 Cadillac CTS-V	400 hp/400 ft-lbs

The LS1 is the engine code most automotive enthusiasts think of and use to refer to the Gen III engine architecture. This is understandable as the LS1 was the first engine released based on the Gen III V-8 and it has gotten a lot of notoriety for its ability to make power while exhibiting excellent street manners and durability. Other than the block material and some of the internal dimensions, most of the Gen III V-8 engines have the same component design and external appearance.

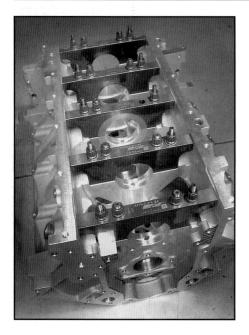

When GM went racing with the C5 Corvette, the GM Racing division developed a 7.0-liter aluminum block to use as a foundation to build a powerful, durable engine. The resulting piece, called the C5R block (PN 12480030), is a high-buck piece with Siamesed, 4-1/8-inch bores and the ability to handle over 1000 hp. It's available from any GM dealer through GM's performance storefront: GM Performance Parts.

THE LQ4 AND LQ9 6.0-LITER GEN IIIs

The Gen III engine many automotive enthusiasts desire is the 6.0-liter and it comes in two varieties. The GM names for these two engines are the LQ4 and LQ9. The LQ9 engine is the high-performance 345-hp version that was first available only in the Cadillac Escalade. The 300-hp LQ4 is available in many full-size Chevy and GMC trucks and SUVs. The external differences between these two engines are slight, but you can still determine the type of engine using available internal and external clues.

Short Block: cast-iron block, cast crank, powdered metal rods, cast aluminum pistons (with coated thrust faces and domes)

Top End: aluminum heads with 72-cc combustion chambers, plastic truck intake, iron heads on '99-'00 LQ4, aluminum on both engines after '01

Fuel/Air/Spark: crank-trigger activated, sequentially fired EFI system, coil-near-plug ignition system

Valvetrain: hollow factory camshaft, hydraulic roller lifters, investment-cast rockers with a roller fulcrum, and beehive valvesprings

They weigh approximately 500 lbs fully dressed and are the same external size as the LS1/LS6. The 6.0-liter LQ4 and LQ9 block part numbers are 12568950, 12568951, and 12568952.

BUILDING A HIGH-PERFORMANCE 6.0-LITER GEN III V-8

You can put together a high-performance 6.0-liter with some simple GM parts swapping. The high-performance LS6 cylinder heads and intake will bolt directly to a 6.0-liter engine (the stock LQ4/LQ9 intake is not designed for high-RPM power, but will make excellent power in the low to midrange powerband).

In fact, bolting the LS6 cylinder heads on a 300-hp LQ4 is similar to the recently released LS2 6.0-liter performance engine in the '04 C6 Corvette. There is an issue with compression ratio on the LQ9 swap, as it already has a 10:1 compression ratio with the 72-cc LQ cylinder heads. Bolting on the LS6 heads, with their 64-cc chambers, will require a piston change to get back to a streetable 10:1 compression.

As a note, the blocks are the same on the 300- and 345-hp 6.0-liter engines, as are many other internal components.

The pistons are beefier on the LQ engines than on the LS1 engines, and they are easy to differentiate from each

6.0-LITER TRUCK ENGINES			
Eng. Codes	Years Offered	Vehicles	Factory Power
LQ4	'99-present	Chevrolet and GMC light-duty trucks/SUVs	started at 300 hp/335 ft-lb now at 325 hp/370 ft-lb
LQ9	'02-present	Escalade and Escalade EXT	345 hp/380 ft-lb
	'04	Silverado SS	

other. The pistons on early LQ9s have a top and side coating, while later versions of the LQ4 pistons are coated.

If you plan on making over 400 hp with the LQ9 or LQ4, it is recommended the engine be disassembled and the bores be honed with a surface plate on the engine before adding some aftermarket forged pistons. This process will ensure bore symmetry and prepare the bore for the new pistons. Many engine builders feel the factory cast-aluminum eutectic pistons are not as robust to high cylinder pressure situations where detonation and preignition have a higher tendency to occur, which is why it is recommended they be replaced with forged aluminum pistons.

QUALITY BUILT ENGINES

In 2002, the Gen III engine architecture was rated as one of the most trouble-free V-8 truck engines in North America, according to J. D. Power survey results. The 5.3-liter truck engine achieved a rating of 9 problems per 100 engines ("problems per hundred" is a J.D. Power standard abbreviated as pph) in 2002. This is impressive, as the Toyota 4.7-liter V-8 had 13 pph and the Ford 5.4-liter V-8 had a 17-pph rating.

In 2002 alone, the GM engine assembly plants produced over 1 million Gen III V-8 engines. On average, it takes about 4.5 hours to build a Gen III engine in the assembly plant, and many plants can build up to 4,000 engines per day. If you do the math, you'll find that millions of Gen III V-8 engines have been produced since 1997.

The GM engine assembly plants use sophisticated systems to eliminate assembly problems and then document these solutions so the other Gen III assembly plants benefit from that one plant's work to improve quality. One way they do this is by testing a part to make sure they are within specification every 60 or so pieces. Every engine is run through a cold-test that checks over 400 parameters in systems like the ignition, oiling, valvetrain, and more to insure the highest quality. There are even high-tech machines that check every threaded hole in the engine block before it enters the assembly plant to ensure the threads are good.

External Clues: 4.8/5.3/6.0-Liter Gen III Truck/SUV Engine

EXTERNAL CLUES FOR THE 4.8-LITER GEN III:

Engine block
    cast iron

Crankshaft pulley
    2.250-inch offset hub (vs. 0.600-inch drop in 'Vette, 1-inch drop in F-car)

Intake manifold
    high rise, front entrance
    came with either cable-actuated throttle body or
    electronic throttle control (ETC) depending on vehicle

EXTERNAL CLUES FOR THE 5.3-LITER GEN III V-8:

Engine block
    cast iron   full-size trucks and SUVs
    aluminum   Trailblazer/Envoy/Bravada/Rainier/SSR

Cylinder heads
    aluminum   all
    for PNs, see chart on cylinder head details on page 28

Intake manifold
    high-rise, 75-mm inside diameter cable-actuated throttle body

EXTERNAL CLUES FOR THE 6.0-LITER GEN III:

Engine block
    cast iron
    6.0-liter cast into side of block on back side of block

Cylinder heads
    aluminum   all, except ...
    cast iron   '99 and '00 LQ4 6.0-liter

Ignition
    Larger coils offset mounted on valve covers

Intake manifold
    high-rise, 80-mm inside diameter cable-actuated throttle body except ETC on all-wheel-drive Escalade and Silverado SS LQ9-equipped vehicles

---

Where Gen III V-8 Engines are Built

General Motors has Gen III V-8 engines assembled in plants located in St. Catherines, Ontario, Romulus, Michigan, and Silao, Mexico. The breakdown of what plants build what engines is as follows:

Romulus, Michigan
- 4.8, 5.3, 6.0-liter and high-output 6.0-liter
- '97-'99 5.7-liter LS1

St. Catherines, Ontario
- 5.7-liter LS1 and 5.7-liter LS6 ('99 and later LS1/LS6)

Silao, Mexico
- 5.3 L (built in a 2:1 ratio to all other Gen III engines)

LS Engine Rebuilding

Some variation of the LS Gen III engine has powered the Corvette since 1997, and the Camaro/Firebird from 1998 to 2003. Each year, about 40,000 Corvettes and over 70,000 Camaro/Firebirds were sold, so there are a lot of LS Gen IIIs out there for hot-rodding.

The only problem with the aluminum block Gen III LS1 V-8 as far as hot-rodders are concerned is that it's not intended to be rebuilt multiple times. GM used centrifugally cast iron liners that are very dense and thin, so they can only be machined 0.010 inch. This leaves a minimal bore thickness for the engine to be sufficiently overbored without being sleeved.

Also, the main bearing caps have an interference fit into the engine block receiving surfaces. This interference fit is used to lock the main caps in place without using dowel pins. Eventually, to maintain this lock, either dowels will need to be installed for use with an aftermarket steel cap and/or the receiving area will need to be re-machined.

Both of these issues are being addressed by aftermarket automotive enthusiast businesses. A cylinder liner company, Darton, is now making sleeves to take the stock blocks up to 7.0-liters and billet-steel main caps are already available. So, this problem isn't a deal breaker, but it does affect how the Gen III LS V-8 is rebuilt.

This last issue was a big one in engine manufacturing for years, but with this new machinery, cross-threading problems have been minimized. This has allowed engine plants like Romulus Assembly, located just outside Detroit, to go from 125 problems per million (ppm) to 0. This technology was quickly integrated into the plants in St. Catherines, Canada, and Silao, Mexico. In general, 99.98 percent of Romulus' engines exit the assembly plant free of problems.

The result of this problem-solving innovation has been high productivity and excellent quality from all the assembly plants, and awards in highly prestigious benchmarks like the Harbour Report — which awarded the Romulus Engine plant the "most productive V-8 Plant in North America" in 2002.

VEHICLE AND GEN III V-8 FACTORY COMBOS

If you have a vehicle with a Gen III V-8 and aren't sure what the engine variant is, this chart should make it easier to determine what peak power level engine is with the vehicle.

Transmission:

LS1: 4L60E 4-speed automatic
T56 6-speed manual

LM/LR/LQ: 4L60E 4-speed automatic
5-speed manual

1997
Corvette
5.7-liter LS1
345 hp at 5,600 rpm
350 ft-lb of torque at 4,400 rpm

1998
Corvette
5.7-liter LS1
345 hp at 5,600 rpm
350 ft-lb at 4,400 rpm

Camaro/Firebird
5.7-liter LS1
305 hp at 5,200 rpm
335 ft-lb at 4,000 rpm

Camaro SS/Firebird Ram Air
5.7-liter LS1
320 hp at 5,200 rpm
345 ft-lb at 4,400 rpm

1999

Corvette
5.7-liter LS1
345 hp at 5,600 rpm
350 ft-lb at 4,400 rpm

Camaro/Firebird
5.7-liter LS1
305 hp at 5,200 rpm
335 ft-lb at 4,000 rpm

Camaro SS/Firebird Ram Air
5.7-liter LS1
320 hp at 5,200 rpm
345 ft-lb at 4,400 rpm

Chevy/GMC truck/SUV
4.8-liter LR4
255 hp at 5,200 rpm
285 ft-lb at 4000 rpm
5.3-liter LM7
265 hp at 5,200 rpm
320 ft-lb at 4,000 rpm
6.0-liter LQ4
300 hp at 4,800 rpm
355 ft-lb at 4,000 rpm

2000
Corvette
5.7-liter LS1
345 hp at 5,600 rpm
350 ft-lb at 4,400 rpm

Camaro/Firebird
5.7-liter LS1
305 hp at 5,200 rpm
335 ft-lb at 4,000 rpm

Camaro SS/Firebird Ram Air
5.7-liter LS1
320 hp at 5,200 rpm
345 ft-lb at 4,400 rpm

Chevy/GMC truck/SUV
4.8-liter LR4
P/U
270 hp at 5,200 rpm
285 ft-lb at 4,000 rpm
SUV
275 hp at 5,200 rpm
290 ft-lb at 4,000 rpm
5.3-liter LM7
285 hp at 5,200 rpm
325 ft-lb at 4,000 rpm
6.0-liter LQ4
300 hp at 4,800 rpm
355 ft-lb at 4,000 rpm

2001

Corvette
5.7-liter LS1
    350 hp at 5,600 rpm
    375 ft-lb at 4,400 rpm
5.7-liter LS6
    385 hp at 6,000 rpm
    385 ft-lb at 4,800 rpm
    Note: Redline reset to 6,600 rpm
    (vs. original LS1 6,000 rpm)

Camaro/Firebird
5.7-liter LS1
    310 hp at 5,200 rpm
    340 ft-lb at 4,000 rpm

Camaro SS/Firebird Ram Air
5.7-liter LS1
    325 hp at 5,200 rpm
    350 ft-lb at 4,000 rpm

Chevy/GMC truck/SUV
4.8-liter LR4
P/U
    270 hp at 5,200 rpm
    285 ft-lb at 4,000 rpm
SUV
    275 hp at 5,200 rpm
    290 ft-lb at 4,000 rpm
5.3-liter LM7
    285 hp at 5,200 rpm
    325 ft-lb at 4,000 rpm
6.0-liter LQ4
    300 hp at 5,200 rpm
    360 ft-lb at 4,000 rpm
    Note: First year for aluminum
    heads on LQ4

2002

Corvette
5.7-liter LS1
    350 hp at 5,600 rpm
    375 ft-lb at 4,400 rpm
5.7-liter LS6
    405 hp at 6,000 rpm
    400 ft-lb at 4,800 rpm

Camaro/Firebird
5.7-liter LS1
    310 hp at 5,200 rpm
    340 ft-lb at 4,000 rpm

Camaro SS/Firebird Ram Air
5.7-liter LS1
    325 hp at 5,200 rpm
    350 ft-lb at 4,000 rpm

Chevy/GMC truck/SUV
4.8-liter LR4
P/U
    270 hp at 5,200 rpm
    285 ft-lb at 4,000 rpm
SUV
    275 hp at 5,200 rpm
    290 ft-lb at 4,000
5.3-liter LM7 rpm
    285 hp at 5,200 rpm
    325 ft-lb at 4,000 rpm
6.0-liter LQ4
    325 hp at 4,800 rpm
    370 ft-lb at 4,000 rpm

Cadillac SUV/EXT
6.0-liter LQ9
    345 hp at 5,200 rpm
    380 ft-lb at 4,000 rpm

2003

Corvette
5.7-liter LS1
    350 hp at 5,200 rpm
    375 ft-lb at 4,000 rpm

5.7-liter LS6
    405 hp at 6,000 rpm
    400 ft-lb at 4,800 rpm

Camaro/Firebird
Discontinued

Chevy/GMC truck/SUV
4.8-liter LR4
P/U
    270 hp at 5,200 rpm
    285 ft-lb at 4,000 rpm
SUV
    275 hp at 5,200 rpm
    290 ft-lb at 4,000 rpm
5.3-liter LM7
    285 hp at 5,200 rpm
    325 ft-lb at 4,000 rpm
5.3-liter LM4
    290 hp at 5,200 rpm
    330 ft-lb at 4,000 rpm
6.0-liter LQ4
    325 hp at 4,800 rpm
    370 ft-lb at 4,000 rpm

Cadillac SUV/EXT
6.0-liter LQ9
    345 hp at 5,200 rpm
    380 ft-lb at 4,000 rpm

2004

Corvette
5.7-liter LS1
    350 hp at 5,200 rpm
    375 ft-lb at 4,000 rpm

5.7-liter LS6
    405 hp at 6,000 rpm
    400 ft-lb at 4,800 rpm

CTS-V
5.7-liter LS6
    400 hp at 6,000 rpm
    400 ft-lb at 4,800 rpm

GTO
5.7-liter LS1
    345 hp at 5,200 rpm
    345 ft-lb at 4,000 rpm

SSR
5.3-liter LM4 (aluminum block)
    300 hp at 5,200 rpm
    331 ft-lb at 4,000 rpm

Chevy/GMC truck/SUV
4.8-liter LR4
P/U
    270 hp at 5,200 rpm
    285 ft-lb at 4,000 rpm
SUV
    285 hp at 5,600 rpm
    290 ft-lb at 4,000 rpm
5.3-liter LM7/L59
    295 hp at 5,200 rpm
    330 ft-lb at 4,000 rpm
6.0-liter LQ4
P/U
    325 hp at 4,400 rpm
    370 ft-lb at 4,000 rpm
SUV
    325 hp at 5,000 rpm
    365 ft-lb at 4,000 rpm

Trailblazer/Envoy
5.3-liter LM4
    290 hp at 5,200 rpm
    325 ft-lb at 4,000 rpm

Cadillac SUV/EXT and Silverado SS
6.0-liter LQ9
    345 hp at 5,200 rpm
    380 ft-lb at 4,000 rpm

PRODUCTION PARTS FOR PERFORMANCE

If there is one great aspect to General Motor's small-block V-8s, it is that they have a lot in common. This is especially true with the Gen III V-8. It means parts off the Z06 Corvette engine, the LS6, fit on 6.0-liter Gen III truck engines without a lot of work. So, this is the chapter that will tell you what other quality original equipment manufacturer (OEM) parts can be swapped to different vehicles and provide real performance. Not only does this chapter show you what factory performance parts to use and how to swap them onto your base engine for a power increase, there are many tips and tricks on how to massage a little more performance out of these same pieces for little or no money.

The components discussed here are arranged in order from the foundation components up to the small details. They include engine blocks, cylinder heads, intakes, camshafts, throttle bodies, MAF sensors, and airboxes. The airbox, MAF, and throttle body are all simple remove and replace (R and R) jobs on many vehicle platforms. The block, cylinder heads, camshaft, and intake require the engine to be removed from the vehicle. But, as you'll see elsewhere in this book, the Gen III V-8 engine is by far the easiest to disassemble and reassemble of any GM V-8 engine ever built — once you know the tricks and tips, which you'll get here.

ENGINE BLOCKS

The Gen III V-8 engine blocks are pretty much externally the same between the aluminum and iron versions. If you are looking to minimize the weight of your vehicle, there is no better way than using the aluminum LS1 or LS6 engine blocks as the foundation for your engine. These blocks are superior to any other small-block alu-

The 1997–99 Gen III block (bottom) had these machined holes for a rear oil passage. This makes them less desirable than the 1999 and later blocks (top) with their open oil passage area.

minum block on the market — period. An advantage to running the iron block would be that it can be bored to 4.000 inch (vs. the 3.893-inch LS1 engine bore) to achieve a 6.0-liter engine.

If you are going to use the aluminum engine block for a big-hp engine, many builders suggest that you avoid the '97-'98 LS1 engine block. These blocks have a shallow oil transfer galley at the rear of the block that limits equal flow of oil to the main lifter oil galleys. This galley is visible only with the rear cover removed. If the engine is complete, the valve covers on it will have

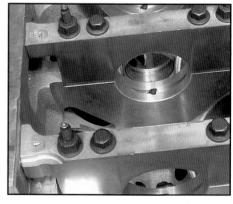

If you're trying to figure out what Gen III V-8 aluminum block to use, look for the ones with these cast-in-place slots in the base of the crank mains. These deal with high-rpm crankcase pressures better than previous block designs.

The 6.0-liter cast-iron engine blocks have incredible capability, as they are identical in design to the aluminum blocks, but the cast iron has more strength. Unfortunately, the added strength will cost you about 65 pounds. Notice the oiling found on early LS1s above and to the right of the camshaft bore. Notice the hole-style oiling found on early LS1s above and to the right of the camshaft bore.

Look for the part numbers on the back of the blocks as a way to figure out what block you're looking at. This is an early cast-iron 6.0-liter block.

their bolts around the perimeter of the cover (post-1998 Gen III V-8 valve covers were a center-bolt design).

If the engine is torn down, the way to tell which block you are looking at is by removing the rear block cover. The '97-'98 blocks have just two holes above the cam bore, while the '99 and later blocks have a large cavity cast into the block above the cam bore.

Overall, the less-desirable early aluminum blocks look the same as the later blocks, but the casting number, located on top of the driver side of the bellhousing mount area on the '97-'98 blocks, is 12550592. The more desirable blocks have casting number 12561168.

The LS1 engine block will serve the majority of performance applications, but the LS6 aluminum engine blocks (casting number 12561168) that came in

the Z06 are the most desirable blocks for hot-rod engines because they are designed to handle high-RPM, big-hp situations. For the most part, they are identical to '01 and later LS1 blocks. Pre '01 blocks have a hole machined through the main webs to improve bay-to-bay crankcase breathing. The hole cures the bay-to-bay oil-vapor pumping issues, but the cast-in ports found in the '01 and later blocks are an improvement on that fix, so they are that much more desirable.

If you are building a big horsepower engine, the cast-iron version of the Gen III V-8 has been shown to easily handle over 800 hp. Most enthusiasts use the 6.0-liter block and the stock 3.622-inch crank, because this is an inexpensive combination good for making power.

The expensive choice for blocks would be to order a C5R aluminum block from GM Performance Parts. They are very expensive (over $6,000), but if you want to build a 4.125-inch bore, 7.0-liter engine, this is the only block available to do it with.

Tip: If you are going to use the high-performance C5R engine block as the foundation for your engine, make sure to grind out any leftover casting sand and sharp burrs. These racing-intent engines usually have a fair amount of rough edges as shipped (the assumption is that a race shop will know to prep them in this fashion, but you may not…).

CRANKS

The same 3.622-inch crank is used in the LS1 and LS6 engine, so there is no reason to be swapping them. The crank is cast, but it has rolled fillets, which means the side edges of the bearing journals are compressed into a soft radius to minimize stress risers in that area. This crank has unusual strength for a cast piece and

GM Part Numbers

There is an interesting point about GM part numbers (PN). The GM part-number superceding process doesn't involve alphanumeric additions to the base eight-digit PN (like some other car makers use). Instead, GM creates an entirely new random eight-digit PN for the next version of a part. The new PN is usually needed to signify the release of an improved version of the part — usually from ongoing development. As a result, it's sometimes hard to follow the next sequence of PNs

released from outside of GM, so these numbers are correct to the best of our knowledge.

Also, it's common for the number cast into many GM components to not be the same as the GM part number the component is sold under. This is because bare castings get a new part number if they are machined. As a rule, the part numbers are correct at the present, though part numbers may change at any time.

The factory cast cranks are extremely capable and common throughout the car Gen III line (left). The truck cranks (right) have a different rear seal surface width.

has a lightening hole drilled through it to improve bay-to-bay breathing and reduce rotating weight. If more cubic inches are desired or if you plan to make more than 550 hp, going to an aftermarket forged crank is a viable option.

The truck Gen IIIs use a variety of cranks, the main difference being the width of the rear main seal surface. The 4.8-liter crank has 3.270-inch stroke, while all the other Gen III truck engines use the standard 3.622-inch crank. If the Gen III V-8 engine is from a 2500 or Heavy-Duty truck, it will most likely have a wider seal pad on the crank. The car and truck seal surface diameters are common, but the heavy-duty trucks have a thicker seal surface. Making things more confusing with the truck vs. car Gen III V-8 crank issue is that in the last few years, many of the truck engines were redesigned to come with the standard, narrow "car" seal pad.

In general, the car crank is considered more desirable because it is lighter.

Tip: Be aware that the 2001 and later Gen III V-8s cranks run a tighter tolerance based on improvements in GM production capability.

RODS

You can use the stock connecting rods if you're building an engine that will make 550 hp or less. If you do plan on using factory connecting rods, the way to go is with the LS1/LS6 rods for car engines.

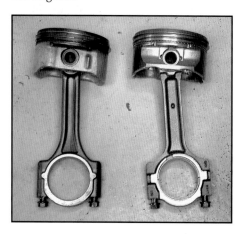

The car and truck powdered-metal rods can handle over 500 hp with little more than the addition of aftermarket rod bolts.

The LS1 and LS6 use the same powdered-metal, cracked-cap rod, which uses a pressed-in piston pin. All of the Gen III V-8 factory rods are 6.096 inches in length and use 8-mm rod bolts.

There are a few versions of factory rod bolts that feature improvements that GM engineers have made over the years. Essentially, avoid the '97-'98 rod bolts, but the bolts used from '99 and beyond have been known to handle over 450 hp without issue. ARP and a few other fastener manufacturers make good replacement bolts for the stock rods and they're good insurance — so it's recommended that you install aftermarket rod bolts no matter what power you're going to make.

PISTONS

There is a difference in the material of the pistons used in the LS1 and LS6. Both are lightweight, flat top eutectic cast aluminum pieces with pressed on pins that can handle being in a 500+ hp Gen III engine. The original LS1 pistons are made by Mahle using an aluminum/silicon alloy called M124. LS6 pistons are made of M142, which has a higher content of copper and nickel than M124. M142 is stronger and exhibits reduced expansion at high temperatures than M124. This helped the Gen III team use tighter bore clearances to minimize oil consumption and piston noise while maximizing durability. Later pistons are also coated to minimize piston scuffing due to tighter tolerances.

Often, in a performance engine the stock pistons are replaced with aftermarket forged pistons, which is not a bad idea. The forgings are more forgiving to abuse, meaning they don't fracture like the cast pistons under detonation, instead usually 'lifting' a ring land, melting through the piston dome, or cracking off a small section of the ring land. A cast piston is more apt to simply self-destruct in similar situations.

In the truck Gen IIIs, the LQ9 piston is the best choice. These pistons are also eutectic cast aluminum, but they have a low-friction coating on the thrust faces of the pistons and floating piston pins. These pistons are not recommend-

The hole in the factory aluminum piston in the number 4 hole on this LS6 engine is from the overuse of a 150-hp nitrous kit. Considering the temperature and detonation abuse it experienced, as shown by the speckled aluminum on the face of the piston, it's impressive that the piston just burned instead of completely shattering.

ed in engines making more than 450 hp, as they are heavier than the LS1 pistons.

VALVES

The lightweight, hollow-stem valves are one of the cooler components in the 2002 and beyond LS6 engines. The hollow section of the exhaust valvestem is packed with a sodium-potassium mixture to help it remain cool, while the intake valvestem is left hollow. These valves are racing-inspired components that will improve throttle response, valve control, and heat management on any Gen III. More than that though, they have GM part numbers, which means they've made it through OEM durability testing and validation.

Tip: The '02 and later LS6 valves are 0.6 mm longer than the previous LS1/LS6 valves to compensate for changes to the '02 LS6 camshaft base circle. If you make the swap to these valves, use them with properly matched components — or for simplicity, just use the '02 LS6 cam and valvesprings with them. The lifters, pushrods, rockers, retainers, and locks are all common.

Valves	PN
'02 LS6 Intake	12565311
'02 LS6 Exhaust	12565312

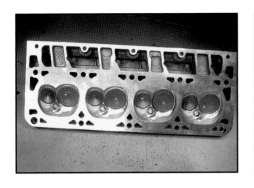

VALVESPRING DETAILS

Engine	Year	Valvespring Color
LS1	'97-'04	natural (PN 12553696)
LS6/385 hp	'01	blue (PN 12565117)
LS6/405 hp	'02-'04	yellow (PN 12565313)
LQ4	'99-'04	natural (PN 12553696)
LQ9	'02-'04	natural (common to LS1 – PN 12553696)

The factory valvetrain works great up to about 6,500 rpm, but if you plan on revving the engine higher than that, plan on adding larger valvesprings and stronger aftermarket pushrods. The valve spacing was standardized early in the engine process for the smallest bore diamter of 96 mm, so all agree there is power to be found in increasing the intake-valve size and interlocking the valveseats.

VALVESPRINGS

GM has literally spent millions developing valvesprings that can handle the valve motion of the Gen III V-8 with a minimum of drama. The Gen III valvesprings are one of the best compromises in pushrod engine technology. They are light and compact, yet perform similarly or better than a multi-coil performance valvespring. The "ovate" spring wire and "beehive" design are key to achieving this performance. Depending on your camshaft specs, the LS6 (PN 12565313) and ASA (American

The "beehive" LS6 ovate-wire valvesprings are impressive. Comp Cams and other aftermarket companies also make high-performance valvesprings of this design that will handle over 0.600 inches of lift.

Speed Association) valvesprings will meet just about any street requirements.

As with all GM components, the development didn't stop the day the Gen III showed up in 1997. To identify valvesprings, they are painted, tinted, and/or have a stripe painted on the length of the spring. Check out the chart above.

An added benefit is if you are using factory valves and valvesprings, the need to shim the valvesprings is greatly reduced. This is important as the valve uses the steel base washer to shed heat, and the more shims, the harder it is to shed the heat into the aluminum head.

CAMSHAFTS

By far, the best improvement you can make on your Gen III V-8 is to install a performance camshaft. For cost reasons, many of the early Gen IIIs had a common camshaft that didn't optimize power, but was used because it simplified the assembly process and reduced cost. In 2001, GM began to proliferate camshafts for the various engines to show power increases.

Probably the most popular camshaft for any Gen III V-8 is the '02 LS6 cam. It is truly an impressive piece and should be — GM engine development engineers utilize supercomputer modeling systems to get an engine combination close and then dyno test multiple cams at fractionally different parameters to isolate which is the best for a specific package. The LS6 cam is a result of that type of development and is a superior product that makes power in just about any Gen III engine combination that it is installed.

If you are looking for a little more aggressive camshaft, the ASA or "hot" cams offered by GM Performance Parts take the lessons learned from the build-

ing of hot-rod engines and the ASA circle-track racing engine and offer them to you through GM Performance Parts.

One of the cool aspects of the Gen III V-8 is the cam can be changed without pulling the entire engine apart. Simply pull the valve covers, loosen the rockers, remove the pushrods, and pull the front drive. Spin the cam one revolution to seat the lifters in the lifter trays, and the cam can be slid out. Lube up the new cam with engine oil, slide it in, and reassemble the engine.

Tip: When swapping a camshaft, always check the valvetrain geometry by putting the lobe at 50 percent lift and visually inspecting whether the rocker tip is in the middle of the valvestem. Also, at max lift the rocker tip should not be off

The factory plastic lifter retainers will drain more oil if you drill 1/2-inch holes on their lower face. This helps to manage the oil better in the engine. The more desirable lifters are '01 and later fully encapsulated versions (left). The early versions have some durability issues in high-hp applications.

the tip of the valve. Use different length pushrods to correct valvetrain misalignment. This is especially important when swapping in cams with different base circles — like the '02 and later LS6 cams.

There's some real power to be had in the way of a cam swap, because GM used common camshafts to simplify the build process of their engines.

Tip: Whenever installing a more aggressive camshaft, it's recommended that the stock pushrods be replaced with more robust aftermarket pushrods. The stock pushrods are optimized for light weight and have a tendency to flex and sometimes break in hot-rod applications.

Tip: On Gen III 6.0-liter LQ4-powered trucks, sliding in the '02 LS6 cam while bolting on the small chamber LS6 heads will net about 400 hp. The higher compression of the engine is bled off by the longer duration of the LS6 cam at low-rpm but pumps up the high-rpmhorsepower. You will need to run Premium fuel, though. The calibration will need to be altered to give the engine the appropriate fuel ratio, spark advance, and transmission line pressure adjustments to handle the newfound power.

As you can see from the cam chart on this page, as Gen III production continued, GM used more aggressive camshafts for increased power production. If you have an older Gen III engine, upgrading to a later cam is an easy way to find "hidden" power.

GEN III CAMSHAFT BUILD SHEET

GM cams	PN	Duration (degrees at 0.050 Inch) intake/exh.	Valve Lift (inch) (intake/exh.)	Lobe Centerline (degrees)
Corvette				
LS1				
'97-'98	12554710	199/207	0.472/0.479	117
'98-'99	12560964	199/207	0.472/0.479	117
'00	12560968	198/209	0.500/0.500	115.5
'01-'03	12561721	198/207	0.467/0.479	116
LS6				
'01, 385 hp	12560950	204/211	0.525/0.525	116
'02-'04, 405 hp	12565308	204/218	0.555/0.551	117.5
Camaro/Firebird				
'98	12557812	198/209	0.500/0.500	119.5
'99-'00	12560965	198/209	0.500/0.500	119.5
'01-'02	12561721	196/207	0.467/0.479	116
Trucks/SUV Vortec				
LR4 & LM7				
'99	12560966	191/190	0.457/0.466	115.5
'00-04	12560967	191/190	0.457/0.466	114
('03-'04 LM7 used 12560967 cam)				
LQ4				
'99-'00	12560967	191/190	0.457/0.466	114
'01-'04	12561721	196/207	0.467/0.479	116
LQ9				
'02-'03	12561721	196/207	0.467/0.479	116
GM Performance Parts				
Hot	12480033	219/228	0.525/0.525	112
ASA	12480110	226/236	0.525/0.525	110

CYLINDER HEADS

The Gen III V-8 heads have small, internal changes throughout the portfolio that make substantial differences in their performance, but they're essentially common. In general, the LS6 and LQ4/LQ9 cylinder heads are what everyone desires if they are building a performance engine (see page 28 for a rundown of all the details on the Gen III V-8 cylinder-head portfolio).

While all performance Gen III V-8 heads are cast aluminum with identical valve guide spacing (there were some iron Gen III V-8 heads made for the ear-

The LS1 (left) and LS6 (right) heads look similar if you don't know what you're looking for — the next few pages will show you the details.

The LS1 chambers (right) are slightly larger than the LS6 chambers (left), but the shaping is more important to the engineers. They were able to get some better mixture motion in the LS6 chambers for additional power production.

ly truck engines that are not thought of as performance pieces), there are differences to justify the desires of performance enthusiasts.

The LS6 was developed for the Z06 Corvette, and the aluminum LQ4/LQ9 heads are a derivative of the LS6 heads — same ports, but 8-cc bigger chamber. If you are building a naturally aspirated (NA) engine, the LS6 heads are the best choice. If you're building a boosted engine, the LQ4/LQ9 head is desirable because of the larger chamber.

As far as performance modifications, the valve spacing limits the valve sizes that can be packaged in the chambers. The biggest valve package that will fit without moving the guides seems to be 2.05/1.60-inch valves, though the valve seats will need to be interlocked, which we're told increases power.

These heads are available with CNC machined intake and exhaust ports, which is really the way to go. GM spent a considerable amount of money to develop CNC ported LS6 heads because they thought CNC'd heads would be required to make 400+ horsepower. When they weren't, these heads were applied to the Corvette racing program. These are available from GM Performance Parts. These heads do not have machining in the chamber area, due to the rules in the series they were created for, but they flow better than many fully CNC'd heads. Some aftermarket companies use the LM7 5.3-liter cylinder heads as a starting point, then CNC machine the intake and exhaust ports and combustion chamber. The reason they start with the 5.3 head is it is cast with a smaller combustion chamber (61 cc) than the LS6 and LQ9 heads, so they can machine the chambers without making them too big.

If you want to do some port cleanup work, here's a tip. Don't grind on the intake ports near the valve, but blend the ports to match up with the ports in the intake.

Many of the road racers look for the LS6 heads with these triangles under the exhaust port between the head-bolt bosses on the side of the cylinder heads. Many racers claim these are good for a 6-to-10-hp lift over the heads that otherwise look identical. The horsepower improvement are due to casting-core differences between sand casting (left) and semi-permament mold (SPM) casting (right), but we aren't able to see any differences.

Tip: The Corvette road racers and other "in-the-know" Gen III performance enthusiasts are always looking for the Gen III heads that have what they call the 'triangle' casting marks on the exhaust port side of the cylinder head as they have shown the ability to make more power than the heads that don't have these marks on them.

These marks are left by the semi-permanent-mold (SPM) casting process used by two of the three cylinder head casting facilities creating heads for GM. Apparently, in random testing the sand cast heads have been about 5 to 7 hp down from the SPM heads. The SPM

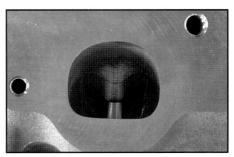

The "D"-shaped exhaust ports are a dead giveaway that you're looking at an LS6 head. The pre-LS6 LS1 heads have oval-shaped exhaust ports. LS1 heads from 2001 and later were common to the LS6 (a positive to the GM method of commonality in the assembly plants). Notice the head on the left are sand cast and the one the right has the markings of being an SPM head — the more desireable piece.

The LS1 and LS6 intake ports look similar, but the LS6 has slightly larger ports for improved flow. This photo is of one of GMPP's CNC'd LS6 performance heads.

heads have shown practically no variation in power production.

FASTENERS

The factory torque-to-yield cylinder head fasteners will handle over 500 hp, but you cannot reuse them. They are one-shot players only! These fasteners are very consistent and inexpensive, considering the job they do. But when GM says to only use them once, they aren't kidding. One torque sequence, then throw them away.

The single-use head bolts now come in a kit with a single part number, which makes sense because you can't reuse these bolts once they are removed (i.e., you'll need a full set every time you take off the heads).

Failing to blow out the blind bolt holes with compressed air to remove any liquid before you torque the bolts can lead to a worthless cracked block like this one.

As a purchasing tip, buy the cylinder-head fasteners for all '97-03 Gen IIIs in a kit (PN 12498545) that has enough fasteners to do both cylinder heads. The '04 block uses all the same length head bolts that need to be purchased in a kit.

Tip: This is important! Make sure you blow out all fastener holes with compressed air before installing fasteners. Many of the tapped holes in the Gen III block are "blind," which means they are closed off at the bottom. Any oil or other incompressible fluid at the bottom of the hole could cause the engine block to crack when the fastener is torqued down. The engine block *will be junk* if fluid does cause a crack! So, avoid this big problem by blowing out all bolt holes.

INTAKE MANIFOLD

Since the Gen III V-8 intake manifold is made of nylon and has a wall thickness of only 3 mm, there is little to be done with the internal shape of the ports. The LS6 intake that came out in '01 is *the* piece to use, as it will flow enough air for 650 hp and beyond. The LS6-style intake became the standard intake on all LS1 engines in 2002, but it's still called the LS6 intake.

The visual way to tell whether you are looking at an LS6 intake is to look for the flat, low-slung floor. The LS1 intake floor has more clearance between the bottom of the intake and valley plate cover on the engine. The LS1 intake floor also has a double swoop in it where it is deeper at the center.

The LS1 (left) and LS6 (right) intake manifolds look similar if you don't know what to look for. The shape of the floor is what gives the LS6 intake away.

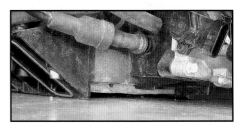

If the intake is mounted on an engine, the best way to determine whether you are looking at an LS6-style intake is by looking between the valley plate and the bottom of the intake. The intake with the "wing"-shaped floor on the top is an LS1 intake, the intake with the flat floor on the bottom is an LS6 intake. As a tip, all 2001 and later LS-engines came with the LS6-style intake.

Otherwise, the LS1 and LS6 intakes look almost exactly alike. There is a rumor this intake was raced in Corvette racing the season before it came out on the production Corvette and went undetected because it looked almost exactly like the LS1 intake. Hmmmmm.

If you don't have any height restrictions and don't have a problem with the visually challenged look of it, the truck intake is a cost effective way to make streetable power. We have been advised that it works in NA engines making over 400 hp below 5,500 rpm,

LS1 ENGINE INTAKE MANIFOLD VISUAL IDENTIFICATION CLUES	
Description	**Visual Inspection**
'97–'01 LS1	non-flat floor of intake, steam tubes running underneath
'01 and later LS6	flat floor, no steam tubes running underneath
Post '02 LS1	flat floor, no steam tubes running underneath

or with a turbo making 700+ hp. The truck intake is a common part from the 4.8-liter to the 6.0-liter, so there are plenty of them out there.

Tip: Some road racers have been using the pre-LS6 steam tubes underneath the LS6 intake to improve cooling in cylinder number 7 (they previously had detonation problems in that hole). While the steam tubes weren't used on factory LS6s, they will fit under the intake by slightly grinding down some of the stiffening ribs on the bottom side

Another way to identify the LS6-type intake (right) is by looking underneath it. The LS6 intake has a flat floor, while the LS1 style intake has a lot of shape, with a single hump down the length of the intake. Also, the LS6-and-later intakes have the square ribbing between their intake ports, while the early intakes have "x" ribbing.

of the intake. Some racers just install the steam tube component and, during rebuilds, find some small indentations where the ribs come in contact with it.

Tip: The 2001 LS6 fuel injectors have higher flow, and to simplify the manufacturing process, the 2001 LS1s received these same injectors, also.

COILS

There are three versions of coils used on the Gen III V-8 that are distinguishable by their external shape or their usage. There are two truck coils many hot-rodders describe by their external appearance — they are called the "round" and "triangle" coils. The LS1-engine coils are more rectangular in shape with the spark plug wire connector at the bottom of the coil. The triangle truck coil looks similar to the LS1 coils but the spark plug wire connector is in the midsection of the coil. We're told by GM engineers that the differences are merely external, as a result of the three different coil suppliers.

The factory coils have about a 60 mJ spark, which can knock you on your can if you get the full blast — so these coils are good for big power. In fact, the stock coils have been known to handle over 1000-hp turbo applications with no problem. They've gotten a bum rap from the blower and turbo crowd as

many claim the coils struggle to handle high-RPM, big-number power. Actually, the problem is not the coils, but with the spark dwell timing.

On boosted engines, the dwell needs to be lengthened at higher RPM but kept near stock levels at low RPM to avoid overheating the coils. Changing the dwell in the production calibration is not easily done, but there are some uplevel and newer aftermarket controllers, like the Big Stuff III system, that will allow spark dwell changes vs. RPM. It can be tough to follow GMs PN scheme, so finding coils using the visual method works best in this case.

COIL VISUAL DESCRIPTIONS

Coil	Visual Description
Car	Rectangular, bottom spark plug wire plug
Truck	Round, spark plug wire connects at bottom of coilRectangular with triangle-shaped side-post plug at mid-section of coil for spark plug wire

OIL PANS

Depending on what vehicle you are installing the Gen III V-8 in, GM has an oil pan for you. If you are installing into

By the time the LS6 came out, the GM Engineers improved the calibration of the engines and eliminated the AIR system inlet into the intake manifold. Because of this, hot-rodders can delete this system when upgrading to the LS6 intake. Use GM PN 12558346 to plug the hole in the exhaust.

The three styles of coils that come on Gen III V8s from the factory are shown here. The LS1/LS6 coil is on the right, and the two styles of truck coils are shown in the middle and on the left. Many engine builders believe the round truck coils perform better in high-horsepower applications than the other two coils.

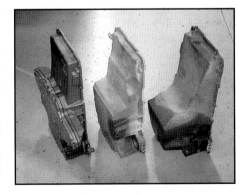

The Corvette batwing oil pan (left) looks much different than the Camaro/Firebird F-body oil pan (middle) and full size truck/SUV oil pan (right). The F-body pan gets the most hot-rod usage by far because of its shallow front section, 5.25-inch deep rear-sump design (flange to bottom), and availability.

These two Corvette oil pans are identical except the one on the right is a two-piece design, while the pan on the left is the early one-piece pan. Use the two-piece pan as it's easier to clean and check oil pick-up height.

a vehicle that came with a Gen III engine, there really isn't any need to swap to a different pan. For instance, the Z06 LS6 engine runs the same oil pan and oil scraper as the Corvette LS1. The same can be said for the LQ9; it uses the same oil pan as the lower-hp LQ4 and smaller 4.8- and 5.3-liter engines.

The Corvette pan is an extremely shallow rear-sump design often described as the "batwing" pan. As with all Gen III oil pans, it's cast aluminum and comes with a factory installed oil scraper tray attached to the main bearing cap bolts. But the 'Vette pans were originally made as a one-piece design, and then refined into a two-piece design. The two-piece pan is more desirable, because it's easier to clean, check the pickup height, and install.

The Camaro and Firebird (F-body) oil pans are a rear-sump design also, but they don't have the kick outs of the batwing Corvette pan. The F-car pans also have a shortened oil scraper because the front of the pan gets too shallow to fit the scraper all the way to the front, as it does on the 'Vette and truck oil pans.

The truck oil pans are rear sumps, but the sump is three inches deeper than the sumps on the car oil pans. This is good for powerful engines, as it is more oil to lubricate and cool, and also provides room to get the oil away from the spinning crank. These pans are sometimes used in hot-rod applications where hood height is not an issue, but usually the F-car pan is selected.

The pans are a structural member of the powertrain, so the transmission mounts to the oil pan and the engine block — delivering forces to both. This was done for improved NVH. We're told you can use an aftermarket oil pan that doesn't have these holes if you really want to. But for those that want to save some money and want a quieter, smoother-riding vehicle, it's good to know the factory oil pan has an enormous amount of development in it.

If you are using the Gen III in a custom application, you might have to trim the sump or crossmember to create clearance. There are some aftermarket pans now coming onto the market, but in general, most hot-rodders are cutting off portions of the stock pans and welding on plate aluminum to fit various applications.

THROTTLE BODY

The factory throttle bodies come either as a cable actuated or as an electronic throttle control (ETC) unit. Both come in multiple inside diameters. For performance applications, usually bigger is better, and smoothing the inside surfaces will show a small increase in performance. Going too big with a cable actuated throttle body can make low-RPM driveability challenging, which is part of the reason GM went with the ETC — it allows minute application adjustments based on wheel speed,

The early 75-mm LS1 throttle body (left) can be easily replaced with an 80-mm LQ4 throttle body (right) for an increase in airflow. The LS6 throttle bodies are 80 mm, but they are electronic throttle control (ETC), whereas the LQ4 throttle body is cable actuated.

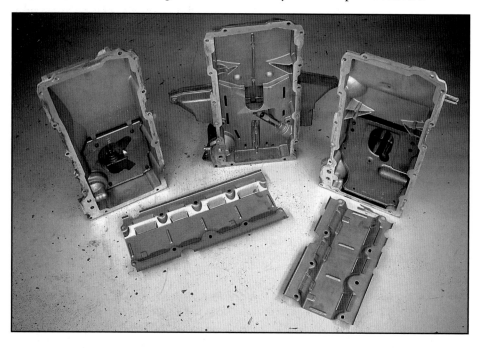

All of the GM oil pans come with crank windage trays and oil containment trays to minimize oil wrapping around the crank and sloshing in the crankcase. Notice the F-body pan is shortened as it won't fit in the shallow front section of the pan, but the 'Vette and truck windage trays are full length.

Transmissions

The Gen III V-8 has been bolted to a multitude of transmissions, which is a blessing for performance enthusiasts. Gen III cars have had 6-speed manuals and electronically controlled 4-speed automatics behind them, so you have those as choices. The 6-speed will bolt in and operates with a factory hydraulic clutch and trans-mounted shifter. The automatic is called the 4L60E inside GM — the 4 is for 4-speed, the L for longitudinal, the 60 is for the series of transmission, and the E is to show that it's electronically controlled. GM has created an improved automatic that has been used in the Corvette, Escalade, and GTO called the 4L65E. If you don't want to swap complete transmissions, the 4L65E guts will fit in the 4L60E case.

engine speed, and other vehicle sensor inputs to make 405-hp vehicles easy to drive.

The most desirable throttle bodies are the 85-mm inside diameter units that came on the Corvettes and trucks. Some of the truck units were cable actuated, so they are sought out for F-cars and hot rods. The 'Vette has had the 85-mm ETC since it first came with the Gen III

in 1997. Various trucks (mostly all-wheel-drive trucks) have come with the 85-mm ETC.

Tip: For improved throttle-body airflow, smooth the transition surfaces up to and after the throttle blade with a 180-grit tootsie roll on a grinder. Be careful not to touch the area where the throttle blade seats in the body, as this will negatively affect idle quality.

Mass Airflow (MAF) Sensors

The simple modification that should be performed to every MAF sensor is the gentle removal of the inside screen. GM obviously saw the light on this after a few years, because the '02 Z06 Corvette doesn't have a screen in the MAF.

Changing to a larger or higher-flowing MAF sensor will often change how the computer interprets the amount of air entering the engine; so check this before installing a new MAF.

Tip: To remove the screen, carefully negotiate two fingers through the back of the MAF (past the wires that read the airflow) until they are touching the screen. Push on the screen until it pops out. Some truck MAFs come with a lock ring that needs to be removed before the screen can be pushed out. You are done with this performance improvement.

Tip: The screen is used to straighten

To remove the screen, carefully push from behind to unseat it from the MAF body. Be very careful not to touch the sensor components, as they are very fragile and easily damaged.

the air coming into it to minimize false airflow readings, but on the LS vehicles with straight intakes, the screen isn't required. On trucks where the air tube approaches the MAF from the side, the screen should be left in unless you're willing to make calibration changes to account for the new readings.

GM is slowly going to all ETC, like the LQ9 (left) and LS6 (right) shown, so hopefully it won't be long before an aftermarket company comes up with an ETC throttle pedal for hot rods. This way, automotive enthusiasts won't have to keep retrofitting back to cable throttle bodies (like the LQ4 unit shown in the middle).

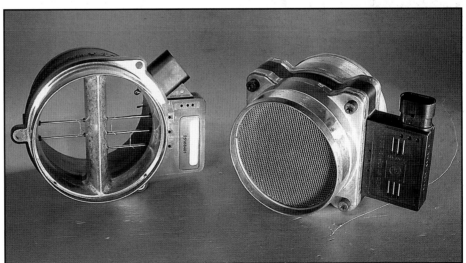

The MAF on the left is from an LS6 engine, while the MAF on the right is from a 5.3-liter truck engine. The LS6 MAF screen is easily popped out, but the truck MAF has a lock ring that must be removed before the screen can be popped out.

AIRBOX

While there are many aftermarket airboxes available, GM has continued to search for power in the factory airboxes over the years. Just swapping a Z06/LS6 intake box and air tube in the place of an LS1 engine airbox won't cause a huge increase in power by itself. But it does allow more air to pass into the engine, which becomes increasingly necessary as other performance parts produce more power with the same engine.

Some of the possible airbox upgrade ideas are listed below:

Corvette: Z06 LS6 5.7-liter Airbox on LS1
Camaro: SS airbox and hood from SLP on LS1 Camaro
Firebird: Ram Air airbox and hood from SLP Firebird
Trucks: Escalade LQ9 6.0-liter airbox in V-8 truck

Tip: A simple way to increase the breathing capability of the stock airbox is to cut holes in the bottom of the airbox. GM doesn't put these holes in because the vehicles have a tough time passing the water ingestion testing (simulating situations like the Alabama porch washer and flooded road crossing) and allow more intake noise to be heard. Since you aren't going to be fording a river anytime soon (are you?) and the intake noise soothes your hot rod soul, opening up the stock airbox with some holes is all good.

The SS and Ram Air hoods are very effective at getting cold air into the F-body intakes. They mate up with the stock airbox and are impressive in their packaging. They are still available new from GM dealers and SLP.

Cooling Equipment

Other good components to swap into a high-performance vehicle are radiators, electric cooling fans, power-steering fluid coolers, and other cooling equipment from the SS Ram Air, LS6, and Escalade. If you are making more power, you'll need to make sure the engine keeps its cool.

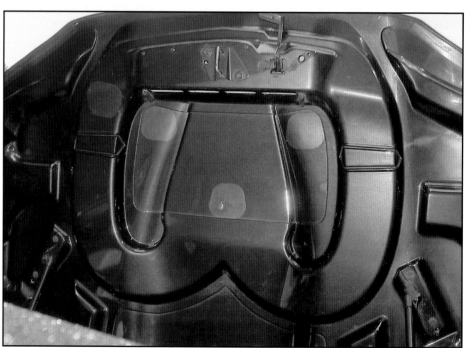

TIPS AND TRICKS TO REMOVE AND REINSTALL THE GEN III V-8

As simple as it may seem, just getting the Gen III V-8 out of a production vehicle can be frustrating if you haven't done it before. Because of this, the following chapter covers as much detail as possible with visual support to show how to remove and reinstall (R & R) a Gen III V-8 from the vehicle it was shipped in. The tips and tricks listed here are a little from the GM manuals, but mostly from the technicians doing this work every day. These techs have discovered ways to simplify the task of pulling a Gen III V-8 engine while minimizing the amount of work and the possibility of damage to the vehicle components at the same time. These steps are offered as suggestions to improve the journey of separating the engine from the vehicle. If anything, using this info will help you look like you know what the hell you're doing when your friends are around.

The R & R of a Gen III V-8 from the Camaro/Firebird (F-car) and Corvette (Y-car) is more involved than the R and R on the full-size trucks (called the 800-series internally within GM). This is because the engine should come out of the vehicle from underneath on the F- and Y-car. GM installs the engines from underneath on the cars, so that's what you need to do, too. For all of these vehicles, including the trucks, being able to put the vehicle on a lift will make the R & R job much easier.

As you can see from the 100+ images used to document each of the three different platforms, the process is thoroughly detailed here visually to make it easy for you to accomplish.

REMOVING A GEN III V-8 FROM AN F-CAR

Having the engine come out from under a Camaro and Firebird seems like a very difficult process when you haven't done it before. But after going through it, you'll see that dropping the engine out from under the car is a straightforward process that doesn't require all the finagling and finesse usually required to negotiate an engine out

Keep the System Sealed

One of the great ways to simplify the R & R of the Gen III V-8 is to keep the many "sealed" systems just that — sealed. So, on the power steering and air conditioning systems, instead of removing the pumps from the vehicle's engine bay, the pros have figured out how to unbolt them from the engine assembly and swing them out of the way, without unbolting any hoses in the engine compartment.

This avoids the hassle and cost of having to purge the air from the power steering system (a major job) and recharging the A/C system. Another reason to avoid disassembling these systems is that many techs believe these systems aren't the same after they've been taken apart in the field.

Here's what it will look like when you successfully remove the engine from an F-car — the engine sitting on a cart underneath the vehicle after a minimum of frustration and expense.

of and back into an engine bay from the top. The only major hurdle with the dropout process is that now a vehicle lift is required to perform this task instead of just an engine hoist.

The tools shown here will make the removal and reinstallation easier. The ratcheting open-end wrenches are for the fasteners in the tight areas. The radiator hook tool or angle pick is used to release the many electrical connector clips and hose clamps. A clutching cordless drill with a 3/8-inch drive will assist in removing the many smaller bolts, and the remote hose clamp depressor is a specialized tool that isn't required, but it helps out with some of the harder-to-reach hose clamps.

1. To make a long story short, the Camaro/Firebird body needs to be lifted off of the front cradle-mounted engine/transmission combo. To start the process, the vehicle needs to be put up on a four-point lift. This under-car shot shows where to place the four pickup points of the lift. Notice the aftermarket long-tube headers and performance exhaust, along with the subframe connectors and driveshaft loop – this car is fast!

2. As a rule of thumb, whenever working on a vehicle, disconnect the battery cables to prevent stray sparks or voltage from damaging the electronic equipment or starting a fire.

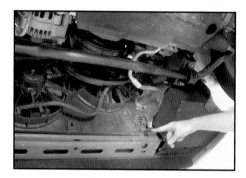

3. The coolant is the first fluid that needs to be drained from the vehicle when removing the engine. If the engine is going to be torn down once removed, now is also a good time to drain the oil. To drain the coolant, open the petcock at the bottom of the radiator on the passenger side of the vehicle (indicated by the finger in the picture). As a note, the Gen III V-8 uses a 50/50 mix of Dexcool and water.

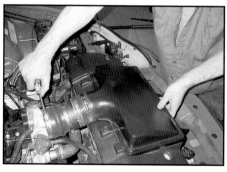

4. The next components to be removed are the air cleaner housing and mass airflow (MAF) sensor. This vehicle has an aftermarket SLP air cleaner box, but it installs in the stock fashion. To remove, unclip the airbox clamps at the front and loosen the rear-most hose clamp.

5. Next, remove the upper radiator hoses using pliers to compress the clamps and sliding them back from the radiator mounting tube. These clamps can be reused.

6. To remove the throttle cable, use the radiator hook tool to push on the locking tab through a hole in the bracket towards rear of the vehicle. With the locking tab released, slide the cable anchor up and out of the bracket.

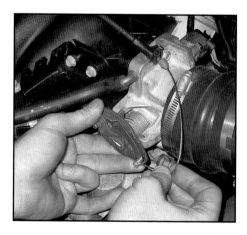

7. Unloop the throttle cable from the throttle body arm and slide the cable end out the access slot to remove it from the anchor point.

8. Removing the fuel line requires a special tool. This hand-held plastic tool works fine, but there are metal hand tools also available from tool retailers. Start by clipping the tool onto the manifold side of the fuel line.

9. Pull the fuel line removal tool toward the vehicle feed line to release the tangs holding it in place. At the same time, push the feed line toward the removal tool. Once the tool is fully seated, you can remove the feed line from the manifold fitting — but be careful, as this line will probably be under pressure. Cover the joint with a rag and release it slowly to gently bleed off pressure.

10. Simply pull the brake booster hose off the vacuum booster by hand.

11. The purge selenoid has a hose connection on it that you can remove by pinching the circular loop to release the clamp (fingers). Try to pull it while gently wiggling it to make it easier to remove. Remove the coil wiring connector first to give yourself more room to take the line apart.

12. The AIR system valve is electronically actuated, so remove its wiring connector by lifting the locking tang and pulling it off (finger). The exhaust gas recirculation (EGR) valve control also has a hose going into the control — pull it off at this time.

13. Using a 13-mm flare-nut wrench, remove these two brake lines from the ABS module. Push the lines toward the engine, as they will be dropped out of the vehicle with the engine cradle. As a tip, there are clips behind the sheetmetal shield that hold the brake lines to the frame down near the exhaust. Remove the 10-mm nut that retains the shield, and then pop the lines out of the clips.

14. Using a socket on an extension, remove the two 15-mm nuts holding the brake master cylinder on the booster, and push the master cylinder toward the engine (shown moved). This allows access to remove the two Torx 50 shock-tower nuts under the master cylinder. You should remove the rest of the shock tower bolts (13-mm hex heads) just before you lift the vehicle off the engine/front cradle/suspension assembly, but do these two bolts now.

15. Using a 7/16-inch socket, remove this bolt holding the intermediate steering shaft in place. The steering knuckle can be removed either here or at the lower point on the shaft. Removing it here is a better idea since it makes it easier to reinstall. Reinstalling it at the lower point on the shaft is also good because there are two flats on the shaft that make getting the steering back together with the steering wheel clocked in the "right" location a 50/50 proposition — you choose.

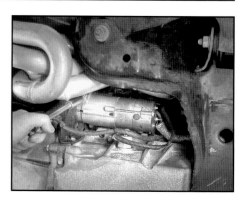

16. Here are all the plugs to unhook on the passenger side of the engine bay to remove the LS1 from an F-body: the two PCM plugs, all the smaller plugs in the foreground, and the plug on the right that is the A/C clutch WOT override. The two PCM connectors each have a 7-mm bolt to hold them in place. Use a socket to loosen them — the bolts are nested so they won't come out of the connectors. To remove the connectors, touch the vehicle to ground yourself, then carefully work the connectors out of the PCM. To remove the PCM, slide it out of its holder and carefully work it past the lower portion of the windshield and passenger-side shock tower.

18. Here's a big timesaver. There are two wire bundles that run into the interior through a grommet on the lower portion of the firewall behind the passenger-side wheelhouse. You need to disconnect these to remove the engine. GM recommends pulling apart half the interior to get to these connectors. Many hot-rodders instead remove the firewall wiring grommet and carefully pull the wiring into the engine bay. There is just enough wire to get the connectors into the engine bay, allowing you to disconnect them without touching the interior. Be careful the plugs coming from the interior don't fall back through the firewall. You can avoid this by zip-tying them to the engine-bay wiring. To reinstall, plug the wiring connectors back together, feed the wiring back into the interior, and slit the grommet to get it back into the firewall.

20. Next, you can remove the two 13-mm hex-head bolts holding the starter in place. Carefully unhook the wiring, taking note of where all the wires go, and set the starter aside.

21. The best way we've seen to remove the connector for the crankshaft position sensor is to slide a straight pick through the tang on the clip next to the engine, then pry the retaining clip open while pulling on it. Also, remove the bolt holding the ground wire on the engine and unclip the O2 sensor pigtail going to the exhaust, which isn't shown, but it's in the same area.

17. Remove the PCM mount (in hands) by taking out the two 10-mm hex-head bolts going into the shock tower sheetmetal.

19. Now, the A/C compressor bolts can be removed. Start with the top two 15-mm bolts on the A/C bracket from the top of the engine bay. The bottom two 15-mm bolts are easier to remove from under the vehicle. Then swing the A/C compressor and adjoining hoses towards the front of the vehicle and hang the pump from the radiator core support with a coat hanger or zip ties so the hoses don't have to be unhooked from the vehicle. This way, you won't have to recharge the A/C system later.

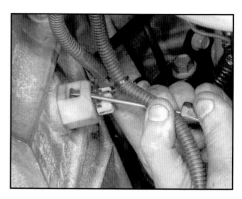

22. Lift the retention tang off the oil level sensor connector and pull it off the sensor.

25. Working from underneath the front subframe and behind the alternator, use a 13-mm flex socket on a 10-inch ratchet extension to remove the constant power wire nut (in hand) that hooks up to the back of the alternator.

23. Release the front sway bar from the chassis by removing the four 13-mm bolts holding it in place. Let the sway bar hang on the engine cradle. A good way to keep from losing the bolts is to put them back in the mounts.

27. Here are the male and female portions of the quick disconnect. You can really see how the release sleeve slides over the little retention tangs to free up the disconnect.

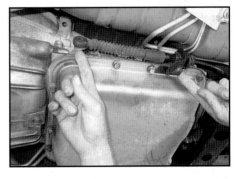

24. There are numerous ground straps tying the powertrain and vehicle together, like this one (finger pointing to it), and they all need to be disconnected before you remove the engine. Watch for them as you go through the removal process, as the ones you miss will be torn off when the lift goes up!

26. The Camaro, Firebird, and Corvette all have a hydraulic throwout bearing line equipped with a quick disconnect at the transmission (it's the copper-colored connector on the braided steel line). This can be removed by using the radiator hook tool to push in on the Teflon release sleeve and carefully pull the disconnect off the transmission.

28. On an automatic transmission vehicle, now is when you would remove the shifter cable from the transmission shift arm and its mount. This is done by prying the end off the shift arm. Then, use the radiator hook tool to pull up on the lock pin (a gray component at the top of the anchor point) in the cable housing to release the lock it has on the mount. Also, on an automatic vehicle, take off the three 15-mm torque converter bolts accessed through the opening where the starter used to be. This can be done through the small access hole in the transmission housing – but it's easier through the hole where the starter used to be.

29. The exhaust Y-pipe now needs to be disconnected and removed. This vehicle is for off-road use, so the catalytic converters have been removed. For on-road vehicles, the exhaust from the catalytic converter on the back also needs to be removed at this time.

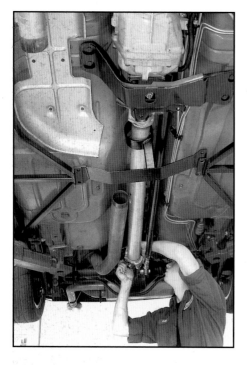

30. Now is the time to remove the driveshaft. Remove the U-joint bolt-on caps at the front of the rear end and slide the driveshaft forward slightly to release it from the pinion. If the rear end is hanging at full droop, getting enough clearance might be difficult. To get the driveshaft loose, you might need to remove the U-joint bearing caps for extra clearance. A good tip is to put the caps back on right away and use electrical tape to hold them in place while you work on the rest of the vehicle so the needle bearings don't fall out of the caps.

31. Here's one trick that will save you considerable time. GM suggests removing the trans to get the rear-end torque-arm connection loose. To avoid removing the trans separately, take out the top bolt on the trans-mounted torque-arm bracket and bend the bracket to the side so the bushing will barely clear the bracket. While this vehicle has an aftermarket torque arm, the stock piece would respond to the same process.

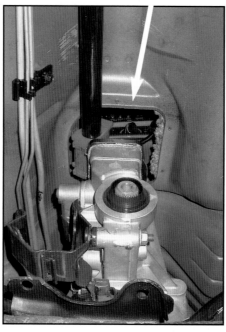

32. Using some raw manpower, work the torque arm a little towards the driver-side of the vehicle. Don't try to do it all at once. Slide the bushing past the clamp anchor on the trans a little and raise the vehicle a little. Then keep following this process until the bushing is above the trans shifter box. This should give you room to drop the engine and trans together.

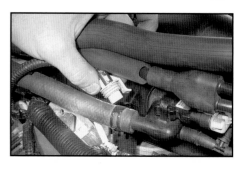

33. Disconnect the oil pressure sender at the back of the intake on top of the valley plate (in fingers). You also need to disconnect the hose plugged into the manifold pressure sender, located just below the finger in the picture.

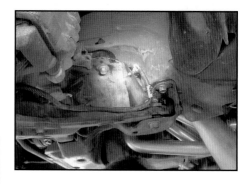

34. Next, remove the front wheel speed sensors. They're located near the rear of the lower A-arm frame mount for both front wheels. To free them up, pull up on the retaining tab and slide the wiring connectors apart.

35. If you are removing an engine from a manual transmission car, you need to remove the shifter now. This requires the boot around the shifter, which snaps in place, to be pulled off using both hands. The stock shifter is held in place by two 13-mm bolts; remove them and slide the shifter out. Aftermarket shifters will require you to remove a little more of the console to access the four 13-mm hex-head bolts that hold many of them in place.

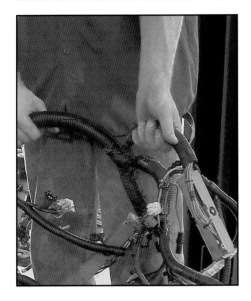

36. I recommend that you pile all the wiring up on top of the engine like this to prevent it getting hung up on something in the vehicle and getting damaged when you raise the body off of the engine.

37. Now is the time to slide the cart under the vehicle so you can set the engine cradle on it. Most shops recommend using a simple wooden utility cart, like this one, with some blocks to shim the engine cradle flat on the cart.

38. Unbolt the remaining shock-tower bolts, and swing the suspension mount down out of the wheelwells.

39. Remove the four 15-mm bolts holding the transmission crossmember in place on the vehicle. This vehicle has subframe connectors tied to the trans mount; most vehicles will not have the black tubing running underneath the vehicle like this.

41. Now the engine should be completely unbolted and unplugged from the vehicle. You are now prepared to start raising the vehicle off the engine cradle. Do this an inch or so at a time, taking plenty of time to inspect for wires, hoses and other components that are hanging up on the vehicle, or that still might need to be removed.

42. As the cradle is being separated from the vehicle, wiggle the steering arm U-joint to slide it off the steering shaft.

43. As you're separating the engine cradle and vehicle, be vigilant about making sure all of the wiring, hoses, and components are disconnected and clear from the vehicle.

40. Lower the vehicle down on the lift until the engine cradle is resting on the cart. Then remove the three 18-mm bolts from each side of the engine cradle (there is a total of six).

44. With the engine out of the vehicle, you can perform many parts substitutions. This vehicle was getting different valve-train components that required the heads to be machined, so they were pulled, and the work was performed.

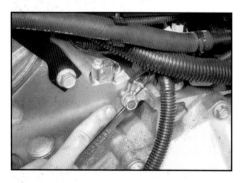

45. The wiring harness that stays with the engine and transmission has these three ground wires bundled together on this bolt at the back of the engine block. Go ahead and remove the bolt.

46. Disconnect the wiring connector hooked up to the temperature sender on the front of the driver-side cylinder head.

47. There is a small hose (finger pointing to it) that runs out from the vacuum-controlled fuel pressure regulator on the intake manifold to the HVAC system inside the vehicle. This hose needs to be disconnected before you remove the engine.

48. The next step is to disconnect the throttle position sensor (TPS) connector and the idle air control (IAC) connector on the throttle body.

49. Each of the eight wiring connectors attached to the fuel injectors needs to be removed. Just pull up on this silver clip (next to the finger on left) and remove the connector from each injector.

50. The four coils on top of each valve cover have a main connector between the two center coils. Pull the plastic lock pin out of the electrical connector (in fingers) and work the two connectors apart.

51. The best way to deal with the power steering pump is to remove it from the engine but leave it on the front subframe that was dropped out of the vehicle — that way you won't have to refill the system later. To do this, you'll have to remove the pulley to access the four 15-mm hex-head fasteners that connect the pump to its bracket. Use this puller (Snap-On, PN CJ117A) to make pulley-removal a snap; it grabs onto a lip on the pulley and pushes on the pump shaft.

52. This is the installer tool for the power steering pump pulley. As you can tell, it is completely different from the puller. It's available from Snap-On (PN CJ113B101).

53. If you plan on removing the cylinder heads from the engine, now is a good time to remove these drain plugs on both sides of the block to drain coolant out of the heads. This is done so the cylinders and more importantly, the blind head-bolt holes in the block, don't fill up with coolant when the heads are pulled. If there is any incompressible fluid — oil, water, etc. — in these bolt holes when you torque down the head bolts, you'll crack the block. This means you'll need to replace the entire engine block!

54. To reinstall the engine, just perform the steps listed here in reverse. After the engine is reinstalled, add oil and coolant. Be careful of air bubbles in the coolant system. It should take about 2.5 gallons of coolant/water mix, but this will probably need to be added a little at a time. The best way is to fill the radiator, then run the engine with the heat on full blast for a few minutes. The coolant level in the radiator should drop; then shut off the engine and add more. If the engine runs hot and doesn't take the coolant needed, it probably has a bubble at the thermostat. To fix this, open the system at the upper radiator hose (make sure the system is not under pressure), allow air to escape, and reinstall. Resume coolant filling.

55. While running the engine during the coolant fill process, check the upper radiator hose to see if it's getting hot. Also, have the heat on in the vehicle — if it blows cold after a few minutes, the system is not filling properly and probably has an air bubble near the thermostat.

REMOVING A GEN III V-8 FROM A CORVETTE

As with the removal and replacement notes on the Camaro/Firebird, the tips shown here are what the pros are doing in the field. Some of the steps shown in the F-car process are similar to those for the Corvette and will not be supported by photography here, but they will be noted so you can refer to the F-car pictures for reference.

Pulling an engine from a C5 Corvette requires the entire drivetrain to come out. Check out this photo sequence if you want to see how it's done.

1. To lower the drivetrain out of a 'Vette you need to remove the shifter inside the vehicle. Getting the interior components removed to access the shifter is shown in the sidebar on the next page.

Corvette Shifter Removal

1. To start, remove the three Torx 15 screws holding the ashtray in place (not shown). This is located just to the left of the glove-box key lock. Then, pull up on the trim bezel around the traction control and remove the two 10-mm nuts underneath the bezel (fingers pointing to holes) that help hold the console in place.

3. With the glove box nut closeouts taken out, remove the two 10-mm nuts holding the console in place. These are located where the fingers are pointing.

5. Undo the three Torx 40 bolts holding the shifter in place.

2. Gently pop up the two nut closeouts at the rear of the glove box with the radiator hook tool to access the 10-mm nuts. These distort easily, so be careful when removing them.

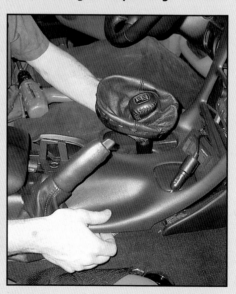

4. Now you'll be able to pop up and slide out the shifter console cover. This is done to access the fasteners holding the shifter assembly in place.

6. Wiggle the shifter mechanism off the shaft at the rear to release it, and then pull the entire assembly out of the console. Now you can lift the body off the powertrain/suspension without damaging the shifter or interior. To lock the shifter in neutral, push down on the little tang in the trans opening — this will prevent the shifter from going into the wrong position when you reinstall it. When you do reinstall the shifter, use one hand to grab the shifter shaft at the rear of the console opening and guide it onto the shifter mechanism.

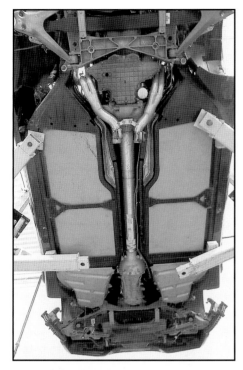

3. The first step is to remove the exhaust components that go over the rear independent suspension (see tip in next caption). Then, remove the exhaust tubes that run down inside the main spar tunnel as shown. As a tip, disconnect the O2 sensor connectors before removing the exhaust tubes.

4. To get the exhaust out from the rear suspension and subframe, remove the sway bar-to-cradle bolts to swing the sway bar down out of the way. This will allow you to snake the exhaust tubes up and over the rear suspension cradle to get them out from under the vehicle.

2. Using a four-point lift on the C5 Corvette requires some special care to avoid damaging the body. Many custom shops have built special spacers to seat into the factory lift holes, but you don't need to go to that detail if you don't plan on doing this often. You can pick up a plastic-body kit from SPX Kent Moore that does the job for you. Or just use some wood blocks on the legs of the lift for where the body swoops down against the frame. Notice the passenger side fender is loose from the body and free to swing out. Make sure this is the case before you put your Corvette on the lift.

5. Get your powered ratchet fired up because the torque tube closeout plate needs to be removed at this time. There are a ton of 8-mm bolts holding this heavy sheetmetal plate in place, and they all need to be removed to get the torque tube out.

6. Remove the brake lines from their clips in the tunnel, as these lines will come down with the powertrain assembly.

7. Remove the quick-disconnect hose fitting for the clutch hydraulic throwout bearing following the process shown in the Camaro/Firebird removal process.

8. A good way to simplify the reassembly is to place the removed components on roll-around racks, like the one shown on the left.

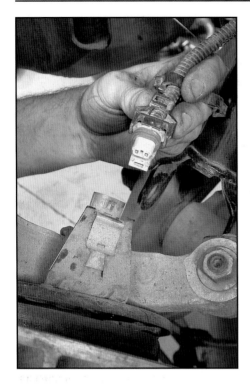

9. Back at the rear of the Corvette, disconnect the anti-lock braking system (ABS) wiring connectors at the calipers and remove the two 22-mm bolts holding the rear disc brake calipers on their mounting brackets.

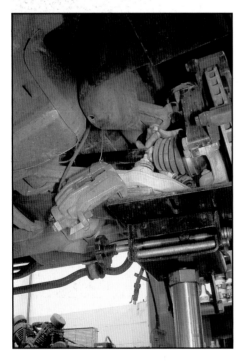

10. Hang the calipers on the lower control arms with some welding wire, zip ties, or a wire hanger, so the brake lines aren't supporting the calipers.

11. Next, you need to disassemble the rear suspension. To start, support the spindle upright with a stand. Then, remove the 24-mm nut/bolt combo holding the lower shock absorber on the lower control arm. Loosen the 18-mm nut holding the upper ball joint in place, rattle the tapered ball-joint shaft with an air hammer or take a 3-lb hammer and smack the upper control arm with slight spring pressure on it to release the ball joint. Then, get out a massive 1-5/16-inch socket and loosen the halfshaft nut in the upright.

12. With all these components loosened from the rear spindle uprights, begin to lower the upright to release the upper ball joint. As you're lowering it, pull the parking brake cable off its caliper. Follow this process to disassemble the remaining uprights (obviously, the half shafts won't exist on the front uprights, but otherwise, the component sets are common).

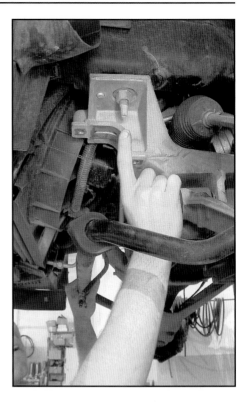

13. Under the front of the vehicle, remove the four 13-mm front sway bar bolts holding the sway bar on the frame. Swing the bar down out of the way.

14. Back in the engine bay, remove the brake lines from the ABS control module that sits in front of the engine.

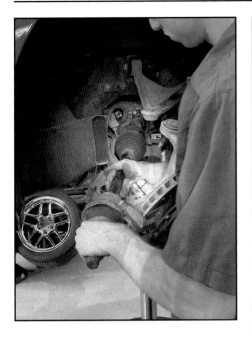

15. Now, remove the half shafts at the rear of the vehicle. Often, this will require rattling the halfshaft through the upright with a pneumatic air hammer. This is done to loosen the splined mating point between the halfshaft and drive hub. Slide the halfshafts towards the center section to get them out of the drive hubs. It's a good idea to mark the shafts as left or right to avoid mixing them up when you reassemble the vehicle.

17. Disconnect the main wiring connector at the rear of the vehicle. This wiring is for the lighting and other electrical components at the rear of the vehicle.

19. If you haven't already, remove the lower 7-mm hex-head bolts holding the passenger-side fender on the vehicle. You need to remove the fender bolts so you can tilt up the fender and remove the PCM and its wiring (in this photo, the PCM has already been removed). There is one 7-mm hex-head bolt inside the fender that most novices break off because they think they've already removed them all. As you can see, it's located up inside the fenderwell and can only be seen after you've removed the inner fenderwell (detailed in the next photo). Now you know!

16. Remove the 10-mm hex-head bolt holding the multiple ground wires on the frame on the driver-side of the frame rail at the rear of the vehicle.

18. Before you drop the suspension/drivetrain combo out of the vehicle, undo the steering shaft knuckle. The finger is pointing to the rack-and-pinion shaft with the knuckle slid off it.

20. The next component you need to remove is the passenger-side inner splash panel. Remove the 7-mm bolts that hold it in place. This gives you access to the A/C bolts and hidden fender bolt — refer to the Camaro/Firebird A/C removal process to see what this looks like.

21. Next, loosen the three nested 7-mm bolts to disconnect the vehicle wiring harness connector from the PCM. Go back into the engine bay and remove the fuel lines and vacuum hoses off the top of the engine. This is identical to the Camaro/Firebird process, so refer to those pictures to see how it's done. Now, remove the PCM from its bracket.

22. Remove the alternator, the three ground wires bundled on one 10-mm bolt on the passenger side of the vehicle, and the radiator hoses at the radiator. All of these processes are the same as that performed on the Camaro/Firebird, so refer to those photos for more detail on these steps. Also, disconnect the heater core hoses from the passenger side of the engine (this is also the same as the Camaro/Firebird process).

23. Remove the battery (you did disconnect the battery cables from the vehicle before starting to remove the engine, right?) by loosening the one hold-down bolt at the base of the battery. Then, remove the plastic battery tray after loosening the four 13-mm hex-head bolts in the middle of the plastic tray.

24. The fuse panel is then removed by taking the two 10-mm nuts off; there's one on top, and one hidden near the bottom of the panel. Remove the one 13-mm nut holding the positive cable ends on the stud and remove the panel.

25. Pull up on the plastic push rivets (similar to those used on the truck radiator shroud discussed later in this chapter) to remove the engine bay closeout panel. Unplug the vacuum line that runs into the engine harness and unplug the six connectors behind the passenger-side wheelhouse.

26. Uncoil the wiring harness and set the wires on top of the engine. This LS6 had a broken valvespring and a dropped valve, which is why the valve covers are off the engine.

27. Disconnect the AIR tube that runs from the exhaust manifolds to the air pump (in hand). Also, unbolt the A/C compressor and hang it on the frame. Finally, disconnect the brake booster hose (refer to the Camaro/Firebird photos).

28. The drivetrain needs to rest on a special stand or series of blocks. There are many companies that have built custom stands to hold a drivetrain/suspension system that's been dropped out of a Corvette. Wheel to Wheel Powertrain offers plans on how to build your own version of one of these stands.

29. Now, set the powertrain down onto the support, remove the four 21-mm nuts in front and rear (eight total) to free the powertrain from the frame, and slowly bump the body up to separate the two systems. Watch for leftover stuff like ground wires, brake lines, wiring, etc.! As you can see, the number of components lowered out of the 'Vette body is really impressive. Basically, if you plan on doing intensive work on the engine, this is the best way to get to it.

REMOVING A GEN III FROM A FULL-SIZE TRUCK OR SUV

Pulling a Gen III V-8 from a GM full-size truck or SUV will probably look familiar to those that have pulled engines from other full-frame vehicles. That's because the truck engines come out the top of the engine bay and over the radiator core support.

Even with that traditional nature, there are plenty of sensors, hoses, and other specific tips and tricks shown here that will make the job go easier when it comes time to pull your Gen III.

Installing the Gen III V-8 back in the engine bay requires basically reversing the removal process shown here. Any different details to the reinstallation are discussed during the removal process.

While the 800-series truck and SUV chassis allows the most access to the Gen III engine, you'll still need to remove it if you really plan on hot-rodding it. Check out the photo sequence that follows.

The first step is not a requirement, but it will make your life much easier. Put the truck on a lift. If you don't have a lift, just plan on sliding underneath the vehicle to pull the starter, torque converter bolts, trans bolts, and a few other things. Disconnect the battery at this time.

The tools required to do this job vary from the standard pliers, screwdrivers, and open-end wrenches to a custom pulley puller and radiator hook tool. The hammer and pry bar are used to persuade various components away from their homes.

1. To start removing parts, loosen the hose clamps at each end of the air tube assembly and the hose clip at the passenger side of the radiator. Weasel it off the air cleaner box and the MAF sensor flanges. Look at the next image for a close-up on how to remove these clips.

2. There are many clips on the Gen III engine that are a little tricky to get loose, like this main radiator hose wiring harness clip. To open it, place the tip of the radiator hook tool (your best friend when removing the hose and wiring clips and connectors) inside the clip section (take a good look at the location in the photo to understand where!), push it down, and pull the clip open with the other hand.

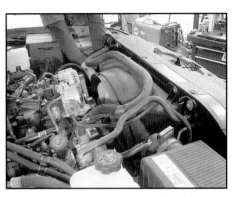

3. The next part to come off is the engine cover, which has already been removed by loosening its 10-mm bolts. Then comes the upper radiator fan shroud. Remove the two 10-mm bolts from the upper edge of the shroud and the four pull pins where the upper and lower portions of the shroud come together.

4. A good way to remove the radiator shroud pull pins is to lightly clinch under the tab with side cutters (don't cut the tab, just use the side cutters to pull up on the tab) and pull up about 1/2 inch to release the clip.

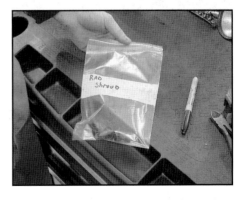

5. To prevent losing all the little parts or forgetting where everything goes, put all the fasteners in Ziploc bags and mark their usage and quantity on the bags.

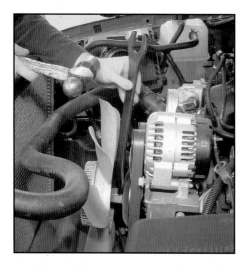

6. Remove the fan next. Use a 36-mm wrench (Blue Point, PN YA9521) to twist the nut against the cranking rotation of the belt (the belt direction is different on the various front drives). Don't remove the accessory drive belt before doing this, as the belt will hold the water pump shaft in place while you loosen the fan nut. You should be able to remove the nut by hand, but if not, refer to the next photo for how to remove "stuck" fan nuts. Remove the lower shroud by taking it off its two resting tabs.

7. If the radiator nut is locked in place, use an air hammer with a chisel attachment to rattle the nut loose. Place the chisel on the back edge of one of the nut faces and push the nut loose.

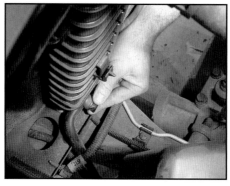

8. The next task is to drain the coolant. Pull the drain tube out of its holder on the side of the radiator and point it down at a bin to collect the coolant. Turn the drain petcock to start the flow.

9. Use pliers to compress the spring clamp holding the upper radiator hose on the engine. If possible, compress the clip until it detents open to make reinstallation a snap (literally). Lift the hose to drain the coolant in the hose back into the radiator. As a note, these clamps are staked to the hoses, so they won't slide back and forth on the hose.

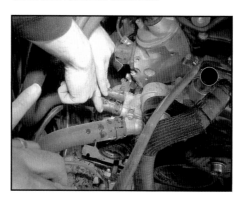

10. Use pliers to compress the clips on the lower radiator hose and two heater hoses and remove. You might need a radiator hook tool to pry between the rubber hose and metal fitting to get these loose.

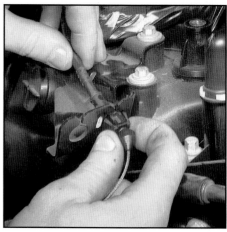

11. Remove the throttle cable by holding the throttle at WOT and unlooping the cable off the throttle blade cam. Depress the two tangs on the anchor of the cable housing to pull it out of the bracket.

12. Take off the upper cover bracket on the intake manifold by removing the three 10-mm bolts. Reinstall the bolts in the intake after the cover bracket is off so you don't lose them.

13. Pull the disc brake booster hose from the brake booster housing (left hand) and start taking off the many ground straps (right hand). This one goes to the firewall.

14. Start removing the wiring harness by pulling the TPS and alternator control plugs. These are traditional plugs and are easily removed.

15. Next, remove the air temperature sender and EVAP solenoid control wire connectors (in hand). Notice the EVAP is removed. To do this, squeeze the connector while lightly pulling up to release it.

16. This main clip needs to be released to get the harness out of the way. The best way to release this clip is to use a radiator hook tool to pry under the small locking tang.

17. Now, remove the main coil plugs on each side of the engine by pulling the side pin out and pulling up on the clip while lifting the lock tang. Now is also a good time to unhook the main alternator power wire (a 10-mm nut).

18. There are two knock sensors under the intake manifold that are connected to a jumper wire that comes out under the intake at the back of the engine. This photo shows how much wiring is running through that area. Because of all this, if you don't know what the connector feels like, you're probably not going to get it unhooked. On the first engine removal, plan on taking the intake off to get to this and a few other connectors back there — once you get them figured out, maybe next time you'll be able to do it blind.

19. Here's a simple task once you've done it, but a hell of a job if you don't know what you're doing — removing the fuel injector wiring connectors. The connectors are nestled down between the fuel rail and intake itself, leaving little space to see what you're doing.

20. This is how the fuel injector connector will look when it's installed in the injector body. The gray clip needs to be pulled up before the connector can be released from the fuel injector.

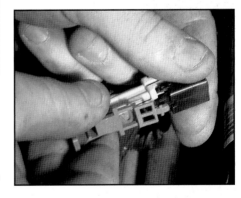

21. To start the injector removal process, work the gray clip up and out of the clip body. Sometimes, it will help to pull the upper portion of the clip off the wire, then you can get a better grip on the clip to pull and wiggle it off the fuel injector.

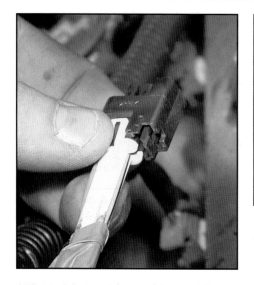

22. You need to depress this little tab on the fuel injector wiring connector as it's worked off the injector. Do this for all eight fuel-injector wiring connectors.

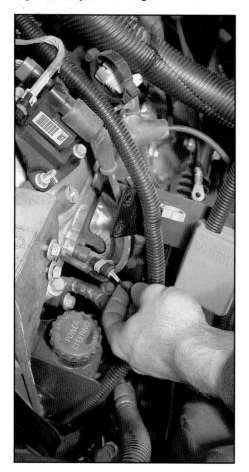

23. Now, pull the water temperature sensor wire connector off the sensor on the driver-side front of the engine block by lifting the lock tab and pulling the connector off.

24. Next, remove the wiring connector for the MAP sender. This is located at the top of the intake manifold towards the rear. Lift the lock tab and pull the connector off.

25. The wiring loom clip on the valve covers is released by pressing on the inside tang, as shown, with the end of the radiator hook tool. The loom has been removed to show where to press on the clip with the hook tool.

26. The reason this method will save you time and effort is because you're not taking out any components you don't have to. When you remove any wiring connectors from the vehicle, place as much as you can on top of the engine to minimize the chances of it being damaged when the engine is removed.

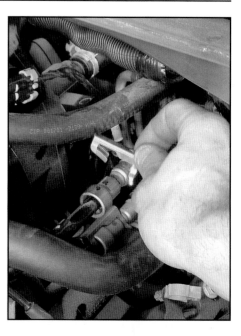

27. Disconnect the fuel feed and return lines next. Start by pulling this lock clip off of both lines with your hand. Store the clips in a bag so you don't lose them — they are not easy to buy.

28. The fuel lines use special connectors that require a special tool to release. This plastic tool and more expensive metal tools are available through most professional tool suppliers. The plastic tools work just as good as the metal ones, but they wear out. If you're only pulling an engine a few times in your life, the plastic version will be more than enough to get the job done.

33. Now, swing the power steering pump towards the inner fenderwell to clear the engine. Use wire or zip-ties to hold it in place until it's time to reinstall the engine.

29. This close-up of the fuel line fitting shows its small tangs that engage the fuel rail hard-line to lock the two fittings together.

31. Remove the power steering pulley to access the four bolts holding the pump onto the engine. This is done to keep the power steering system together — it's easier to remove the pump from the engine than it is to take the whole system apart and put it back together. Use a special puller tool (Snap-On, PN CJ117A) to pull it, and a special install tool (Snap-On, PN CJ113B101) to reinstall the pulley.

34. Perform the same swing-away process on the A/C compressor. First, remove the two 15-mm hex-head bolts on the side of the A/C pump and remove the bottom two 15-mm bolts. Then, push the A/C compressor up and over towards the passenger side of the engine bay to clear the engine. Use wire or zip-ties to hold it out of the way.

30. Remove the front accessory drive belt by relaxing the tensioner belt with a 15-mm wrench and pulling the belt off by hand.

32. Next, remove the four 15-mm hex-head bolts in front (three hold the pump, one holds the wiring bracket, which needs to be removed so you can move the wire while you remove the pump) and one bolt in back holding the pump on. Bag the fasteners for safe keeping.

35. Next, you'll need to remove the starter. To do this, remove the two 13-mm bolts and the 10-mm bolt holding on the flexplate access cover. Getting the cover off helps you maneuver the starter out from under the vehicle. Patiently work the starter down and back against the wiring and trans cooler lines to get it out. It might help to remove some wires and move the transmission lines by pulling them out of some of their clips.

36. With the starter out, use a straight pick to depress the hidden tab on the oil-level wiring connector to remove it from the oil pan. While you're down there, remove the 10-mm bolt that's holding the harness on the front of the oil pan.

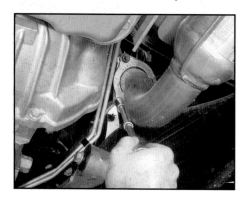

37. Next, unbolt the three 15-mm fasteners from the exhaust collector that connects the manifold to the exhaust Y-pipe. To make this job easier, use a long extension to access these fasteners.

38. Remove the three 15-mm bolts that hold the flexplate and torque converter together. You can reach them through the area on the passenger side of the automatic transmission where the starter was, or struggle through the small access plug in the bellhousing.

39. You can now remove the 15-mm bolts that hold the transmission to the engine block. The bottom bolts are easily accessed, but the top bolts are practically impossible to reach.

40. One of the methods to reach the top bolts on the transmission is to use a looooonnnnnggggg extension on a ratchet. In this case, the torque required to loosen the bolts was too much, so we decided to remove the intake to access the bolts and connectors at the back of the engine (oil pressure, knock sensors, etc.).

41. To get the intake off, you'll need to loosen the 10 nested 8-mm bolts and a few hoses and electrical connectors. The intake gaskets are a one-piece component, and it usually takes just a few pries on the intake-to-cylinder-head mounting flange to release the intake. Carefully vacuum around the intake before you remove it to avoid trash from falling into the intake ports.

42. Before you separate the connector for the oil-pressure sender (shown) and knock sensors, push the wiring loom back towards the firewall. Remember to tape over the intake ports to prevent objects from falling into the engine. This engine was being completely rebuilt, so this precaution was not taken.

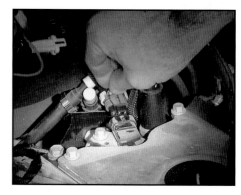

43. Once the cam sensor sender connector is pulled off, the 10-mm bolts holding a few wiring brackets can be removed, and you'll be able to get to the remaining 15-mm transmission-to-engine bolts.

44. There are three 15-mm engine mount bolts on each side of the engine that you need to remove before you can pull the engine from the vehicle.

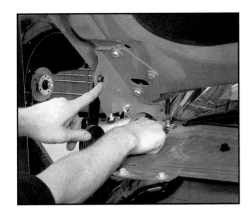

45. You'll need to remove the hood to get the engine out. To make it easier to reinstall, remove these two 13-mm bolts. This way, you won't have to realign the hood on the vehicle when you go to put it back together. Use two people to lift the hood off the vehicle because it's big and heavy.

46. In this case, we were lucky enough to have a forklift to lift the engine out of the vehicle, but you can do it with an engine hoist. Attach a chain to the front and rear of the engine and lift it out. Wiggle the engine a little to get it free of the transmission and other components. Watch for wires still connected to the engine while you slowly lift it out of the vehicle.

RUNNING A GEN III V-8 IN A PRE-GEN III V-8 VEHICLE

The Gen III LS1 V-8 is a great engine to install in past model vehicles because it is compact, has a simple external shape, closely mimics a Gen I/II small-block Chevy in its external dimensions, and it looks cool. The photos show an LS6 installed in a late-model Chevy S10 pickup. To install this engine, the owner had to build small engine mount adapters, which are also available from multiple sources. Headers needed to be fabbed up, along with a larger radiator. The inlet tube was fabricated and an open element air filter connected to the end. The engine runs on a GM controller, but the calibration has been altered using LS1Edit to make it work in the S10.

This little S10 is a hoot to drive, yet it idles like a stocker, gets 20 mpg, and is easy to service. This setup is so straightforward, it's shocking GM didn't build the thing in the first place.

As can be seen by the wiring rat's nest in the engine bay, wiring up the Gen III so that it works in concert with the rest of the vehicle's controls is a challenge. If you're not electronically minded, find someone who is, or plan on buying an aftermarket wiring harness. Also, the calibration will need some work to run the S10 dashboard and other components, but these challenges are surmountable. Once this owner got through these details, this truck ran like a new hot-rod from the get-go.

S10 pickups like this one are great to add Gen III V-8s to. They're plentiful, inexpensive hot-rod toys that are a hoot to drive with a hopped-up LS1 under the hood.

There are many components that require custom fabrication, like this air cleaner tube. This one is made of 4-inch aluminum tubing and an open-element K&N air cleaner. The radiator is a custom unit, necessary to get the inlet and outlets to match up to the LS1 inlet/outlets. You'll need a slim electric fan to clear the front of the engine. Otherwise, it looks like GM should have built them this way.

BOLT-ON POWER

Knowing all the technical aspects of the Gen III V-8 engine is interesting, but more than likely, the information you really want to know is how to improve its performance. That's why this chapter is about aftermarket components that can be bolted on to the stock Gen III LS1 V-8 engine for power increases. In the following pages, you will see the performance gains of some of the most popular components and combinations of components used to increase power on the Gen III V-8. The chapter starts with simple external bolt-ons and progresses to big-hp, highly involved engine combinations. To put some data behind the combinations, most have their power output documented with dynamometer testing.

Note that all dyno results shown here are standard corrected, not the OE-standard of SAE corrected. Standard correction is to 29.92 inches Hg at 68 degrees F, while SAE correction is 29.23 inches Hg at 77 degrees F. Usually, standard correction data will be about 10 percent higher than SAE corrected, due to the lower temp and higher density of the standard correction. Also, most of the testing was performed without the FEAD, or front engine accessory drive, installed for simplicity. The alternator, A/C compressor, and power steering supposedly consume about 35 hp.

As you will see, the Gen III V-8 responds positively to many different external performance components, like airboxes, exhaust systems, and intake manifolds. There is no one component that unleashes 50+ hp, but the careful selection of a few components combined with some knowledgeable tuning can produce impressive power gains. This chapter starts with some of the more simple modifications, like adding a freer breathing airbox. Then, you'll see some of the better combinations being tested in the dyno rooms of LS1 developers. Chapter 6 shows you exactly how to upgrade the top end of a Gen III V-8 for a 100+ hp gain, while Chapter 7 shows you all the details needed to build a 500+ hp normally aspirated, stock-block Gen III V-8.

WHERE DOES BOLT-ON POWER COME FROM?

If you have ever wondered why GM, or other vehicle manufacturers, "restrict" power output by not using parts like the aftermarket offers, there is one big reason and a lot of smaller ones. First, most of the simple bolt-on performance components that produce power without major changes do so for a simple reason. When GM engineers begin the development of a certain powerplant, they do so with many external components that don't have the final durability, refinement,

packaging, piece cost, and noise, vibration, and harshness (NVH) canceling devices on them. Some of the more common components like this are the air intake and exhaust systems.

In fact, many of these base components and systems are changed over the course of the GM development and durability evaluation process to meet the extensive requirements for creating production-level powertrains. Many of these requirements conspire to "consume" horsepower — or so most hotrodders would believe. Actually, GM would do anything to keep the power output as high as possible, but an even more important issue to them being a successful automobile company is that they not alter the requirements needed to exceed their extremely high quality and durability expectations.

Essentially, if GM were building racecars, then noisy, short-fuse power would be okay. But they're building highly refined street vehicles that most of the public wants to drive without hearing the engine running for hundreds of thousands of miles. So, the powertrain engineers work backwards to end up with quiet, smooth vehicles.

NOISE CANCELING

A good example of this is GM adding sound canceling devices, called

Helmholtz resonators, into the intake tubes to minimize the valvetrain and intake air noise that emanates from under the hood. Since the GM engineers started the powertrain development process with intakes that didn't have the final noise canceling features in them, the base computer calibrations have values in the tables and some simple learn features to run the engine in the "noisy" mode.

This is where the aftermarket comes in. They reverse engineer components, like intake air tubes, that don't have these noise-canceling and power-consuming features. Also, they don't have to adhere to the same technical specifications as the production engineers do on cost, packaging, materials, durability, crash testing, and other parameters. This freedom allows the aftermarket manufacturers to increase the airflow into the engine.

With the less restrictive air inlet, the mass airflow (MAF) sensor reads higher airflow into the engine and the powertrain control module (PCM) looks up the required fuel ratio in a different area of the calibration to increase the fuel being injected into the engine. And since the calibration has the values in it or a learn function, the powertrain experiences an increase in power.

The main negative from the installation of many of these performance components is the vehicle will experience an increase in NVH. But since most automotive enthusiasts *want* to hear the powertrain doing its thing, as they equate this with increased power production, this works out to everyone's advantage.

HOT ROD DEVELOPMENT

There is another subject that should be discussed regarding the aftermarket industry. Unlike the time- and money-consuming durability testing and validation GM performs on all of their production components, the aftermarket sees much of their component evaluation done in the field in backyard garages all over the world.

As this book is being written, GM is spending about $400 million a month on warranty claims, so they can't afford to sell anything they aren't confident will work impeccably in practically any situation on the road. If your aftermarket component fails, you will sometimes get a new component. But often, the consumer understands they are developing their own powertrain and sometimes they will exceed the capabilities of the part. When this happens, they'll need to step up to a more durable component or buy a replacement part and do something different so as not to repeat the situation that failed the part.

Neither situation is better than the other by itself. If the factory warranty matters to you, then you need to honor GM's wishes to maintain it. If you aren't concerned with voiding the warranty or having a few failures along the way to engineering a "better" powertrain, then making major changes to the powertrain will be very satisfying.

There are many more components on the market than the components shown in this chapter (see the sidebar Gen III Power Parts on page 76) and more on the way. This overview is intended to show some of the potential of the Gen III V-8 with regard to aftermarket components.

Note: If you are comparing dyno charts within this chapter, you'll notice the power figures don't correspond for various upgrades. That is because the parts were tested on different engines. You should pay attention to the test-bed engines being used to test the parts, as they will have a strong influence on the outcome of the test. For example, a high-flow airbox will probably add more power to a fully built race motor than it will to a bone-stock engine.

AIRBOXES

Whether you own a Camaro, Firebird, Corvette, or full-size GMC or Chevy truck, all will respond positively to the installation of an aftermarket air intake tube and air filter. This is a good first modification, as any other power increasing additions need more air to make power, which the performance airbox and air filter will provide.

Installing an aftermarket air filter and tube usually can provide a lift of anywhere from 7 to 15 horsepower on a Gen III V-8 engine. The systems being sold vary in the horsepower they provide based on their design and the vehicle platform. Most of the Camaro and Firebird aftermarket companies sell just an airbox lid and air filter, while most of the aftermarket Corvette airbox companies sell a complete replacement tube and air filter unit that installs in place of the factory airbox. For the full-size GM trucks and SUVs, most aftermarket companies sell replacement tubes, airboxes, and air filters.

Many of the production GM airbox engineers attribute much of this power

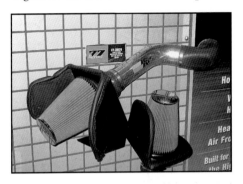

The aftermarket air tube/open-element air filter setup is probably one of the most popular modifications made to Gen III-powered vehicles.

The F-body cars usually require only a lid that doesn't have the ribbing and noise-canceling chambers of the production airbox lid in combination with a low-restriction air cleaner. These are very easy to install.

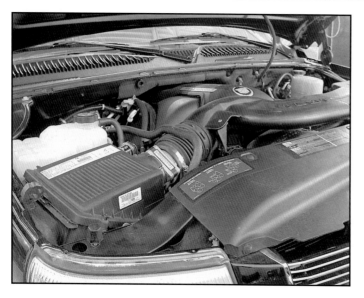

Installing an aftermarket air filter system is probably more involved on a full-size GM truck or SUV than many other Gen III-power GM vehicles, so that's the one we'll detail. Here's what the stock air filter system looks like.

Once the stock airbox system is removed, the K&N system is mocked up in place. With many aftermarket air claner systems, you need to drill a mounting hole into the radiator support, which is easy with a cordless drill. As a note, for those considering removing the screen on the MAF sensor on full-size vehicles, be aware GM put the screen in as an airflow straightener. On the 'Vette and F-body cars, with their straight-on intake tubes, this screen isn't required. But on the trucks or other cars where the intake tube makes a 90-degree turn, the screen does an important job of calming down the intake air coming through the MAF.

Gen III Power Parts

Here are some of the many components to personalize your Gen III V-8 engine in the search for higher performance, and some sample companies offering them. For contact info, see http://sema.org

Airboxes/Lids	K&N, Airaid, Whisper, Donaldson, LGM, Direct-Flo, Texas Speed, Breathless
Factory-Replacement Air Cleaners	K&N, Green, VaraRam, Holley, Crane
Cat-Back Exhausts	Borla, Corsa, Flowmaster, Gibson, Random Technology, SLP, Hooker, DynaTech, Flotech, Mac, B&B, Bassani, GHL, Edelbrock, MagnaFlow
Performance Catalytic Converters	Random Technology, MagnaFlow, DynaTech
Long-Tube Headers	SLP, Stainless Works, Hooker, More Performance, FLP, TTS, MAC, DynaTech
High-Flow Throttle Bodies	Comp Cams/Wilson, Shaner, BBK, TPS
Fuel Regulators	Aeromotive, Kinsler

High-Flow MAFs	Granatelli, Pro-M Racing
Spark Plug Wires	GM Performance Parts (GMPP), MSD, Taylor, Moroso
Performance Gaskets	Fel-Pro, GMPP, Mr. Gasket, TKO, ROL
Performance Fuel Rails	Comp/Wilson
High-Performance Rockers	Comp Cams, SLP, Crane, Jesel, T&D
High-Rate Valvesprings	Comp Cams, GMPP, SLP, Crane
Rev Kits	Agostino Racing Engines, Comp Cams, Crane
Lightweight Valve Locks/Retainers	Comp Cams, GMPP, SLP
Larger Valves	Ferrea, Manley
Camshafts	GMPP, Comp Cams, Crane, Lunati
Pushrods	MTI, Trend, Smith Brothers, Comp Cams

increase to the elimination of various noise canceling equipment in the intake tract, being able to spend some more money for a smooth inlet tube, and going to an open-element air filter. To get the full power increase possible, shield the air cleaner from the hotter underhood air so it will breathe cooler ambient air for the maximum power increase.

While open-element air filters work great in performance applications, there are plenty of reasons why GM doesn't sell their vehicles with these types of air filters. The biggest issue is the noise generated by the intake air rushing into the engine and the valvetrain noise emanating out of the intake tract. While performance enthusiasts find this noise music to their ears, much of the public doesn't enjoy listening to it.

Other issues to be aware of include

what GM calls water ingestion. This refers to the ability of the air filter housing and tube to allow the engine to breathe in air without ingesting water that is either standing on the road or falling from the sky. The automobile manufacturers perform extensive testing to make sure their vehicles can be driven during heavy rains without causing the

engine to suck in a deadly amount of water. This is not to say the aftermarket air filter systems won't pass these tests, just that they haven't been through this testing.

Usually, performance enthusiasts enjoy a little noise from the engine bay and understand the quirkiness brought on by the use of certain performance

Gen III Power Parts (continued)

CNC-ported GM Cylinder Heads	GM Performance Parts (GMPP), ET Performance, CNC, SLP
Specialized Cylinder Heads	GMPP, AFR
Top-End Engine Power Packages	More Perf., MTI, SLP, (heads, cam, intake, headers, etc.)
Performance Intakes	GMPP, Comp Cams/Wilson, Edelbrock, Holley/Weiand
Stroker Rotating/Reciprocating Kits	Lunati, Katech, SLP
Forged Pistons	CP, JE, Lunati, Diamond, Katech, Mahle, Speed Pro, Ross, Arias, DRP Wiseco, Probe
Performance Piston Rings	Speed Pro, Total Seal
Performance Steel Connecting Rods	Oliver, Crower, Scat, Callies, Carrillo, Manley
Steel Crankshafts	Lunati, Scat, Callies, Crower
Performance Fasteners	ARP, B&B
High-Performance Fuel Pumps	Walbro, Bosch
GM Controller Reprogramming	Hypertech, LS1-Edit, Superchips, DiabloSport, FastChip, TTS
Aftermarket EFI Controllers/kits	ACCEL, Electromotive, MoTeC, SuperSquirt, F.A.S.T., Big Stuff 3, Holley, Speartech, Howell, Gen III Performance
Higher Flow-Fuel Injectors	Bosch, Holley, MSD, F.A.S.T.
Nitrous Oxide Systems	NOS, Nitrous Express (NX), TNT, ZEX
Supercharger Kits	Magnuson, ProCharger, Vortech, Paxton
Turbocharger Kits	1/4-Mile Performance, Wheel to Wheel Powertrain

components, so these issues are not a problem, but it is important you know they exist.

INSTALLATION NOTES

In general, installing an aftermarket air filter housing and inlet tube on a Gen III V-8-powered vehicle usually requires little more than some wrenches, screwdrivers, a radiator hook tool, and possibly a drill to create a mounting hole.

Most aftermarket performance airboxes on the LS1-powered cars are a direct bolt in, requiring no drilling or additional components.

Gen III LW/LR/LQ V-8-powered trucks and SUVs have similar hose clamps and connectors as the cars, but also often have a few fasteners holding the rather large airbox and tubing in place. The aftermarket airboxes usually use a fastener or two to hold them in place, but often not the factory fastener holes — so new holes will sometimes need to be drilled in the radiator core support or fender support to hold the performance airbox in place.

In general, the performance increases these units provide for the amount of work required to install them makes these a popular addition to these vehicles.

POWER PRODUCTION AND DYNO TEST DETAILS

As a note, these dyno figures, and the other dyno figures shown in this book, are standard corrected, not the SAE corrected figures used by the automobile manufacturers. In general, the standard numbers usually are about 10 percent or so higher than the SAE numbers. Also, many of these tests were performed without the accessories, which means there were no losses from the alternator, A/C compressor, and power steering pump. These accessories can consume 35 horsepower or more.

INTAKE MANIFOLD

GM has spent considerable engineering and tooling money to develop a cost-effective, free-flowing, lightweight, nylon intake. Since the stock intake has such

The power increases from aftermarket air cleaners are usually felt from midrange to peak power. Some improvements in mileage could be experienced also.

The dyno test shown here compares the stock airbox with a K&N open element air filter, airbox, and inlet tube on a LQ9 6.0-liter V-8-powered '02 Cadillac Escalade with CNC-ported heads, an LS1 cam, Smith Bros. pushrods, and low-restriction shorty exhaust headers. The higher-flowing heads, cam, and exhaust really show the advantage of the performance intake system. A stock engine would also show an increase, just not as much.

K&N KIT DYNO

| RPM | BASELINE | | | K&N KIT | |
	Torque	HP		Torque	HP
3,000	372	213		381	218
3,100	372	220		382	226
3,200	373	227		383	233
3,300	377	237		388	244
3,400	382	247		393	254
3,500	389	259		400	266
3,600	397	272		408	279
3,700	404	285		415	292
3,800	408	295		419	303
3,900	410	304		422	317
4,000	411	312		425	324
4,100	413	322		429	335
4,200	416	333		431	344
4,300	417	341		432	354
4,400	418	351		435	364
4,500	**420**	360		**436**	374
4,600	419	367		**436**	382
4,700	417	373		434	388
4,800	414	378		431	394
4,900	409	382		426	398
5,000	403	384		421	401
5,100	398	387		414	402
5,200	393	389		409	405
5,300	387	390		402	406
5,400	380	**391**		396	407
5,500	373	**391**		389	**408**
5,600	365	389		381	406
5,700	357	387		372	404
5,800	347	383		363	401

The latest high-tech component to come out of the aftermarket for the Gen III V-8 is the F.A.S.T. replacement intake manifold. This three-piece design has shown the promise of releasing up to 15 hp on an LS6, and 7-10 hp on an early LS1 engine with no other changes. The intake has nitrous nozzle bosses built in, should you decide to add nitrous in the future.

Cat-Back Exhausts

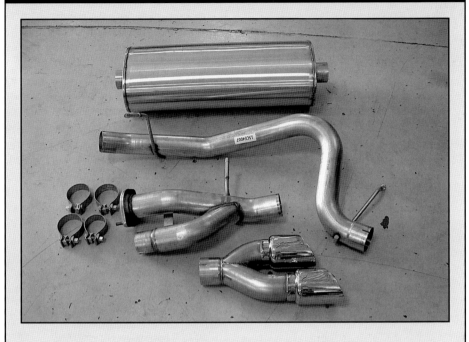

Most cat-back exhaust systems come with everything needed for installation.

Bolt-on exhaust system upgrades have been around for years in the form of cat-back systems. This term refers to the exhaust system from the rear flange of the catalytic converter (the "cat") on back to the tailpipe (the "back"). When first introduced, cat-back exhaust systems provided a lift in power output of 15 hp or more across the powerband with a stock engine. But today, the automobile manufacturers and their exhaust suppliers have, in general, gotten the most out of the stock cat-back exhaust with a stock engine.

So, for a stock engine, most aftermarket cat-back exhaust systems are a "see and hear it" component vs. being a "feel it" piece. For many, this doesn't matter because they like the more aggressive exhaust note, different outlet locations, and personalized tips of the aftermarket cat-back systems.

In many ways, cat-back exhausts are like aftermarket air cleaners in that they allow more power to be released if/when an engine is modified for performance. This is because the performance cat-backs will usually allow a modified engine to flow more exhaust gases than a stock system, but with the same system pressure as the stock exhaust system — resulting in more power output. You don't want the backpressure to be much less than stock, as the calibration is designed for a certain amount. Too little backpressure, and the engine will not run smoothly.

Aftermarket cat-back systems usually use the stock exhaust hangers. This allows them to leverage all the lessons learned by GM in how to keep the exhaust on the vehicle and keep it rattle-free.

thin wall thickness, porting the stock intake passages is not an option. The F.A.S.T intake manifold is an ingenious revision to the one-piece, nylon production intake manifold. F.A.S.T has tooled up a three-piece intake that produces a noticeable lift in an LS1's power output.

The F.A.S.T. intake can be ordered with either the factory opening, or set up for a F.A.S.T./Wilson 90-mm billet throttle body for high-horsepower applications.

INSTALLATION NOTES

The F.A.S.T intake manifold bolts onto any Gen III V-8 just like the production intake, and the throttle body/inlet tube mounts in the stock location too. It is probably a 30-minute job for an experienced hand, and maybe an hour or so for someone who has never pulled an intake manifold. While that hour or so might sound optimistic, remember the Gen III intake doesn't have a water crossover or distributor. Simply remove 10 bolts, remove some wires and hoses, pry off the stock intake, clean the port gasket face area, install the new intake with new gaskets, tighten down the bolts, and reinstall the wires/hoses. Done.

PERFORMANCE CAMSHAFT AND VALVETRAIN COMPONENTS

Changing the camshaft on a Gen III V-8 holds a lot of potential for a variety of reasons. First, the initial Gen III engines had common camshafts for manufacturing simplicity and cost containment. This led to compromises in power production, but that's good for performance enthusiasts, as there is power available with just a cam swap. Second, the stock LS1 and truck/SUV intake and exhaust systems have the ability for increased flow, especially on the 4.8- and 5.3-liter truck engines, as those systems are built to handle up to the 6.0-liter engine

INSTALLATION NOTES

If you are new to cam swaps, consult many sources before making a

The F.A.S.T. intake makes power across the meat of the powerband. This component is very new to the market, but we're told its true potential becomes apparent with the addition of other performance components that allow more airflow into the engine. Some of these components include CNC-ported cylinder heads, a more aggressive camshaft, a freer flowing exhaust, and other similar components.

The baseline dyno tests were performed with a stock LS6 5.7-liter engine, Comp Cams camshaft (210/216 intake/exhaust duration, 0.566/0.588 inches intake/exhaust lift), long-tube headers with 1-3/4-inch primaries, and a Donaldson Blackwing air cleaner. The F.A.S.T. intake tested here was used in the initial development testing.

F.A.S.T. INTAKE DYNO

RPM	BASELINE Torque	HP	F.A.S.T. INTAKE Torque	HP
3,000	403	231	404	231
3,100	403	238	402	237
3,200	402	245	400	244
3,300	402	253	401	252
3,400	405	262	403	261
3,500	408	272	408	272
3,600	413	283	416	285
3,700	421	296	424	298
3,800	428	310	431	312
3,900	433	321	435	323
4,000	437	333	439	334
4,100	440	344	445	347
4,200	444	355	449	359
4,300	448	367	454	372
4,400	451	378	459	385
4,500	454	389	462	396
4,600	**457**	400	**464**	406
4,700	**457**	409	**464**	415
4,800	**457**	418	463	423
4,900	455	425	461	430
5,000	454	432	460	438
5,100	452	439	459	446
5,200	449	444	458	453
5,300	445	449	453	457
5,400	439	451	448	461
5,500	432	**452**	441	**462**
5,600	424	**452**	432	460
5,700	415	451	421	457
5,800	406	449	412	455
5,900	398	447	404	454
6,000	390	446	397	453
6,100	382	444	389	452
6,200	375	442	381	449
6,300	364	436	373	447
6,400	356	430	363	443
6,500	347	429	355	440
6,600	339	426	348	437
6,700	330	421	339	433
6,800	321	416	330	428

change. Valvetrain combinations can be confusing and cause considerable damage if miscalculated, so the more data you can gather from knowledgeable sources, the higher the chances of increased power without any problems.

The worst situation would be the valves hitting the piston tops while the engine is rotating. This is catastrophic to the engine operation. The best way to avoid this is pull the cylinder heads, put a dime-sized dollop of modeling clay on the lowest point of the intake and exhaust valve faces where they might hit the pistons, and reinstall the head. Then, slowly cycle the engine through a full combustion rotation and remove the head to measure the thickness of the clay where the valve contacted it. This thickness should not be less than 0.160 inch.

A cam swap on many of the early Gen III V-8s results in a noticeable power increase. The cam swap is extremely straightforward and takes just a few hours.

The Gen III cams are straightforward to remove, just pull the valve covers, relax the rockers, pull the pushrods, rotate the cam 360 degrees to nest the lifters in their retainers, and slide the cam out. Use a long 3/8-inch extension slid up inside the gun-drilled cam for leverage when you're removing it.

Before installation, lube up the new cam with engine oil on the lobes and bearing surfaces. Also, with any performance Gen III cam substitution, you should install aftermarket pushrods to handle the increased forces from the more aggressive cam lobes.

Aftermarket Valvespring Install

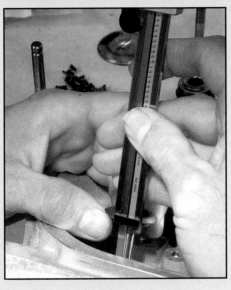

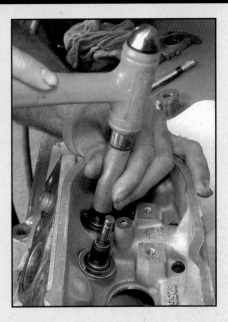

Should you decide the stock valvesprings aren't enough for your latest 0.580-inch-lift cam, here's how to swap to new valvesprings. While this swap involves the tried-and-true multi-coil valvespring (right), there are stock-design, beehive-shaped performance valvesprings (left) available from companies like Comp Cams. Both valvesprings should be installed with the following process.

2. Using a micrometer, measure the valvespring height from the valvespring seat to the retainer face. You can use shims if the stem height is longer than the valvespring, but you want to use as few shims as possible on an aluminum head so the valvespring can dissipate heat through the base as efficiently as possible.

4. When factoring the valvespring compressed height, make sure you factor in the valvestem seal height into the measurements so the retainer doesn't crash into the seal. Here it is being installed with a special tool.

1. The key starting point is to assemble valvesprings, retainers, locks, and valves that all work together.

3. Many valvespring manufacturers will provide a recommended valvespring seat height to provide the appropriate valvespring force on the valve. To achieve this height, shims are often used under the valvespring bucket seat.

5. A standard valvespring compressor will require an extension to clear the tall valve cover rail, but otherwise it will install valvesprings in a similar fashion to past small-block V-8s.

Long-Tube Headers

Bolting on a set of long-tube headers like these will release impressive power from any Gen III V-8. On the Gen III-powered cars, most of the long-tube headers require the engine to be removed from the vehicle to install them, but a ZO6 can pick up 25 hp with long-tube headers and some calibration work. You can install a set of long tubes on most of the full-size trucks and SUVs without removing the engine. Remember, there are two O2 sensors in each collector on most long-tube headers. If you choose to run without cats, you'll need to pick up some off-road-only load simulators, or sims, to prevent the PCM controls from shutting down the operation of the powertrain. There are two O2 sensors in each tube because the PCM compares the readings before and after the cats to make sure they're still effective.

If you want to unleash hidden power in your Gen III V-8, long-tube exhaust headers are a sure bet. The stock exhaust manifolds and catalytic converters are designed to provide low emissions at startup over the life of the vehicle with an eye towards low piece cost. Maximizing exhaust gas flow at high RPM is something the GM Powertrain engineers want, but the emissions, cost, durability, and NVH issues come before peak power. Short-tube headers are better than the stock cast-iron manifolds, but only slightly – the real power gains are in long-tube headers.

Bolting on headers is not as simple as a cat-back system or an aftermarket airbox. They often require new smaller cats (to fit under the car) and a new exhaust system all the way back to the tailpipe. Many of the brackets, wires, and hoses that are close to the stock exhaust need to be modified, moved, or protected from the bulkier exhaust and heat of the headers.

If you live in a state that operates to California-level 50-state standards, the responsible thing to do is run a street-legal set of headers and exhaust system. For an exhaust system with a set of headers and relocated cats to be street-legal in these states, it needs to have attained an Executive Order, or EO, from the California Air Resources Board (CARB). There are header and exhaust systems on the market that make good power. Some suppliers are listed in the

sidebar "Gen III Power Parts on pages 76 and 77."

If you install a set of headers, plan on having to add fuel and timing advance to take full advantage of the increased exhaust flow. There are a few handheld tuning devices that can do basic recalibration work, but by far the most flexible system is LS1-Edit. For more on calibration work and the various tuning systems, see Chapter 10.

This is what a street-legal long-tube header exhaust system looks like. Notice the smaller-than-stock catalytic converters and tight packaging to get everything to fit under the vehicle. An emissions legal part like this doesn't necessarily make less power than an off-road exhaust, it just means the supplier spent the time and money to pass emissions testing. These systems do release power, so many consider them worth the effort to get on the vehicle.

POWER PRODUCTION AND DYNO DETAILS

Camshafts are the brains of the engine, so the cam choice you make will seriously affect the power production. If you go with a mild street cam, the idle quality and powerband will be smooth and predictable. If you go with a more race-oriented cam, the idle will probably need to be higher, and the powerband will be peakier — which means most of the gain in power will be at the upper reaches of the RPM band. Neither is necessarily better than the other, you

just need to decide what you are looking for from the vehicle.

The cam used here would probably be classified as a hot street grind. It has a good idle quality, but leaves no doubt that the engine is a performance piece. The driver would feel the power increase from this cam swap. Also, the addition of a set of better-flowing CNC cylinder heads would only make this engine come to life even more, as can be seen in the adjoining dyno numbers.

The baseline dyno engine was an LS6 5.7-liter engine, long-tube headers

with 1-3/4-inch primaries, and a Donaldson Blackwing air cleaner. In the chart on page 83 the middle test adds the cam to the engine, and the test on the far right uses the cam and a set of W2W Power Pak CNC-ported cylinder heads.

Here are the specs on the cam:

Camshaft specs	Intake	Exhaust
Duration (deg)	212	222
Lift at 0.050 inch	0.557	0.549
Lobe separation	116 degrees	

CAM/HEAD DYNO

RPM	BASELINE		WITH CAM		WITH CAM AND HEADS	
	Torque	HP	Torque	HP	Torque	HP
3,000	339	194	371	212	390	223
3,100	344	203	372	219	388	229
3,200	347	211	371	226	383	233
3,300	350	220	371	233	378	238
3,400	354	229	372	241	376	243
3,500	358	238	376	251	378	252
3,600	363	249	381	261	384	263
3,700	368	259	388	273	392	276
3,800	372	269	394	285	401	290
3,900	376	279	400	297	406	301
4,000	379	289	404	308	409	312
4,100	383	299	408	318	413	322
4,200	386	309	411	329	417	334
4,300	390	320	415	340	423	347
4,400	393	329	418	350	430	360
4,500	396	340	421	361	436	373
4,600	399	350	424	371	441	386
4,700	**401**	359	426	381	446	399
4,800	**401**	366	**428**	391	447	409
4,900	**401**	374	**428**	399	449	419
5,000	400	381	426	406	449	427
5,100	398	387	423	411	448	435
5,200	396	392	420	416	447	443
5,300	393	396	417	421	**450**	454
5,400	389	400	412	423	447	460
5,500	383	401	409	428	446	467
5,600	379	404	403	430	443	473
5,700	375	407	398	432	439	477
5,800	369	408	391	431	435	480
5,900	364	408	384	431	429	482
6,000	359	**411**	379	**433**	423	**484**

this application as it has shown the capability to handle 750+ hp all day long with no problems, while the aluminum blocks require modifications and maintenance to handle these power levels.

The supercharger in this test is a ProCharger D1SC belt-driven centrifu-

The key with any centrifugally supercharged engine is to have a very robust mounting system for the blower. The side loading on the front drive brackets can cause flexing, which leads to misalignment of the pulleys and excessive wear on the drive belt.

SUPERCHARGERS

One of the simplest ways to increase the power to the Gen III V-8 is to install a supercharger. For full-size trucks, the best choice is the Magnuson, and it's discussed in Chapter 8. Here, we'll be discussing one of the many centrifugal superchargers available for the car version of the Gen III V-8.

The engine run here could be built with a 5.7-liter LS1 aluminum engine block or a 6.0-liter LQ cast-iron engine block. The key changes here are this engine has had an aftermarket Lunati crank with a 4.000-inch stroke installed in place of the 3.622-inch stock crank to increase the engine size to 408 cubic inches (or 383 ci if you start with a 5.7-liter block). The iron block was used in

Using a 6.0-liter truck block, this 800-hp, supercharged, air-to-water intercooled Gen III powers a street killer F-body. The iron block can handle this kind of power with no prep work; you just end up with about 60 lbs more over the nose as compared to the aluminum LS1 block.

This supercharged engine is going into an F-body car, so it required some tight packaging on the blower drive. A custom crank pulley was created from billet aluminum to tuck the blower tight to the engine. Often, a centrifugal blower drive system will require this kind of custom machine work for your specific application.

gal supercharger. The engine requires only a small handful of performance components to create a true 800+ hp giant. This engine will need to run on 100 octane street gas.

INSTALLATION NOTES

The 4.000-inch stroker crank drops in without any block modifications required (like grinding on block surfaces to clearance the increased stroke crank). This engine has aftermarket rods and pistons, so checks were done to make sure the rods cleared the cam (they should), and that the number-8 piston is machined to clear the crank sensor wheel.

The ProCharger D1SC supercharger kit comes with all the necessary components for installation. If there is any improvement that every supercharger system like this can benefit from, it's stronger brackets to hold the centrifugal supercharger on the engine. Bracket flex often shortens belt life, increases belt slippage, and accelerates supercharger bearing wear. You'll never go wrong increasing the stiffness of the supercharger bracketry.

POWER PRODUCTION AND DYNO NUMBERS

The centrifugal supercharger system has the capability of making considerable power when set up properly. They can be sensitive to belt alignment and fueling issues, but with those handled, they usually make good power. Mileage usually suffers with centrifugal supercharger systems.

Parts used:

- Iron block 6.6-liter (408-ci) engine (3.990-inch bore x 4.000-inch stroke)
- ProCharger D1SC centrifugal supercharger, mounting flanges, tubing, etc
- GM LS6-type intake
- CP Forged aluminum, full-dish pistons to achieve 9.0:1 compression
- Oliver billet steel 6-1/8-inch connecting rods
- GM CNC LS6 cylinder heads with 2.02/1.60-inch valves
- Block modified for ARP 1/2-inch head studs

- Aftermarket Comp Cams camshaft (W2W grind)
- Comp Cams valvesprings (PN 266618)
- Lunati 4.000-inch forged crank
- SLP 1-7/8-inch primary headers and full exhaust
- Modified stock controller or, if you're building a street rod use an aftermarket controller (ACCEL, Big Stuff, Electromotive, F.A.S.T., etc.)
- Stock oil pump with ported outlet and higher-pressure pop-off spring
- BBK 85-mm throttle body
- LS6 85-mm MAF sensor
- 42-lb/hr fuel injectors
- Max supercharger boost of 11.5 psi

SUPERCHARGER DYNO		
RPM	Torque	HP
3,000	548	312
3,100	553	326
3,200	562	342
3,300	576	361
3,400	591	382
3,500	610	406
3,600	627	429
3,700	644	453
3,800	661	478
3,900	676	502
4,000	689	525
4,100	702	548
4,200	717	573
4,300	733	600
4,400	746	625
4,500	755	647
4,600	762	667
4,700	767	687
4,800	776	709
4,900	**781**	729
5,000	779	741
5,100	762	740
5,200	744	736
5,300	731	736
5,400	722	743
5,500	718	752
5,600	715	762
5,700	715	776
5,800	711	786
5,900	711	798
6,000	710	811
6,100	704	817
6,200	698	824
6,300	689	**826**
6,400	678	**826**
6,500	660	816

NITROUS

While there are many different types of nitrous systems available for the Gen III V-8, the system shown in this chapter is a simple Nitrous Express (NX) 150-hp, wet-flow, single-shot system. While there are port-injected, dry flow systems and injector-ring systems available, the single plate wet-flow system is by far the easiest to install and yet still provides a substantial power increase when the nitrous is flicked on. Usually, wet-flow systems are preferable for up to 150-hp systems. Dry systems that get the additional necessary fuel through larger fuel injectors are usually used for 200+ hp systems.

One drawback of the nitrous system's affordability is that the nitrous bottle needs to be continuously refilled. This lightweight bottle is equipped with a remotely activated electric opener and heater, so you can arm the nitrous while you drive down the road.

INSTALLATION NOTES

This NX nitrous system, which was installed on a '01 Pontiac Firebird, came with all the components to install. The one tricky step is drilling a hole in the intake. This can be done with the intake still on the vehicle by removing the intake tract and placing a vacuum suction tube just below the drilling to catch the chips. Check the pictures for hints on where to mount the solenoids and nozzle.

POWER PRODUCTION

If you've ever driven anything with nitrous, you know what a hoot it is to press the happy button. If you haven't, you really need to try it. A big power boost is a precarious chemistry experiment, but increases of 150 hp and less are very manageable and very fun. There still is the potential to burn a piston if the fuel solenoid doesn't open to help out the nitrous, but the chances of this are low with a more conservative setup.

If you don't know, nitrous is like renting instead of buying because the bottle will need regular refills to keep the engine pumping and bumping. This isn't the end of the world, just a fact of life with laughing gas horsepower.

Adding a nitrous-oxide injection system to your Gen III V-8 is an affordable way to add some serious power. This nitrous system, a 150-hp kit from Nitrous Express (NX), is called a wet-flow system because it injects both nitrous and fuel into the intake.

Hard Core Power

Open Plenum Intake

If you want a bad-ass engine in your street rod, hot rod, or racecar, order GM Performance Parts' new open plenum intake manifold (PN 88958675). For the street, Edelbrock's dual plane intake will offer impressive driveability and power production.

GM Performance Parts is now offering an open-plenum intake manifold for the Gen III V-8 (PN 88958675). It is designed to be used with a performance carburetor or throttle body and injectors (the manifold is cast with injector bosses). On a stock LS6, this intake has helped produce over 450 hp on a dyno.

Edelbrock has released a dual-plane intake manifold for the Gen III intended to provide street manners with the simplicity of a carburetor.

Both of these intakes will work with a carburetor. The GMPP intake will work with an EFI throttle body, as it is equipped with injector bosses for aftermarket EFI controllers.

Stand Alone Ignition Systems

If you use a carbureted intake system, firing the ignition coils becomes an issue. There are currently many companies working to offer control boxes that will read the factory crank and cam sensors and fire the factory coils (Edelbrock, MSD, GM, etc.). These products should be available soon, as the market is asking for them now. Also, GM Performance Parts will soon be offering a funky-looking, but functional distributor drive/mechanical fuel-pump drive for Gen IIIs.

Stand-Alone EFI Controllers

Many aftermarket companies are offering stand-alone electronic fuel-injection systems that will plug into the factory engine sensors and run the engine with your own calibration. The Gen III V-8 really shines here as the factory crank and cam sensors, along with many other sensors built into the

This distributor/fuel-pump drive offered by GM Performance Parts is a simple solution to the ignition system issue. It's being used in racing, but will work perfectly on a street rod, muscle car, or off-road vehicle.

(continued on next page)

Hard Core Power (continued)

(continued from previous page)

engine, make running an EFI controller a simple "plug-and-play" affair. Some of the companies offering these products include ACCEL, Electromotive, F.A.S.T., Big Stuff, MoTeC, and others.

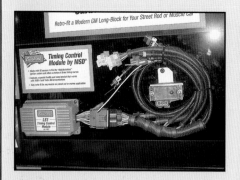

Edelbrock has enlisted MSD Ignition to create a stand-alone ignition system that reads the crank- and cam-trigger sensor outputs to drive the factory coil-near-plug ignition system. Look for more ignitions like this in the near future.

Stroker Kits

The Gen III V-8 lends itself to adding a bigger stroke crank because of the copious room in the crankcase and raised camshaft. With no modifications to the block, you can install a crank with up to a 4.000-inch stroke in place of the 3.622-inch stock crank. This will yield about a 10 percent increase in displacement (from 346 to 382 ci on an LS1). Some strategic grinding on the bottom of the cylinder liners will allow up to a 4.250-inch crank in an LS1 block, which will attain 406 cubic inches — a 17 percent increase in displacement on an LS1. Obviously, a stroker kit should be accompanied by increased airflow capabilities to take advantage of the increased displacement.

Tip: When swapping in aftermarket pistons, make sure the number-8 piston has been machined to clear the factory crank sensor wheel.

Sleeving Stock Blocks

There are a few ways to get more than 406 cubic inches out of an LS1. One is to cut away much of the inside of the block and add sleeves to get up to 4.160-inch diameter bores (the stock bores are 3.897 inches). There is great debate over the streetability of these engines. We can say this modification is drastic and costly, yet it seems to be gaining popularity.

Though it's expensive, you can choose the C5R block from GM Performance Parts. These blocks come with 4.125-inch bores and are designed for high-performance applications. These are expensive to work with, but probably only a few thousand more than a sleeved block (what's a few thousand when you're building a $15K+ engine?) and are designed to handle the power you'll undoubtedly be making.

If 383 ci is not big enough for you, you could install these sleeves in a machined-out block to achieve a 4.125-inch bore. Combine this with a 4.000-inch stroke and you could have one of the few 427-ci LS1-based engines.

If you don't have a Gen III V-8 engine in your car but want to install one, there are multiple ways to procure one. GM Performance Parts sells brand new aluminum 5.7-liter LS1 and LS6s, and 345-hp 6.0-liter iron-block crate engines. If you're willing to buy used, there are many recycling companies offering pull-out engines and transmissions (like this one shown). These usually come complete with the front drives and other required components, which can be a big time saver when building a car from scratch.

100 HORSEPOWER
ANYBODY CAN INSTALL

The engine assembled here with SLP components was evaluated on a dynamometer before being installed back in a vehicle to verify the performance increase. You don't need a dyno to feel an extra 100 hp — it's dramatic! This engine was assembled and dyno tested at Wheel to Wheel Powertrain, in Warren, Michigan (www.wheeltowheel.net). The dyno results listed later in this chapter tell the potential of the Gen III and the effectiveness of these parts. Going from 370 hp to 470 hp (standard correction) without touching the short block is very impressive. As you probably can tell, these are dyno headers, used so Wheel to Wheel could record exhaust gas temperatures across all the cylinders.

There are very few engine upgrade packages that provide more real "bang for the buck" performance on the Gen III V-8 than the addition of CNC-ported cylinder heads, an intake, a camshaft, a pair of long-tube exhaust headers, and a modified engine control calibration. In this chapter, we'll show you how to bolt on these pieces, offered by SLP in New Jersey, to add 100 hp to the power production of a stock 340-hp LS1 V-8 engine (the power numbers are higher than this on the dyno because there are no accessories, and a set of headers was used in place of the stock manifolds).

For simplicity, this chapter will focus on the disassembly process once the engine is out of a vehicle. For details on how to remove from a vehicle, see Chapter 4. The reassembly is not fully detailed, as most of it is just the reverse of the process detailed here. The few different steps in the reassembly process are detailed towards the end of the chapter.

SLP POWER

All of the pre-'01 LS1 Gen III V-8s will respond with power to the addition of GM '01 and later LS6-type components, so SLP includes the dropped floor LS6-style intake manifold with their CNC-ported LS6 cylinder heads, cus-

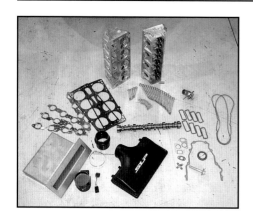

The components used for this upgrade all come from SLP (www.slponline.com). The SLP components used here include assembled CNC-ported cylinder heads, a special roller camshaft, LS6-style intake, roller timing chain, 160-degree thermostat, MAF sensor, cold-air box for the vehicle, various single-use gaskets and fasteners, along with long-tube exhaust headers (a few components not shown). All the aluminum-reinforced gaskets and seals required in the process of replacing these hard parts are available from GM or SLP. Also, SLP offers a calibration to go with these components. It needs to be flashed into the vehicle's PCM to take full advantage of the potential of this package.

tom-ground hydraulic roller camshaft, and assorted other performance-adding components. The LS6 made 405 hp in the '02 Z06 Corvette, so picking up a few ponies is where the CNC-ported heads and matching cam make the difference.

The part that makes the addition of these parts so attractive is they require no modifications to the LS1 short block. Also, SLP offers a revised engine calibration to take advantage of the additional performance components. This new calibration can be added to your factory controller by filling out an information card and sending SLP the controller from your vehicle in the mail.

MORE AIR

This power package makes real power in a very unspectacular way. There isn't a supercharger hanging off the top of the engine or some other wild looking external clue that the power is going to

increase 100 hp over the entire power-band. The heads obviously flow more air, but increased flow volumes in the port and chamber combination do not always equate to power. As the saying goes, "we don't race flow benches." For this reason, the combination of the CNC-ported cylinder heads, camshaft, valvesprings, intake, cold-air box, and calibration all add up to the performance improvement.

A LIFT

The engine work performed here was done with the engine out of the vehicle, which we recommend. For detailed information on how to remove a Gen III V-8 engine from a production vehicle, refer to Chapter 4. These changes could be made with the engine in the vehicle, but the tight confines of the engine bay make a simple job very difficult. As you'll notice in Chapter 4, a four-point (not a drive on) vehicle lift is required to raise the vehicle up over the engine/suspension cradle assembly to access the engine. Obviously, not everyone has one of these lifts in their garage, so you'll have to determine a solution to this to get to the engine. Believe us — removing the engine is worth the effort vs. doing the swap with the engine still in the vehicle.

SPECIAL TOOLS

There are very few special tools required to do the installation of these

performance components. In Chapter 4, we showed you how to remove a Gen III V-8 without buying many special tools. Simple hand tools like a radiator hook tool, wrenches, pliers, and screwdrivers were used in inventive ways to get many of the special connectors and linkages apart.

Engine reassembly does require a special tool: a bolt-stretch angle socket. This tool clips on to a 1/2-inch breaker bar and is used to read how much the bolt is turned. The tool has a "zero" bar that is rested against something solid, then the dial is rotated to read zero on the pointer. The engine assembler then uses the breaker bar to turn the fastener a specific angle, like until the dial pointer is aimed at 76 degrees, to add 76 degrees of stretch to the bolt — which results in more clamping force on the components that are bolted together. Adding "angle" to the clamping fastener is more accurate than torquing, which is why it is used. There are many companies offering these tools. The most common we have seen is from Snap-On, PN TA-360.

In the case of the Gen III V-8 aluminum cylinder heads, the fastening process looks like this. The 10 head bolts per head are first torqued to 22 ft-lbs. Then, most engine builders use a Sharpie pen to mark each bolt head with a vertical line — this is done so if the builder gets mixed up in the midst of the torquing procedure, the lines will help

Dollars Per Horsepower

In case you're wondering, the SLP components discussed here (CNC heads, intake, cam, headers, and custom calibration) total up to around $3,500, which is a fair amount of money. Wheel-to-Wheel charges about $5,000 to do the buildup, dyno, and installation work. But the power gain these components provide, which is about 100 hp and 70 ft-lb of torque across the powerband, brings the cost to about $85/hp, which is a fair price for a new design.

The $/hp ratio is used by many in the automotive aftermarket to gauge whether a component, system, or service will be deemed a good value by the market. In general, $45/hp is the killer deal everyone shoots to meet or be below in the installed power area. The threshold for successful sales seems to be $90/hp – this package just below the mark.

So, this kit provides the kind of power many consider to be of value. The real value is in the extra 100 hp, which is the kind of dramatic lift in performance that anyone can feel — stopwatch or not.

Parts to Increase Power
100+ HP on an LS1 Engine

Description	SLP Part Numbers
SLP CNC-ported cylinder heads	1250399
SLP camshaft	12504
SLP timing chain	55002
SLP long-tube headers	30052
LS6 intake manifold kit	30041
PCM calibration	call
160 degree thermostat	100223
SLP cold airbox kit	21033
SLP MAF sensor	23606

You'll also need these components from GM:

Intake Gaskets	
Car (5.7 liter)	12559612
Truck (4.8/5.3/6.0 liter)	17122608
Oil Pan Gasket	12558760
Engine covers	
Front	12558013
Rear	12574293
Front cover seal	12561244
Valley Plate Gasket	12558178
Water Pump Gasket	12559271
Head Gasket	
5.7 liter	12573949, 12558809-10
4.8 liter	12573329
6.0 liter	
Valve Cover Gasket	12558178
Exhaust Gaskets	
Car (5.7 liter)	12561912
Truck (4.8/5.3/6.0 liter)	12558573

them remember where they are in the process. From there, all the head bolts receive 76 degrees of stretch in the GM-specified sequence. Then, the eight long head bolts get 76 degrees more stretch, following the radial torquing sequence recommended by GM. As a final step, the two shorty bolts at the ends of the head receive only an additional 34 degrees of stretch. This is for an aluminum engine block; the head bolts for iron-block engines receive 90 degrees at first, then 90 degrees on the long bolts and 50 degrees on the shorties.

It was said earlier in the book a few times but needs to be reinforced here — the factory head bolts are single-use only. Do not reuse them, because the clamping load they provide the second time they are stretched is not the same as the first time.

TIPS FOR SUCCESS

Upgrading just the top end of a Gen III LS1 V-8 is a good way to start off modifying these engines. The top end of the Gen III engine is very straightforward and making changes here provides a dramatic change in the power output of the engine. Some tips to maximize your pleasure include the following:

1. Make sure you drain the coolant out of the top end of the engine by removing the two drain plugs at each side of the engine block (one is above the starter). This will keep coolant from drooling into the cylinders and blind-tapped head bolt holes. This is critical, as any fluid in the blind holes increases the risk of cracking the block when the head bolts are reinstalled and torqued.

2. Perform the top end work in a clean area.

3. Blow out the blind tapped head bolt holes with pressurized air before reinstalling the head bolts and torquing them in place. If you don't and there's oil, coolant, or other incompressible liquid in those holes, you could crack the block — which would force you to replace it.

WHY CNC PORTING?

Up until the late 1980s, any ported cylinder head was done by hand. The skilled artisans that did the grinding to create high-flowing cylinder head intake and exhaust ports were sought out for the feel and control they displayed in creating shapes that made power. The only problem with this situation was that getting a ported head was very expensive and each one was a little different. Then came the CNC-machining center, and everything has changed.

The term "CNC" stands for computer numerical control. It describes a machining center that is run by a computer. In days past, a mill or a lathe needed to be operated by a skilled tradesman to perform its duties. While skilled tradesmen still set up the CNC machining centers, the computers run the machines during the actual operations. This allows the employee to do more valued work while the CNC machine whirs along.

Early CNC machines operated in just three axis: what many would call the X, Y, and Z axis. These machines were good at making simple components in large lots.

Then, four-axis CNC machines started to become available and more intricate machining could be performed. Intricate components and areas, like combustion chambers, could be machined to very tight tolerances. The extra axis came from splitting the normal axes at a 45-degree angle, which gave the machining center and computer another angle to approach a component from.

The big leap came when five- and six-axis CNC machining centers became available. Now, a CNC machining cen-

Bypassing the Throttle Body Coolant

Some performance enthusiast magazines have touted bypassing the throttle body coolant hoses to prevent "heating up the incoming air." While on all-out performance engines this has been shown to make a difference, if you are driving your vehicle in multiple seasons, this will probably hurt cold-start characteristics and not be worth the added quirkiness. But you decide...

ter could articulate a spinning cutting tool and the object being machined, like you'd do with human hands. Complex, hard-to-reach shapes, like the port of a cylinder head, could be machined to within thousandths of an inch.

When CNC machines first appeared, many head porters feared their profession was going to be eliminated. Instead, CNC machines have made great head port creators like rock stars. Their port jobs are digitized and copied in CNC machines onto an untold amount of cylinder heads for performance enthusiasts all over the world to enjoy.

VEHICLES THAT RESPOND

This SLP component package will work on any Camaro or Firebird built between 1999 and 2003 with a V-8 engine called out by the GM regular production order (RPO) code LS1. The LS1 engine in the F-body cars was initially rated at 305 hp and 335 ft-lb of torque (SAE corrected), and the SLP package should bump that number into 440 hp and up (standard corrected).

The SLP cylinder heads are fully CNC-ported, which means the intake, exhaust, and combustion chambers have been machined. Beyond the cool look of the heads, the valve sizes have been increased to 2.020 /1.575 inches and the factory valves are replaced with Manley stainless-steel units. The valvetrain is also upgraded with SLP titanium valvespring retainers and performance valvesprings.

The heads are milled to end up with 63.5-cc combustion chambers, which will raise the compression ratio to 10.7:1. This means you'll need to run premium fuel, but that's no problem, right?

3. The LS1/LS6 low-profile intake manifold is held in place with ten 6-mm diameter bolts with 8-mm hex-heads that go into the block. The bolt holes in the block are open to the crankcase, so you need to use some thread sealer when you reinstall them (they come with sealer on them from GM, but they'll need a reapplication the second time around). Once these are loosened, it's easy to pry off the O-ringed intake with a screwdriver.

1. The LS-1 V-8 engine has very few hoses on its exterior, but the few that are left once an engine is removed from a vehicle will need to be pulled off the intake. This Gen III V-8 is an '01 LS1, but the entire Gen III engine family is similar except for a few hoses, wires, and sensors, so most of this info will apply to any Gen III V-8. You can easily remove these PCV hoses that connect the valve covers by pulling them off the valve cover vent tubes by hand.

2. On the LS1 and LS6 intakes, the throttle body is connected to the cooling system by a water hose, which heats the body for improved start-up performance. To remove the hose, use pliers to release the clamp and a screwdriver to work the hose off the tube, or you can use one of these cool clamp/hose pullers from Snap-On.

4. The Gen III V-8 has two knock sensors that bolt to the block deep inside their "nests" in the intake valley cover plate. You need to remove the wiring connectors to prevent the wiring harness from being damaged in the process of tearing down the engine. The first step is to gently pry the rubber grommet loose using two screwdrivers, as shown.

5. There's a special tool available to remove the knock sensor wiring connector from the sensor bolted to the block, but the pros at Wheel to Wheel Powertrain have figured out how to remove the connector using two screwdrivers. By pinching the connectors at the widest point of their base, the two retaining tabs that hold them are relaxed and the connector can be removed from the sensor.

6. Early Gen III V-8s came with this tubing apparatus to vent any steam pockets in the cooling system from both the front and rear. The LS6 intake (which became standard on both the LS1 and LS6 in 2002 and beyond) has more drop in it for a larger plenum area, so GM eliminated the tubing under the intake. To make this work, the rear vent holes are blocked off and the front steam vents are tied together with a tube (the front ties into the throttle preheat system). To remove the vent tubing, loosen the four 6-mm bolts with a 10-mm hex-head socket.

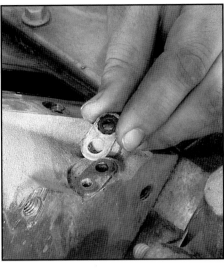

7. Be careful not to lose these steam vent tubing seal plates — often they stick to the engine and appear to be part of the block. If you lose them, the steam vent mounting blocks won't seal against the engine block.

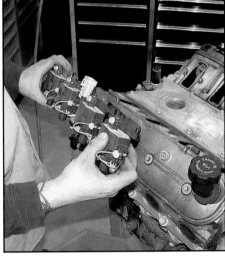

8. Each spark plug on the Gen III has its own coil, with four coils mounted on each valve cover. GM has used two methods to mount the coils to the valve covers. One system, shown here, has the coils mounted on a single bracket. In the other method, used from 1997 to 1998, the coils are mounted separately to the valve cover (these valve covers have perimeter bolts on the valve covers unlike later versions that have the four bolts down the center of the valve cover). To remove the bracket-mounted coils, you'll need to remove the 6-mm diameter bolts with a 8-mm hex-head socket.

9. The valve covers are a dead giveaway to how old the engine/heads are — the perimeter-bolt valve covers were built from 1997 to 1998, and the center-bolt valve covers were built from 1999 to present.

10. The rocker assembly on the Gen III is ingenious in how easy it is to install/remove. Simply loosen the 8-mm diameter bolts with an 8-mm hex-head and the entire system lifts off as a unit. If you are running a CNC-ported head, a good idea is to put sealer on the rocker anchor bolts that are above the intake ports, as the porting process usually removes a lump of material in the intake port that exposes the bottom of these bolt holes.

11. Now you can remove each of the pushrods. If there is one part that always needs to be upgraded for performance applications in the Gen III, it's the pushrods. Buy good replacements and sleep easier.

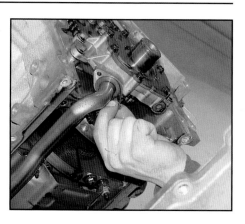

12. There are ten 11-mm diameter bolts with a 15-mm hex head (on the '97-03 engines, there are 2 short bolts and 8 long bolts per cylinder head ; the '04 blocks use all short bolts) to clear the water passages in the block at each end of the cylinder head that hold each Gen III cylinder head on the block. There are also 5 M8 bolts with 10-mm hex heads to seal the intake port area. These bolts are not to be reused! *They are a torque-to-yield design.* The bolts are torqued to 22 ft-lb, a torque that is minimally affected by the variations in friction from the type of lubricant used on the fastener threads or mating surface of the bolt head to cylinder head boss. Then, a torque angle gauge is placed on the wrench and the fastener is twisted to a predetermined angle.

13. The harmonic balancer is also the crankshaft pulley, which eliminates one step of the disassembly process. If you use a deep-throat puller, don't let the center push bolt of the puller seat in the end of the crank, as it will probably damage the threads in the crank. Instead, you can use a big socket or an adapter for the puller to seat against. When reinstalling the harmonic balancer, make sure to torque the bolt to 37 ft-lbs and twist it 140 degrees.

14. There are ten 10-mm hex-head, 8-mm diameter bolts to be removed from the main portion of the oil pan, and two 10-mm hex-head, 6-mm diameter bolts at each end of the oil pan that bolt to the front and rear covers. You need to remove them all to get the oil pan off the engine. The oil pan is a stressed member on the Gen III V-8, but it doesn't use dowel pins or any other type of locator, so the installation process requires some detail to get the front and rear covers and oil pan to all find their homes.

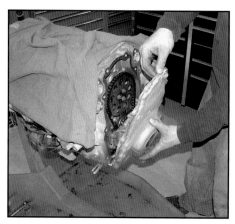

15. The front cover is removed after the water pump is removed (six 8-mm-diameter, 10-mm hex-headed bolts). The front cover is held in place with eight bolts that have a 10-mm hex head and an 8-mm diameter. You'll probably need to use a little coercion to free the cover from the block. Do not reuse this seal; it's a compression design that can only be used once. The rear cover is pressurized, so it's held on the engine with more 8-mm diameter, 10-mm hex-head bolts — 12 to be exact. The front, rear, and top cover, along with the oil pan, all use the same length 8-mm-diameter bolts.

16. When you're increasing power production on the Gen III, it's important to increase the oil flow and pressure in the engine. You can do this by adding a stiffer bypass spring and/or porting the outlet of the oil pump. Either way, the oil pump pickup tube will need to be removed. Once the oil pan is off, remove the one 6-mm diameter bolt with a 10-mm hex head at the bottom of the oil pump. You'll also need to remove the one 8-mm-diameter stud (not shown), which has a 13-mm hex-head nut that holds the oil pump tube tab at the bottom of the engine. Removing both of these will release the pickup tube.

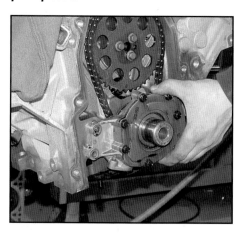

17. The Gen III has its oil pump driven off the front of the crankshaft, which becomes obvious after the cam cover/water pump front cover is removed. Taking the four 8-mm-diameter, 10-mm hex-head bolts off frees the oil pump for rework. Reinstalling the oil pump requires centering the bare oil pump body on the crank. This is done by installing four bolts to 45 in-lbs and centering the pump with two 0.002-inch feeler gauges.

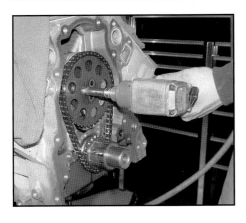

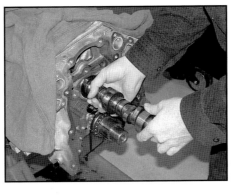

18. The cam gear is held in place with three 8-mm-diameter, 10-mm hex-head bolts; and don't worry, it self centers.

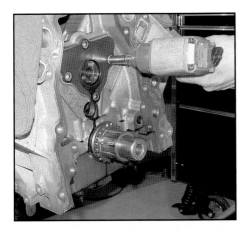

20. Probably one of the most ingenious aspects of the Gen III is that spinning the camshaft one revolution with the upper valvetrain removed pushes all the lifters up into their retainers and allows the cam to be removed — with the lifters still in the engine. The lifters won't stay in the retainers forever, so install the new cam sooner than later. The cam is hollow, so W2W slides a 6-inch-long, 3/8-inch socket extension in the hollow portion of the cam to lift and pull it out of the block a little. Then, once it's far enough out of the block to grab, they pull it out like this. Once the cam is out, you'll have torn down the top end of a Gen III V-8 engine. Now you can add the components to easily make over 450 streetable horsepower.

22. SLP provides a shim to place inside the oil pump pressure bleed-off spring bore to increase the line pressure in the oiling system. Here, the shim is being pushed into the bore of the oil pump pop-off spring. Install the spring and shim by first releasing the factory pop-off spring. Remove the threaded 8-mm Allen plug on the side of the oil pump body. Then, slide the shim inside the bore, apply a few drops of red thread locker on the threads of the Allen plug, and reinstall it in the pump body.

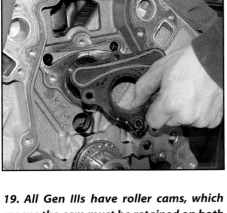

19. All Gen IIIs have roller cams, which means the cam must be retained on both ends (unlike cams with flat-tappet lifters, which hold the cam in place by the spinning of the lobes). Under the cam gear is the cam plate, which is held in place with four 8-mm-diameter, 10-mm hex-head bolts. When you're reinstalling these bolts, they should have a few drops of blue Loctite placed on the threads before they're torqued to 18 ft-lbs.

21. When increasing the power on a Gen III V-8, the oil pressure/flow needs to be increased to ensure there is sufficient oil for lubrication and cooling. To address this, disassemble the oil pump to modify it for increased oiling. Unbolt the seven 6-mm-diameter, 10-mm hex-head bolts, remove the cover plate, and slide out the gerotor gears. Mildly radius the inlet and outlet of the pump body with a grinder and clean it thoroughly. Once the body is reinstalled properly on the crank, lube all the parts liberally with engine oil before reassembling the pump body.

23. The SLP camshaft is a 234/228-degree grind with 0.576/0.571-inch lift on the intake/exhaust valves. This is all on a 112-degree centerline with 113 degrees of lobe separation. If you don't speak camshaft, this means the cam is a street-grind roller lifter cam that'll work with the stock hydraulic lifters, provide a slightly lopey idle, and will make good power across the RPM band, yet still be acceptable to drive every day. The cam journals should be lubed with standard 30-weight engine oil. The lobes should receive a good slathering of the SLP-provided lobe lube. Apply a thorough coating here to ensure a smooth startup. As a note, roller cams don't need high-performance moly-based lube at startup, especially since the moly ends up everywhere inside the engine.

24. While this pump is shown being reassembled on the bench, the oil pump needs to be centered on the crank before being reassembled. When that is done, reassemble the pump body and bolt on the front plate. The 8-mm bolts that hold the oil pump front plate in place need two drops of blue Loctite to minimize the chance of them coming loose in the future. Torque them to 18 ft-lbs. As a note, almost all the small fasteners on the Gen III V-8 are 8-mm bolts of various lengths and almost all of them are torqued to 18 ft-lbs.

26. Reinstall the Gen III V-8 cam cover plate at the front. The four 8-mm fasteners on the front plate should receive two drops of blue Loctite before being torqued in place at 18 ft-lbs.

28. Apply a few drops of engine oil to the crank snout and place the bare oil pump body over the snout of the crank (this oil pump will be disassembled in the next step). The four 8-mm fasteners will need a drop or two of blue Loctite on them before they're finally torqued to the 18 ft-lbs, but don't do that yet. To align the pump body to the crank, attach the disassembled pump body on the engine with two fasteners torqued to an initial force of 45 in-lbs. This low torque level will allow you to center the pump body on the crank to avoid uneven wear in the pump.

25. The best way to install the hollow cam the final third of the way is with a long 3/8-inch-drive extension slid up inside the cam. This provides leverage as the cam is negotiated past the last few cam journals in the block. Up until that point, the cam can be installed by hand, as shown.

27. The Gen III V-8 comes from the factory with a roller timing chain, but it's recommended that you use a more robust performance timing chain, as the stockers have been known to fail in hi-po applications. Luckily, SLP offers a stout roller timing chain and gear combo that bolts in place of the stock unit with no modifications.

29. GM sells a special tool to center the oil pump, but there's an easy way to get this done without buying the tool. Slide two 0.002-inch-thick feeler gauges far enough into the pump so they are between the pump body and crank snout 180 degrees apart. Sweep the feeler gauges around the snout diameter — this will center the oil pump on the crank snout — while keeping them 180 degrees apart. With the feeler gauges still in place, apply two drops of red Loctite to the uninstalled bolts and torque them to 18 ft-lbs to lock the pump in place. Now, remove the initial torqued bolts, apply Loctite, and reinstall at 18 ft-lbs.

Degreeing the Camshaft

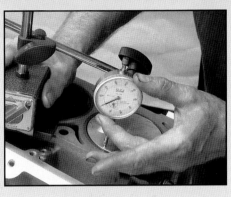

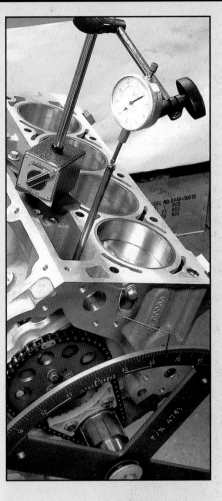

It's recommended that any time you install a different cam in an engine, you degree it, just to make sure it's installed to the manufacturer's specifications and allows sufficient clearance for the valves. This is critical, as even if the best cam is installed four degrees retarded when it should be two degrees advanced, it isn't going to run right and could damage the engine. Degreeing will also ensure that the camshaft is installed properly in relation to the crank and piston movement so the valves won't hit the pistons. The following is a basic breakdown of this process.

1. With the crank and cam gears lined up at the "dot" and the timing chain linking the cam to the crank, install a degree wheel on the crank and a pointer on the front of the engine. In this case, the degree wheel is from Moroso and the pointer is a piece of welding wire.

2. Set the number-1 piston (it would be the front hole of the driver-side if the engine was installed) to TDC by rotating the crank. Use a dial indicator or a piston stop to tell you when it reaches TDC. Move the degree wheel and/or pointer so it reads zero. If you're using a piston stop, rotate the crank 360 degrees. If using a dial indicator, go over TDC to the other side and come back to bring the piston up to TDC again and read the degree wheel.

3. If the degree wheel stops on a value that is 10 degrees different from the initial value, move the pointer 5 degrees towards where the initial value was located. Cutting the difference in value readings in half is how you home in on the true location of the cam in reference to the crankshaft rotation. Next, rotate the crank 360 degrees back the other way again and continue syncing up the cam and crank. Once the values come up the same, go to the next step.

4. Install the dial indicator on a lifter/pushrod combo on the intake lobe and cycle the crank to the full lift point of the camshaft. To check the camshaft, watch the dial indicator while rotating the crank a given amount down from full lift on both sides of the cam lobe. For this example, we'll assume that value is 0.050 inch on each side. At 0.050 inch down from full lift on each side, record the degree values at each point. To determine the intake lobe peak lift centerline, divide the sum of these two values by two. Compare this number to the intake centerline number on the cam card to determine if the cam is properly placed in reference to the crankshaft. If it is advanced or retarded, adjust it using a special cam gear or key.

30. Once you bolt the oil pump back into place, you can reinstall the oil pump pick-up. Apply a light coat of lube to the o-ring before installing. then, use some red Loctite and torque the 8-mm fasteners on the oil pump to 18 ft-lbs and the 6-mm nut on the center main stud to 106 in-lbs.

31. Install the new front cover gasket loosely and then install the harmonic balancer to center the cover around the crank. GM designed the Gen III LS1 V-8 so many of the components find their own home, which means it has few external locators. Then, snug the fasteners on the cover to 89 in-lbs in a radial sequence, and finish by torquing them in a radial sequence to 18 ft-lbs to get everything properly located. See Photo 34 for details on checking alignment before final-torquing the cover fasteners.

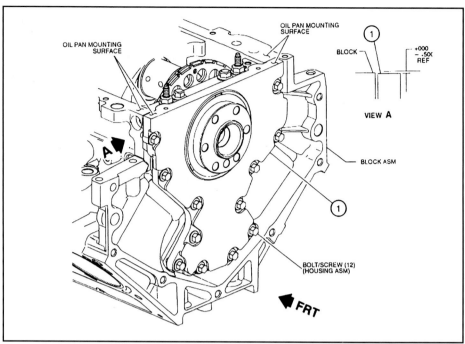

32. While the front and rear covers on the Gen III V8 essentially 'self-locate', this illustration shows how to measure the exact tolerances the GM manufacturing process recommends. (Illustration courtesy of GM)

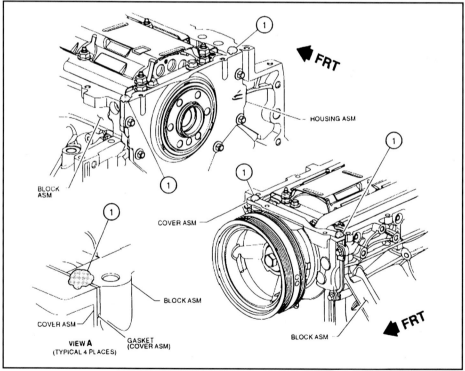

33. The Gen III V-8 was designed to have only planar mating surfaces. This means there aren't angular mating points, which can lead to oil leaks — like the common leak point for small-block Chevys where the oil pan seal arc meets the block rail. While the use of liquid sealer is rare on this engine, it is needed where the front and rear covers mate with the engine block and oil pan. Put four approximately 3/8-inch dollops of sealer at the four corners and then install the oil pan. (Illustration courtesy of GM)

34. The oil pan is then installed on the engine block with the fasteners hand-tightened in place to help locate it. The oil pan needs to be aligned before final torquing. To do this, the two long 6-mm fasteners at the rear corner of the oil pan that thread into the rear cover are torqued to 9 ft-lbs. The oil pan is a stressed member in the powertrain, so the back surface of the pan needs to be aligned with the rear face of the rear cover. The two surfaces need to be aligned within 0.020 inch (0.500 mm), with the oil pan always forward of the rear face of the cover. Now final-torque the twelve 8-mm bolts to 18 ft-lbs in a radial pattern.

36. This is critical! *Blow out all the head bolt holes with pressurized air to make sure no incompressible fluid (oil, water, coolant, etc.) is in them. You will crack the block if you torque down the fasteners with any incompressible fluid inside — making the block junk. Cover the bores to keep any fluid from landing in them when you blow out the holes.*

38. The SLP CNC heads install just like the stock heads, but it's probably not a bad idea to check valve-to-piston clearance with some clay on the dome of one of the pistons to make sure the cam/head change hasn't put you in the danger zone. Put about a 1/2-inch dollop of modeling clay (don't use Playdoh, as it will spring back and give you a false reading!) on the intake and exhaust valve head, bolt the cylinder head on with the old head gasket and four head bolts, cycle the valvetrain through one revolution. You must use either a solid lifter or a checking valvespring so the lifter doesn't collapse and give you a false reading. Remove the head and measure the depth of the clay by plunging a micrometer through the thinnest portion. It should be more than 0.120 inch on the exhaust valve and 0.090 inch in the intake, or you'll need to add valve reliefs in the pistons.

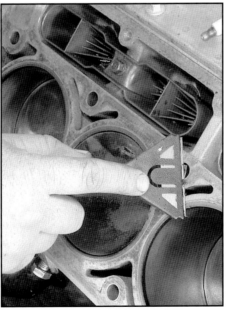

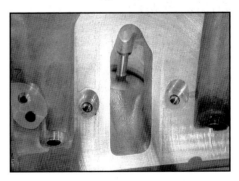

35. There are two different head gaskets used on the Gen III V-8. The 1997-'98 Gen IIIs used a head gasket that can be used on all Gen IIIs, but many hot-rodders believe it cannot withstand the same abuse as the 1999-and-later head gasket. The early head gasket can be identified because it has a cutout at the lower edge between 1 and 3 or 5 and 7 (depending on what bank you're talking about) on the lower edge. An important caveat here is the later head gasket cannot be used on the 1997-'98 head. Using this later gasket on older Gen IIIs will result in a substantial water leak — so make sure you get the right head gasket for your application.

37. Take a few minutes to make sure the engine block and cylinder head mating surfaces are free of anything that might prevent a tight seal between them. A good way to do this is to scrape the head surface with a razor blade. Suck the debris away using a vacuum cleaner tube placed close by.

39. Here's where power is made. The Gen III V-8 "cathedral" intake ports are highly refined from the factory, but they do respond to specific porting work. While port development is still a black art, the act of creating CNC ports is a science. Once a port shape has been created, the CNC machines can duplicate them with impressive accuracy at a reasonable cost. There are many sources for CNC-ported cylinder heads.

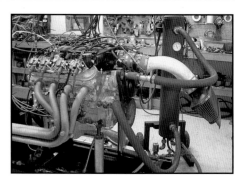

40. Many of the critical fasteners, like the head bolts, on the Gen III V-8 use bolt stretch instead of torque to make sure they have the proper clamping load. To help minimize bolt stretch variation, it's recommended you apply lube to the backside of the fasteners as is being done here. Do not apply any lube, thread sealer, or thread lock to the threads of the 11-mm head bolt fasteners.

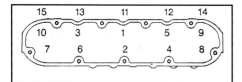

41. The process of setting the proper clamping load on the head bolts goes like this. All of the new 11-mm head bolts are torqued to 22 ft-lbs (30 N-m) in the factory recommended sequence (1 through 10). Using a Sharpie pen, apply a vertical line to all the head bolts to use as a reference when applying the twist to the bolts. Then, install the bolt torque angle meter tool (GM PN J36660 or Snap-On PN TA-360) on a breaker bar and add 76 degrees of rotation to each bolt — again in the factory recommended sequence. Add another 76 degrees of rotation to the long bolts (1 thru 8), while the two short bolts per head get only 34 more degrees rotation (bolts 9 and 10). Torque the top five 8-mm bolts to 22 ft-lbs beginning with the center bolt (bolts 11 thru 15).

42. Install the LS6 intake manifold with new gaskets (available from GM, SLP, and other parts houses). This brings up a good point: don't reuse any Gen III V-8 gaskets because they are all of the compression-carrier design. This means the aluminum surface of the gasket takes the torquing load to control how much compression the embedded silicon sealing surfaces experience. This maximizes sealing control and minimizes the need for re-torquing to maintain the clamping load – but they are one-use items.

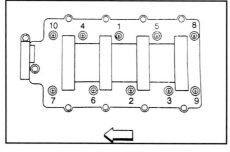

43. The lightweight intake is made of nylon, so it does not require a lot of torque to lock it in place. Many of the intake bolts are exposed at the bottom of the threaded hole, so apply thread sealer/lock to all of their threads. Make a first pass on the fasteners at 44 in-lbs following this sequence. Make a second pass over the fasteners to come to the final torque of 89 in-lbs.

DYNO RESULTS

In the chart to the right, the engine on the left is a relatively stock 2001 SS 5.7-liter LS1 with only a set of headers, and the engine on the right has been modified with the complete SLP Stage III kit, including the heads, cam, intake, and headers.

With the addition of a few hot-rod parts, the power improvement to the LS1 is very real. Most of the additional power comes from upgrading to the latest performance components that let the engine breathe.

	SLP DYNO			
	'01 SS		SLP SS	
RPM	**Torque**	**HP**	**Torque**	**HP**
3,000	347	198	403	230
3,100	349	206	401	237
3,200	352	214	399	243
3,300	355	223	399	251
3,400	357	231	399	259
3,500	359	239	403	268
3,600	361	247	408	280
3,700	365	257	414	292
3,800	368	266	422	305
3,900	372	276	428	318
4,000	374	285	432	329
4,100	373	291	435	340
4,200	374	299	440	352
4,300	375	306	445	364
4,400	378	317	450	377
4,500	381	326	453	388
4,600	**382**	334	456	400
4,700	381	340	**459**	410
4,800	381	348	**459**	420
4,900	380	354	**459**	428
5,000	377	359	457	435
5,100	375	364	456	442
5,200	371	368	452	448
5,300	365	368	449	454
5,400	360	370	445	458
5,500	355	**372**	441	462
5,600	347	370	437	466
5,700	340	369	432	**469**
5,800	335	369	425	**469**
5,900	328	368	417	468
6,000	323	367	409	468
6,100	—	—	402	467
6,200	—	—	394	465

500+ HORSEPOWER NA STREET-RACER BUILDUP

I f there is any doubt remaining about the power potential of the Gen III LS1/LS6 engine architecture, the following real-world engine buildup should clear that up. Simply put, there is no other production 5.7-liter small-block pushrod V-8 engine design in the world that is as easy to build and responds to a set of race-inspired CNC-port cylinder heads and an aggressive camshaft with a streetable 500+ hp.

Now, this engine *will* have the hardcore lopey idle and need for premium gasoline that any high-performance, naturally aspirated engine would exhibit, but the powerband and peak numbers will more than justify those realities. This chapter will show you the details required to assemble any Gen III V-8, while presenting a standard combination of parts to create 500 hp.

POWER PARTS

The Gen III V-8 engine upgrade components used here were originally developed from GM Powertrain components by the people at GM Racing. The aftermarket industry then refined this package. This engine is being built by Wheel to Wheel Powertrain (W2W), in Warren, Michigan, for use in a road racing Corvette, but it isn't much different from the street Gen III V-8s they build every day for hot rod daily drivers.

The big difference between their street engines is this one has some aftermarket components in the short block, like a forged crank, billet rods, forged aluminum pistons, and other performance pieces.

Many of the 500+ hp street engines W2W builds don't have anything changed in the short block — a testament to the Gen III V-8 capability. But the aftermarket additions are shown because it's a good thing to show how aftermarket components are integrated into the Gen III in case more than 530 hp is desired — as that seems to be the limit for some factory components like the pistons and rods. In this chapter, you'll see the machine work and finesse needed to assemble a 500+ hp Gen III V-8 engine. Then, whether you choose to build this engine with the stock short-block or add even more aftermarket performance components, you'll have enough info to understand what it will take to get the engine together.

While W2W does have some tricks and refined processes they perform to extract the maximum performance and durability from these packages, almost all of the processes shown here can be repeated by anyone with similar results. And W2W is quick to give this engine design its due — they acknowledge the ease with which power is unleashed from the LS1/LS6 Gen III V-8 as a direct result of the excellent engineering by the people at General Motors Powertrain and Racing.

EXTERNAL PUMP OILING SYSTEM

As you will see, the engine built in this chapter is assembled with a dry sump oiling system that uses a two-stage external oil pump as the scavenge pump with the factory oil pump on the pressure stage to make sure oil flows to the engine in high-G cornering situations. This system is being used because the vehicle and driver this engine will service run hard through corners and experience high G-loads for sustained periods. If you are building an engine for a more street oriented application, you can save the money this system costs and use the factory wet-sump oiling system instead.

The term "dry sump" comes from the fact that the oil is not stored in the bottom of the engine anymore. There is an external oil sump holds more oil than would normally be used in a production oil pan, which allows the oil to cool and let the air percolate out of it. Storing the oil somewhere other than the bottom of the engine allows the oil pan to be much more shallow, which allows the engine to be mounted lower in the vehicle. Since the oil is not allowed to sit in the bottom of the engine, the chances of the oil roping around the crank, eating horsepower, and getting more air whipped into it, are minimized.

The choice between the dry-sump and wet-sump system usually is driven by how oil needs to be drawn out of the engine, not how oil is pumped into it. The two-stage external oil pump is actually two oil pumps that run off a common shaft. Each pump, or stage, draws oil from a different area of the oil pan. Many dry-sump systems use a three-stage pump, with one of the stages pressurizing the oil and the other stages sucking it out of the engine. The system used here is designed this way because of the rules in a road racing series mandating that the factory oil pump be used in the oiling system.

Dry-sump systems are mostly used in engines that will go in vehicles that can achieve high lateral grip for extended periods, like a road race car. They are expensive, but are good insurance the engine won't starve for oil at the end of a long cornering experience, which

would obviously result in a more expensive problem. Wet-sump oiling systems don't have the same amount of oil and control of the oil in the oil pan as the dry sump systems, which can lead to starvation of oil to the oil pump.

W2W has built 500+ hp Gen III V-8 engines with both the dry and the wet sump oiling system for the street and have never had a problem with durability in either case. It does depend on how you drive the vehicle, but in general, if you do not drive multiple race laps with the car on a road race track, the wet sump system should be acceptable.

SIMPLE PERFORMANCE

W2W uses either the LS1 or LS6 engine as their starting point to build this 500+ hp engine. The only real difference between the LS1 and LS6 engine short blocks is the pre-'01 LS1s didn't have as-cast "windows" between the mains in the bottom end of the engine block for high-

rpm air and oil-vapor flow. If you plan on spending sustained periods of time at high rpm, the later LS6 block (casting number 12561168) is the correct choice as it has better crankcase oil control.

Beyond the block, since the cylinder heads, camshaft, and intake are being swapped out, it doesn't matter whether you start with an LS1 or LS6 engine or even a 4.8-, 5.3-, or 6.0-liter iron-block truck engine. Most performance enthusiasts prefer the aluminum block LS1/LS6 engine for the weight savings, but the iron-block engines are similar in design and cost less if weight is not that big of an issue for you. Obviously, the smaller-displacement engines will make less overall power, while the 6.0-liter should make just a little bit more power than the 5.7-liter LS1 engines.

The CNC cylinder heads W2W prefers to use are the GM Performance Parts CNC heads. There are two versions, the more aggressive 11.2:1 compression head (PN 88958622), or the just

GM-Spec CNC Heads

General Motors' cylinder head port and combustion chamber guru, Ron Sperry, did the CNC development for this GM Racing cylinder head. Sperry recalls, "We were looking for more than peak flow, as these engines needed to have a solid powerband from 3,500 rpm to redline. To do this we did improve the intake port overall flow, but kept as much of the original directional shaping in the short side radius of the intake port and into the combustion chamber. GM Powertrain spent a considerable amount of time and money on this area with high-powered computer simulation and real-time flow mapping thinking a CNC-head would be needed for the '01 Z06 engine, which it wasn't. So I really believe there is very little left on the table as far as performance in this area." Sperry worked with Lingenfelter Performance to develop the CNC program to create the cylinder heads.

Sperry adds, "The rules we were working with at the time didn't allow a change in the valve

angle, intake or exhaust port exit location, spark plug location, or valve spacing, which definitely limited what we could do — but we were still able to find some gains. Basically, we removed the bottom of the rocker bosses that intrude into the cathedral intake ports, refined the port shape and combustion chamber, and cut weight out of the head wherever possible." Bringing in Sperry was the right choice, as he had a big hand in the design of the original LS1 and LS6 ports and chamber. If anyone would know what was left on the table in the creation of the production cylinder head, he would.

"If anything, having to work with such restrictive rules kept the heads stock enough that anyone can purchase them from GM Performance Parts and bolt them on with a new camshaft, pushrods, and valvesprings and make some power," concluded Sperry. We'd have to agree. If the valvetrain would have to be moved around or other changes were

made to make power, upgrading the engine would have been a lot more involved than it is.

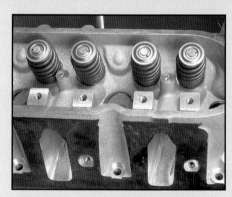

The often-copied GM CNC'd LS6 cylinder heads (the 53-cc chamber head is PN 88958622 and the 64-cc chamber head is PN 88958665) have been on the market for a few years, yet are still the benchmark of CNC'd Gen III heads. Look for more improvements and options from GMPP Gen III heads in the near future.

High-Performance for Corvette Road Racing

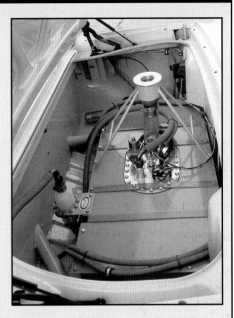

The original Motorola Cup Corvette road-racing series had cars that were essentially stock vehicles pulled off the Bowling Green, Kentucky assembly line midstream. They arrived at raceshops as unpainted chassis with powertrains and a body in white — which means it was unpainted. Obviously, this car is ready to race — but only after a lot of work.

The engine package in this chapter was created for the Gen III small-block V-8 engine by the GM Racing organization to offer to Corvette racers in a road racing series originally called the Motorola Cup. That series has gone through a few sponsors and owners over the years, which might explain why you're not familiar with it, but the engine package that was developed for it has gained a strong following as it is a simple-to-build, street-stompin' engine.

The initial rules package for this series required stock engine architectures. So stock pistons, cranks, rods, intakes, and oiling systems were used. This was a challenge for the racers, but it helped create very durable street engines equipped with wet sump oiling systems. To get the maximum power, it got to the point where the heads were being severely milled to increase the compression ratio, and small valve reliefs were machined into the tops of the factory cast aluminum pistons. This added considerable expense to the engine build and reduced the durability of the engine, so the rules in this class were eventually loosened to allow more performance-oriented components. These rules changes allowed aftermarket performance internal components and external oil pumps, but they all still needed to bolt into or onto the stock engine block.

The outside envelope of the 'Vette had to remain stock in this series, along with the wheelwells and wheel openings.

The engine that's put together in this chapter was originally for the Motorola Cup series. Notice the polished aluminum dry-sump oil tank mounted up against the firewall. This is how the dry sump systems got their name — the stored oil sits in this tank before being pumped through the engine and immediately sucked out.

The interiors were gutted to reduce the weight of the vehicle and to add the required rollcage and racing seat. A lightweight fake dashboard covers the otherwise empty area under the windshield.

A racing fuel cell fed by a dry-break fuel filling system fills the trunk. The filler mates up to a hole in the trunk lid to allow quick refueling during racing.

Lightweight racing wheels cover massive aftermarket rotors. The stock A-arms are mounted on solid bushings and the suspension supported by coilover shocks. The factory anti-lock braking (ABS) system is disabled for racing.

released 10.5:1 compression heads (PN 88958665). Ron Sperry, the GM Racing engineer that originally designed much of the Gen III V-8 cylinder head ports and chambers, did the development of these CNC-ported heads.

The 8622 heads have a small 62-cc combustion chamber, while the 8665 heads have close to the production 65-cc chamber. Both heads have 250-cc intake ports, 85-cc exhaust ports, and can support north of 500 hp. They come with the impressive LS6 factory valvetrain — hollow-stem stainless-steel valves (sodium- and potassium-filled on the exhaust side), chromium-silicon (Cr-Si) ovate beehive valvesprings, and other equipment.

The milling of both of these heads means they will probably need different length pushrods to maintain good alignment of the pushrod tip and rocker cup. The 8622 heads often end up with a 7.325-inch pushrod, while the 8665 heads mostly run with the factory-lenght pushrods. Maximum lift is considered to be 0.570 inch.

There are plenty of CNC cylinder heads available, but W2W's feeling is the GM people, especially Sperry, probably know best how to maximize performance with CNC-ported heads. After all, they understood what they had to start out with, and had a tremendous amount of technology available to make the improvements.

Besides these heads, this engine is loaded with aftermarket components for increased durability and performance. The forged steel Lunati crankshaft used here is the stock 3.622-inch stroke of race rules, but the cranks can be ordered with up to a 4.125-inch stroke to increase displacement. If a longer stroke is desired, sometimes the block will need to be clearanced for the big end of the rods to clear the bottom ends of the bores and bottom of the engine block. This usually depends on what brand rods you are using — often there is no clearancing required. Also, a groove will need to be machined on the number-8 piston so it will clear the reluctor wheel on the crank.

A nice touch is that the Lunati crank comes with the GM factory 24x crank trigger reluctor ring installed on it, so the factory crank trigger will work with-

out any modifications.

The 3.897-inch diameter (for a 3.901-in bore) forged aluminum JE pistons used here offer advantages in durability and performance production over the factory eutectic cast-aluminum pistons for a 500-hp engine. They are machined to accept a standard hot-rod/racing ring package of a 1.5-mm top, 1.5-mm second, and 3-mm oil spacer/separator ring pack.

The production eutectic cast-aluminum pistons are a low cost alternative to the forged aluminum pistons, which is good if you are building tens of thousands of 400-hp mass-production engines. But, since this is a performance engine and saving a few pennies on each piston isn't the main concern, forged pistons are a good choice. This isn't to say cast pistons won't work on the street, but the owner of this engine was willing to spend the money for a little increase in insurance against a failure.

The reasoning against eutectic cast-aluminum pistons for peak performance applications is based on experience. These pistons are less forgiving to the

Parts List for a 500+ hp Gen III LS1/LS6 V-8

Component	Description	GM Part Number
Engine Architecture	General Motors (recommended) Gen III V-8 5.7 L	LS6 — '01-today LS1 — '99-00
CNC Cylinder Heads (complete)	GM Performance Parts, 11.5:1 Comp Ratio 10.5:1 Comp Ratio	88958622 88958665
Camshaft	GM Performance Parts LS6 ('02-04) "Hot" Showroom Stock Or W2W Cam	12565308 12480033 88958606 call for latest
Intake	LS6 Gen III V-8	88894339
Valvesprings	GM LS6	12556531
Valves	GM LS6	
	intake	12565311
	exhaust	12565312

Optional Aftermarket Components

Crank	Lunati
Rods	Oliver
Pistons	JE
Dry Sump Oil Pump	Dailey Engineering
Oil Pan	ARE
Valvesprings	Comp Cams
Ti Valvespring Retainers	Comp Cams
Long Tube Headers	Wheel to Wheel/Stainless Works
Airbox	Blackwing

The parts list is a showcase of GM Powertrain, Racing, and Performance Parts cooperation to create a true 500+ hp all-GM Gen III performance engine. This engine would be exhilarating in everything from a street rod to a muscle car to a full-blown racecar.

pounding of detonation and preignition, and have a tendency to break into pieces instead of just lifting a ring land or melting slightly, as forged pistons usually do when stressed beyond their limit. While many enthusiasts think they aren't going to come close to causing one of these issues, we all know that high-performance engines live in danger.

Peak horsepower is made with the air/fuel ratio and ignition timing set where the engine is just on the edge of detonation, what many hot-rodders call the "rattle of power." Near this fine line, a forged piston offers a considerable

safety net, which is why their cost should be considered the price of entry when building a powerful engine.

W2W likes to use JE or CP pistons in these engines. If you are going to use the stock rod and crank, W2W recommends JE PN 194884. These pistons are set up to work with the stock LS1 6.094-inch rod length, 0.944-inch piston pin, and 3.625-inch LS1 crank. If you are going to use an aftermarket rod and piston, W2W recommends the JE PN 194883 pistons so they can use a 6-1/8-inch connecting rod and a 0.927-inch floating piston pin with locks.

CONTROLLING IT ALL

As with any Gen III V-8, the engine is run by either the production powertrain control module (PCM) controller, or by an aftermarket electronic controller. A F.A.S.T. electronic controller runs the engine being built in this chapter with a program developed by W2W. At the time this engine was built, the F.A.S.T. controller was not yet reading the 24x crank trigger, though it will be able to by the time this book is published. Because of this, W2W installed one of their 4-point magnetic pickup systems. The pickup sticks through the bellhousing on the oil filter side of the block to read four magnets embedded in the W2W-modified flywheel.

By the time this book comes to market, pretty much all the aftermarket controller companies should be able to plug in to the factory crank trigger senders to run the engines, but right now only a few can run off the factory crank triggers.

Take a look at the last chapter in this book for more details on how to alter the calibration on the Gen III factory controller. Also discussed in Chapter 10 is how the aftermarket is modifying the factory calibrations to work with performance components and how to get a Gen III running on an aftermarket controller.

EVERY LAST DETAIL

Simply put, this chapter, and complimenting info throughout this book, thoroughly documents the procedure needed to build a 500+ hp Gen III V-8 street engine. By that, we mean the information presented elsewhere in this book is not repeated in this chapter, but referenced here for you to find. This way, space is not wasted covering information that is already shown. Some examples of this are the processes of degreeing a camshaft, aligning the stressed-member oil pan with front and rear covers, and installing an intake manifold. From there, attaining the pleasant roar of a small-block Chevy Gen III V-8 coming from under your ride's hood is up to you.

Aftermarket Cranks

The aftermarket crankshaft manufacturers have quickly stepped in with forged steel replacement cranks of every kind of stroke imaginable to handle 500+ hp engines and build big cubic-inch engines. There are some factory type components needed on these aftermarket cranks, so before you slap your forged arm into the Gen III V-8, check for these.

The factory crank is center drilled to reduce its weight and improve the bank-to-bank breathing capabilities of the engine. Since crankcase oil breathing is a challenge for the deep-skirted Gen III block, unless the engine has a multistage dry-sump oil pan, your aftermarket crank should probably be drilled. So to keep all that oil inside the engine, a plug (GM PN 24502262) needs to be installed in the rear of the crank. It should be installed about one inch (24.4 mm) deep into the crank center bore as measured from the throwout bearing seat face.

The next part you'll need if you're going to use the factory crank sensor — which you should, as it is impressive — is the crank reluctor wheel, often called the trigger wheel in the aftermarket. This part is available from GM Performance Parts, PN 12559353, and must be installed in an exact location on the crank. Katech Engine Development offers a cool reluctor installation tool if you want to check the location, or you can refer to the illustration shown and measure the location to see if in fact it is 123 degrees from the six o'clock position.

Aftermarket forged or billet cranks can get expensive, but if you are making more than 650 hp, they should be installed. The aftermarket cranks are good to add cubic inches, as cranks with up to 4-1/8 inches of stroke can easily be installed in the Gen III block.

GM uses a 24x crank reluctor wheel on their cranks for the crank sensor to read. While some engine builders remove these, it really doesn't make any sense, as the crank signal has a lot of resolution, which means the computer will better see where the crank is in its rotation vs. the 90-degree inputs of standard race-type crank sensors.

BLOCK PREP

The process of building a legitimate 500+ horsepower 5.7-liter LS1 street engine is fully documented here for you to recreate. If you're going to be running aftermarket components, you'll need some professional help with some of the machine work, but other than that, just swapping in these components will net you a 500+ hp V-8 engine — check out the dyno figures at the end to see for yourself!

1. If you plan on running forged pistons and moly-faced rings, the bores need to be honed to establish the proper bore surface for these components. The bores will be enlarged only about 0.0005 inch from the honing, so their diameters will stay essentially 99 mm. A set of 3.897-inch forged JE pistons was ordered to fit this bore size and they're measured and matched to each of the eight cylinders. The honing improves the concentricity of the bores because it is done with a deck plate installed. The deck plate simulates the head being torqued to the block, so the resulting bore will be more concentric (round) when the engine is assembled — allowing the piston and rings to seal better for more power and better oil control. When GM hones the blocks at the factory, they do so without using a torque plate.

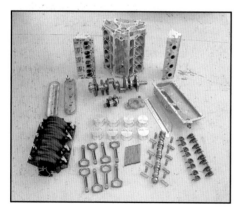

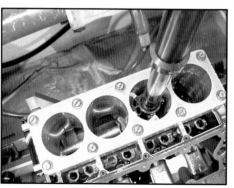

2. Boring and honing are machining processes performed to get the cylinder bores to the proper diameter and concentric over the length of the bore with the required finish. The boring process involves spinning a cutting tool inside the bore, while the honing process consists of rubbing stones on the surface to end up with the proper setup for making power. As an example of the complexity of these processes, the honing process requires a seemingly endless amount of stones and

Installing high-performance parts is good insurance when building a performance engine. Many enthusiasts choose to install aftermarket components like these — a Lunati forged crank, Oliver billet steel rods, and JE forged aluminum pistons for increased durability. If you don't plan on doing any long, sweeping corners, you don't need the dry sump, multi-stage oil pump either — the stock oiling system will work beyond 500 hp.

oils to rub on the bore surface, and the honing tool has a gauge that shows the drag on the stones as they're spun and reciprocated up and down the bore. A good hone operator will know what combo of stones, oil, and drag to use for a certain type of engine (blown or normally aspirated), piston (cast or forged aluminum), and ring package (moly-filled, chrome, mild-steel, etc.). Sound involved? Good, because it is — find someone good at this and let them do it for you.

Bolt Stretch?

GM engineers decided to use torque angle to get the critical fasteners in the Gen III engine to the proper clamping force. Torque angle is the engineering term for the act of applying a light torque force to the single-use factory fastener, then rotating the fastener a pre-determined angle of degrees to stretch it. Torque angle is used on the fasteners that hold the crank main caps, rod end caps, cylinder heads, and other key areas to attain the required clamping force.

Usually a component comes loose because either the fastener wasn't tightened enough to keep it from backing out of its threads, or the fastener was tightened so much that it lost its ability to hold the component (called plastic yield in the engineering world). Either one of these is bad.

GM uses torque angle because it's a good way to create the appropriate clamping force on components, even with the many variations that occur in the production assembly process, like a pneumatic-assisted wrench losing its calibration or a burr on a thread leading to a false torque reading.

Because of the bolt stretching, GM recommends not reusing its production fasteners, like the head bolts. If you're using aftermarket fasteners, like those available from ARP, this stretch information is often invalid, as the fasteners are more robust than the production fasteners. Consult with the fastener manufacturer to ensure you install them with sufficient clamping load to keep everything together.

You can purchase a torque angle gauge from Snap-On and other tool sources. The Snap-On part number is TA-360. The GM tool PN is J 36660.

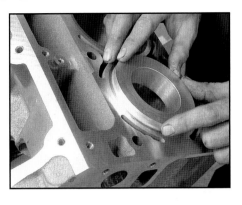

3. The problem with the ring depth-setting tool is that you can't see whether the ring is seated up against the tool. For this reason, you want to...

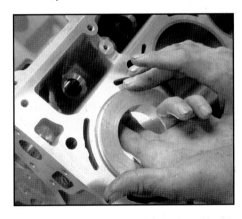

4. ... reach up under the ring depth-setting tool to pull the ring firmly up against the bottom of the ring depth tool.

RING FITTING

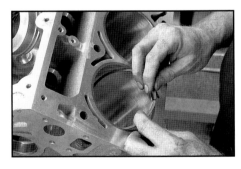

1. Setting the proper ring gaps is critical if you want your engine to make good power, last a long time, and not burn excessive amounts of oil. The following is a complete breakdown of the process of setting ring gaps for a traditional ring pack. The first step is to set the first or second ring gently in the bore it will be used in.

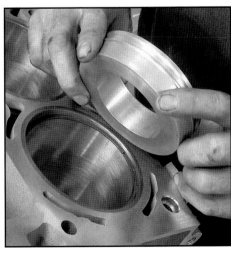

2. Then use a ring depth-setting tool, like this one shown here, to set the ring in the bore perpendicular to the bore centerline at a specific depth in the bore. This depth is usually 1 inch below the deck height.

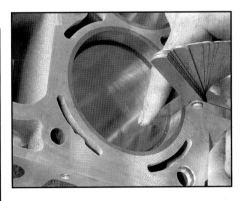

5. With the ring set in the proper location, pull the depth tool out of the way and measure the gap with a variety of feeler gauges. The thickest feeler gauge that fits in the gap between the ends of the ring is its gap. Write this number down and keep the rings organized so you know what rings have what gaps. Now it is time to file the ends to increase the gap, if required.

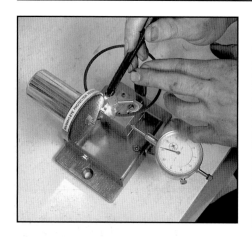

6. A ring filing machine is a small grinding apparatus that requires care and knowledge to use correctly. You want to file the ring gap to the proper width and make sure the ground edge is perpendicular to the ends of the ring. With the wheel static, mate the face of the ring gap up with the grinding wheel. Clamp the ring in this location and pull the ring end back before starting the grinding wheel motor. Start the electric motor and grind off a small amount of ring. Then remove the ring from the machine and install it in the cylinder to be remeasured. Repeat as needed to achieve the proper ring gap on all of the top and second rings. Tape the ring sets together and mark with the bore number as you progress.

BEARING CLEARANCE

1. You'll need to remove the rod cap in preparation for creating the proper rod bearing clearances. Begin this process by placing the rod in an aluminum rod clamp and using a large breaker bar to loosen the rod bolts. Don't use a standard bench vise for this job as any nick or ding in the rods caused by the vise will become a stress riser that could cause the rod to fail prematurely. The rod clamp is made of soft aluminum and has a wide, flat surface to spread the clamping load out over the rod surface without damaging it.

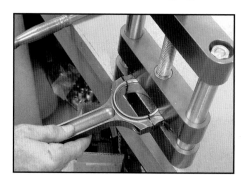

2. With the rod bolts loosened, flip the rod around in the rod clamp, reclamp it on the cap portion of the rod, and then slightly wiggle it up and down until the rod cap comes loose.

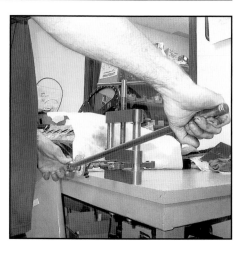

3. You should establish the rod bearing clearances and then the main bearing clearances at this point. See Chapter 9 to see how main bearing clearances are established. For the rods, use the standard cut-and-paste manner of measuring bearings in the rods against the diameters of the crank journals to create the appropriate clearance between bearing and journal.

4. Achieve a 0.0025-inch rod bearing clearance by assembling the rods with the bearings crushed in the big end of the rod. Using a micrometer, or in this case, a hone measureing tool, measure and record the smallest inside diameter (ID) of the rods. Then, measure and record the outside diameter (OD) of the crankshaft journal. You can set the clearances for each rod bearing by changing to different ID rod bearing halves. Side clearance should be 0.012 to 0.018 inch as measured with a feeler gauge with the rods installed on the crank.

HANGING THE PISTONS ON THE RODS

1. The pistons for this project are forged aluminum, with spiral locks and floating pins. Hanging them on the connecting rods is a little different from hanging the production pressed-on pistons and pins. The floating pins are better for performance as they eliminate the fear that the production piston/pin "press" is not robust enough to keep the pins in place during high-rpm, high-power situations. These are key internal components, so it's critical that the assembly area and tools are clean and that the parts are all present before you start.

2. The first step is to install the set of spiral locks on one side of the piston. Spiral locks are tricky to work with at first, but they are a basic component, so you'll get it down. Essentially, get one end of the lock in the piston groove, hold it in place with one finger, and then work it around with your other fingers until it's all in the groove. Install the second spiral lock in the same groove in the same manner (use two for insurance).

3. W2W recommends brushing on a light — and they mean light — coat of straight 30-weight oil on the piston pin boss. They also brush a very light coat of 30-weight oil on the pin and the pin bore in the rod just before installation. Essentially, their feeling is that this area usually has very little oil on it when the engine is running, so why glop a bunch on and encourage the oil to solidify or worse at startup?

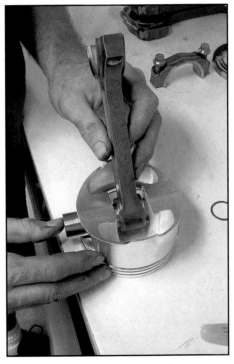

4. With all the components lubed up, it's time to start assembling the rods and pistons. It's a good idea to assemble the piston/rod combo, install the rings on the pistons, and install the piston/rod combo in the engine in one sitting. This will minimize the amount of dust and dirt attracted by the oiled-up components. You don't want too much gunk shoved in the engine during the assembly.

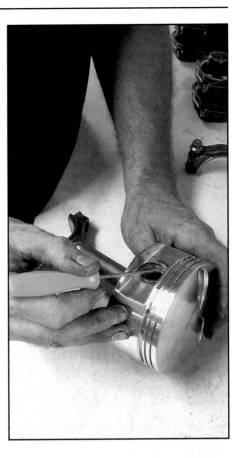

5. With the pin pushed through the piston, install the other pair of spiral locks in the piston to lock the floating piston pin in the piston. Make sure you have matched the piston and rod for each bore (remember, the rings are set for a certain bore and the rod bearings are set for a certain journal).

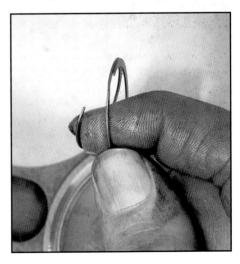

6. This is what the spiral locks look like up close. Notice the angle cut on one end. This is so the locks can be pried out of the lock groove on the piston.

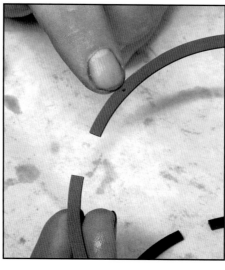

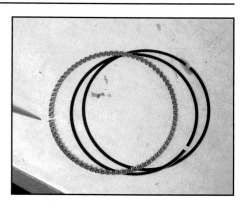

7. Just in case you need to remove a spiral lock from a piston, here's how it's done. First, you'll need a small 90-degree pick or screwdriver to get up under the lock in the groove. Pry the tapered end of the lock up and over the groove edge and continue to work the lock out with another small screwdriver. Getting started is the hardest part; after that, it usually just takes some simple prying.

INSTALLING RINGS ON PISTONS

1. Now that the pistons are on the rods, it's time to get the gapped rings installed on the pistons. Like the rod/piston assembly process, you should have clean tools and a clean area to work in.

2. Most rings are identified by a dot on the face and the location of the taper on the inner edge of the ring in relation to the dot. The rings are usually installed with the dot facing up. To identify which are the top rings, start with the dot facing up and look to the inside edges of the ring. In general, the top rings will have the taper on the upper, inner edge, while the second rings will have the taper on the lower, inner edge.

3. Some engine builders like to use a ring spreader to install the rings, while some think it's acceptable to work the ring onto the piston by hand. This W2W engine builder chose to install the rings by putting one end of the ring in the ring land and working it onto the piston with his hands. Before doing this, wipe the rings with a light coat of 30-weight oil. As a note, the reason some engine builders prefer to use the spreader instead of the hand method is that they feel the spreader minimizes the chance of putting a "twist" in the ring that hurts the ring's ability to seat flat in the ring land. You decide.

4. Most engine assemblers have a ring gap clocking method that they follow, and W2W is no different. While the rings can move around in the ring lands once the engine is running, the startup positions are considered very important. In this case, the rings are clocked as such on the piston from recommendations in the GM Powerbook. As a note, GM Powertrain does not clock the top two rings in the production build of the Gen III, but the oil ring spacers and spreader gaps are clocked to themselves and to the top and second ring. For more on this, see Chapter 2.

INSTALLING THE CRANK IN THE BLOCK

1. With the clearances determined earlier in the buildup, now is the time to install the crank. To start, the upper half of the main bearing shells are wiped down with a light skim of 30-weight oil on the outer surface and pushed into the appropriate place in the block. Before this step, all of these bearings were cleaned in the solvent tank to insure no packing materials or other debris ended up in the engine — you should wash all new components in solvent.

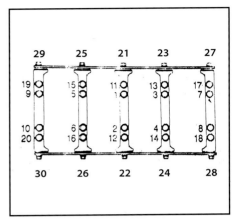

2. Once you place the crankshaft in the engine, it's a good idea to spin it over to make sure it clears the engine block and there is no binding. If there are no issues, you can continue with the installation process. If there is interference, stop and check the bearing clearances again. Issues usually have to do with the overall crank diameter and the thrust bearing clearance.

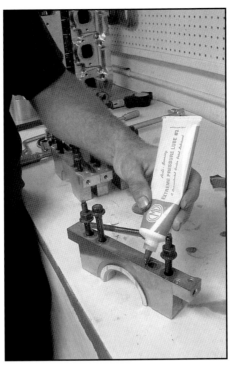

5. As was discussed earlier, the Gen III V-8 engine uses bolt stretch to create the appropriate fastener-clamping load on the critical components. Because of this, it's important to add a light skim of grease where the bolt head seats on the main and/or under the head of the bolts.

7. This illustration details the GM recommended main-cap torquing sequence. Once all the caps are fully nested in the block, start by torquing fasteners 1-20 to 22 ft-lbs, and then loosen them. Push the crank forward to full thrust. Re-torque fasteners 1-10 to 15 ft-lbs, then add 80 degrees of torque angle. Then, torque fasteners 11-20 to 15 ft-lbs and loosen them to hand tight. Re-torque them to 15 ft-lbs and add 53 degrees of torque angle. Now torque fasteners 21-30 to 18 ft-lbs, doing them as pairs per each main cap. The side bolts can be reused but need to be cleaned and have a small bead of sealer put under the head of the bolt because they thread into the crankcase.

3. Remember to give the bottom bearing shells a light coat of Pro Lube engine assembly lube before you snap them into the main caps.

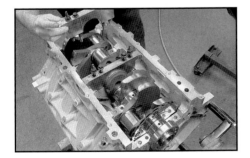

4. Drop the main caps in place on the engine block. Notice how the deep-skirted Gen III V-8 engine block allows for main caps with four vertical bolts and two horizontal bolts. The factory main caps are powdered metal and can handle up to 550 hp, while aftermarket billet steel main caps can handle over 650 hp. The factory caps don't have dowels, but many of the aftermarket caps do. The factory caps nest into the sides of the block for an almost swedge-like fit.

6. Begin the torquing procedure by hand-tightening all the fasteners down in the torquing sequence recommended by General Motors. Refer to the torquing chart shown above.

8. During the torquing portion of the process, the extreme-pressure lube applied to the bottom of the fastener head helps minimize friction that would otherwise result in a false torque reading.

9. Fasteners need to have stretch added to them in order to do their job correctly. A large breaker bar is used to twist the fastener with this degree-reading socket attachment (Snap-On PN TA-360 and GM PN J 36660) between the socket and breaker bar. By resting the stretch socket stop on an immovable part of the engine block (left hand, holding stop against engine block), the amount the fastener is twisted, or stretched, can be exactly measured in degrees.

11. The Gen III V-8 uses a key on the snout of the crank to drive the oil pump and lock the crank gear in place — but it does-n't hold the harmonic balancer on pro-duction cranks. On this Lunati crank, the front drive will be keyed to the crank. Hammer the key in place with a shot-filled mallet.

1. Coat the cam liberally with engine oil. W2W has their own cam created for this engine based on their experience (W2W PN 8606). The basic information on this cam is it has 239/241 degrees intake/exhaust duration at 0.050 inches lift and 0.570/0.570 inches of lift. Spread a light coat of 30-weight oil around the cam journals before you slide the cam into the engine.

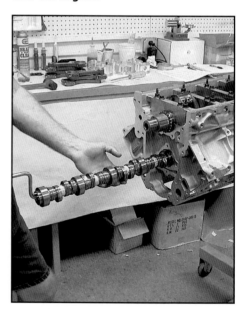

10. The crank endplay should then be checked. This is performed by mounting a dial indicator on one end of the crank and prying between one of the crank throws and a main cap with a screwdriv-er. The endplay should total 0.003 to 0.004 inch.

12. Knock the crank gear onto the crank snout using a 1-1/2-inch inside diameter round aluminum tube and shot-filled mallet. The tube needs to be aluminum too so the gear face isn't marred in the process — remember, the oil pump slides over this area. Also, the key slot in the gear needs to be indexed over the key so it all goes on smoothly.

2. Install the oiled-up camshaft now, along with the timing chain. The LS1/LS6 Gen III camshafts are hollow in the cen-ter, which makes them light and easy to install. Slide a 3/8-inch extension up inside the cam for leverage and control to help you negotiate the cam past the engine block cam journals.

INSTALLING THE CONNECTING RODS/PISTONS

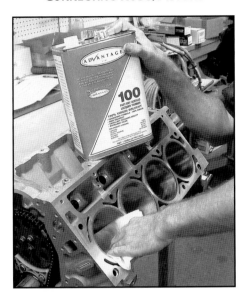

1. Lightly wipe down the bores with a non-linting towel soaked in 100 percent virgin fast-dry acrylic lacquer thinner. Then drool a small amount of 30-weight engine oil into the bores and spread it evenly around every inch of the bore with your clean hand.

2. Wipe a very light amount of 30-weight oil on the rings and thrust faces of the piston.

3. With the bore glistening with freshly spread oil, rotate the crank journal until it's at the bottom of its stroke. This gives you the maximum amount of room to work when guiding the big end of the rod down inside the bore.

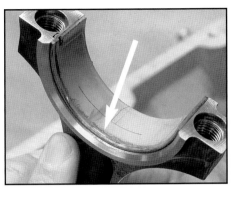

4. Make sure you have the rods/pistons installed with the proper clocking in relation to the pistons, because the bearings are chamfered on only one side to clear the rolled fillet on the crank. Getting this switched around will result in drastic metal-on-metal wear. By the way, the fine scratches in the bearing face are from the bearing ID measuring device on the rod bore machining station and are not a concern for the engine.

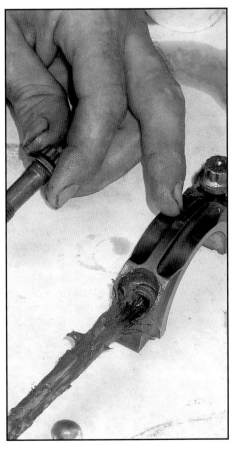

5. Since the rod bolts are set on their final clamping load with torque angle, coat the bottom of the rod bolt heads with a very light coat of extreme-pressure lube.

6. Load the piston into a ring compressor of the appropriate bore diameter to help get the piston into the bores. As a tip, wipe down the ring compressor with the lacquer thinner and oil, just like the bore, before loading the piston into it.

7. Be patient and careful during the initial push on the piston, as this is when the rings go past the ending of the ring compressor and into the engine block bore. Sometimes, the rings will get caught up on this transition. You can try wiggling the assembly to see if you can get past this point, but usually it's best to just pull the piston/rod combo out of the bore, pull the piston through the ring compressor, and restart the process. Often, this problem is caused by the ring compressor not being fully seated on the deck surface of the block.

8. With the piston in the bore, remove the ring compressor and switch to a light mallet to tap the piston down in the bore while guiding the big end of the rod onto the crank journal.

9. Snug down the rod bolts after you've slid the piston/rod combo into the bores and installed the rod cap. Do this after you've wiped a light coat of Pro Lube engine assembly lube onto the bearing surface.

10. Torque the ARP 7/16-inch rod bolts in the steel Oliver rods to 30 ft-lbs. The stock rod bolts would only be torqued to 15 ft-lbs.

11. Place the bolt stretch attachment on a breaker bar and add an additional 40 degrees of torque angle into the ARP bolts to achieve the appropriate clamping load on the rod cap. The stock rod bolts would get 60 degrees of torque angle.

PISTON TALK

If you plan on using the stock short block with heads that have been machined more than 0.050 inches and a camshaft similar to the one used here, be prepared to spend some money buying aftermarket pistons with valve reliefs or having small valve reliefs cut in the stock pistons. The early Motorola Cup rules this engine was originally created for required stock pistons, but they didn't limit valve reliefs, so the engine designers put as much compression, valve lift, and duration in the engine as possible. The piston on the left with the valve reliefs is a remnant from W2W's days of supplying these early racing engines. The piston on the right is a stock unit.

Actually, if you need valve reliefs, W2W recommends installing a set of aftermarket forged aluminum pistons. This is because the cost difference between a set of stock pistons with the valve reliefs machined in them and the forged aluminum pieces is a few hundred dollars — a small price for a lot of insurance towards keeping your engine together. W2W has used heads milled about 0.040 inch, which nets a 62-cc chamber size, on the street with no problems. They've also cut heads up to 0.060 inch, which produces about a 57-cc chamber size, and had no problems in racing applications.

PISTON: IN THE HOLE OR POPUP?

The next important step is to check how much the piston comes out of (or stays down in) the bore during the crank stroke. This is a good parameter to check even if you haven't changed anything on the stock short block. Here's how you do it:

1. Locate the dial indicator on one side of the top of the piston at TDC. With the crank held in place, push on the thrust face of the piston and set the dial indicator at zero.

2. Now, push on the other side of the top of the piston and read the dial indicator.

3. Divide this number by two and pivot the piston back until the dial indicator reads that number.

4. Zero out the dial indicator.

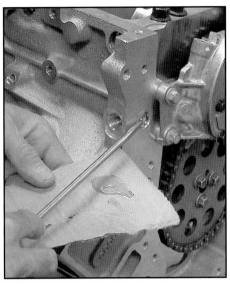

5. Rotate the base until the indicator is reading the block deck height. In this case, the piston is popping 0.010 inch out of the bore. This is normal as the Gen III V-8 is designed as a negative deck-height engine. This means the piston is meant to stop its upward motion slightly above the deck face. Doing this increases the squish effect of the piston approaching the combustion chamber, focusing the combustion pressure in the chamber for maximum force transferred to the piston. You should degree the cam at this point, following the procedure on page 95.

OILING SYSTEM AND WATER PUMP

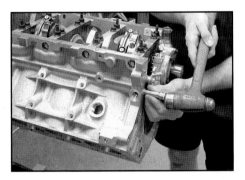

1. The modified factory oil pump has been located and mounted to the front of the crank snout (see Chapter 6 for tips on the factory oil pump locating process). The pressurized oil flows down the side of the engine block in a large main gallery. A welsh plug needs to be installed in the block 2.5-mm deep with a tolerance of +/- 0.3 mm to get the oil to flow down this gallery (shown being installed). When an engine is torn down, this plug is removed to clean the main oil gallery with a brush. Notice the custom W2W billet outlet on the factory pump — this is used to mate up with the internal passage that has been ported to increase oil flow out of the pump and mate up with the custom dry-sump oil pan.

2. To make sure the engine block oil gallery plug stays in place during extreme power production, you should apply a liberal coating of JB Weld onto the rim of the welsh plug. If this plug did come loose during operation, the oil pressure in the engine would drop to zero, because all the oil would pour back into the pan.

3. The fabricated ARE dry-sump oil pan has a receiver on it to plumb the oil from the dry-sump reservoir to the pump. This fitting has two O-rings on it to seal the two fittings together. W2W recommends putting a light skim of 30-weight on the O-rings so they'll slide into the hole with little resistance.

4. This timing-chain dampener, GM PN 88958607, was originally designed for the production LS1/LS6 Gen III V-8 engine but didn't make it past the bean counters. It works very well to minimize chain activity/movement in high-RPM situations. W2W likes to use it in all of its performance engines to improve durability and power production over the life of the engine. The only problem with this is that some of the blocks don't have the holes drilled and tapped. But the part does come with a template to help you install it on an undrilled block. Apply blue Loctite to the threads and torque the fasteners to 18 ft-lbs.

5. A plastic insert that many call the "barbell restrictor" is used to stop the pressurized oil from the oil pump from continuing down the main oil gallery. The barbell redirects this oil into the oil filter. The oil then comes back up through a different passage to the main gallery. The other end of the barbell keeps the oil from going toward the back of the block. Install the barbell restrictor by lightly lubricating it with 30-weight oil and pressing it into the bore at the back of the engine block. It needs to be installed with the O-ring going in last — you should still be able to barely see the O-ring when the restrictor is properly installed. The rear cover plate locks the barbell restrictor in place.

6. This engine is set up with an external-scavenge dry-sump oiling system. The system is great at getting oil out of the engine that isn't lubricating or cooling at that moment, which is good to keep oil from roping on the crank and doing other power-eating activities. Before you install the oil pan, the front and rear covers need to be installed (see page 116). The –12 AN fitting at the front of the oil

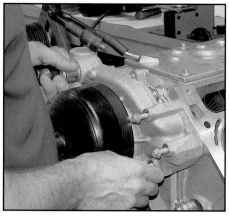

pan (on the left) is plumbed to the bottom of the dry-sump oil reservoir for uninterrupted oil flow to the stock oil pump, which provides oil to the bearings and other critical components. The two threaded holes toward the rear of the oil pan are for the oil pickups. This pan is not a stressed-member like the factory pan, so it doesn't need to be aligned like the factory pan. Note the custom billet aluminum front drive spud on the crank snout for the racing harmonic balancer and front drive pulleys.

11. The water pump can then be bolted into place. Apply 18 ft-lbs of torque to the fasteners.

BUILDING CYLINDER HEADS

7. Then bolt the valley cover in place. This is as simple as it sounds — just install the cover with the preformed seal and torque the fasteners to 18 ft-lbs in a radial pattern. This is the later '02 LS6 valley cover, which you can tell by the vent valve near the right side.

9. A good trick to improve the oil control in a hot-rod Gen III V-8 is to drill these 1/2-inch drain holes in the lower face of the lifter retainer trays above each lifter. On a production engine, having engine oil pooling here is acceptable, but on a high-rpm engine, having oil lying around only costs you power and causes the oil to foam and get hot.

8. The lifter trays, with four stock roller lifters installed in each, should now be dropped in the engine. These lifter trays are very cool in that they hold the lifters in place on the roller cam. Also, if you want to make a cam change once the engine has been assembled, rotating the cam one revolution will push the lifters up into the trays, allowing quick cam changes

10. The lifter trays are held in the engine block with 6-mm bolts torqued to 106 in-lbs.

1. The cylinder heads are easy to assemble because they're designed to be easy to manufacture. Since the 2002, the stock LS6 intake valves are hollow and the exhaust valves are sodium/potassium filled, which is a high-performance option on many hot-rod engines. These valves will work great in many demanding applications. Make sure you check the valvetrain geometry because the '02 LS6 valves are 0.6-mm longer than previous LS valves to account for the smaller base circle on the '02 LS6 camshaft.

Rear Seal Installation Tool

If you're tearing a Gen III V-8 completely, the rear cover will need to be removed. This isn't tricky, but reinstalling it is, as the seal has a bi-directional seal lip on it. "Bi-directional" just means there are two seal lips on the production seal. One points in towards the engine and the other out towards the transmission. Because of this, the seal should be slid onto the engine with the assistance of an installation tool.

GM has a tool available, as does W2W Powertrain. The W2W version is a simple installation tool that centers the seal on the crankshaft seal surface. This helps you avoid the common problem of cocking the seal on the crank and possibly causing a leak.

W2W also offers a seal-to-cover installation tool for both the front and rear covers. This is useful if you plan on having a dry sump or vacuum pump pulling on the crankcase as

the factory seals have been known to allow a high level of air past them — which often can be heard as a high-pitched whistle when the engine is running. W2W uses this tool to install TKO's performance seal and hasn't had any problems, even at quite aggressive crankcase vacuum levels (in the 20-inch Hg range — which is dramatic!).

The factory seal has two lips, one angled inward, one angled outward to minimize oil leaks. If a Gen III V8 crankcase is being evacuated at a high vacuum, a more aggressive seal will be required to prevent air from being sucked past this seal point. This seal is from TKO and held up against 20 inches of vacuum in an oil pan.

The seal installation tool should be slid into the seal before the cover is installed on the engine. This is how you make sure the inner angled seal lip isn't folded under, allowing a rather substantial oil leak.

The rear cover on the Gen III has a seal that needs to be pressed into it. The factory seal will last a long time so this seal is only replaced if a dry sump oiling system or a vacuum pump is going to be used to pull a vacuum on the crankcase.

W2W offers a tool, along with GM and a few other suppliers, that seats the seal in the cover with a male/female combination of machined parts that is pulled together by tightening down a through-bolt.

Once the cover is installed on the engine, the install tool can be removed. This tool is from W2W, but these are readily available at multiple engine builder tool outlets.

Oil Pan/Front and Rear Cover Installation Tips

Reinstalling the oil pan and front and rear covers is kind of tricky as these three components "find their home" as the combination is bolted together. This is another area in which the GM Powertrain Engineering and Manufacturing people got together to simplify engine assembly by minimizing the number of precision machined, external locating points required. The usual locating points include dowel pins and machining pads. Without them, engine assembly is easier because the covers and oil pan can be finessed to fit as a combination without having to relocate dowel pins.

While this is great for production, you're probably wondering how to do this at home. Well, W2W has a method they use everyday with great success and are kind enough to share here. First, they recommend installing all the front and rear cover bolts to the point they touch the front and rear covers. On the front cover, install the harmonic balancer to center the cover around the crank. With the

bolts hand-tight, the covers will locate on the seal surfaces – what GM calls finding their home. To check their location, measure and make sure that both the front and rear cover oil pan flange are within 0.020 inch (0.500 mm) of the block oil pan flange on both sides. This is so the oil pan will seat properly to the flange portion on the covers. Then torque the fasteners on the front and rear covers down to 18 ft-lbs in a radial pattern starting from the inner bolts. In general, the covers are easy to get positioned properly because they are seated on the crank seal surface.

Then, apply four small dollops of sealer at the mating point of the cover, block, and oil pan — two at the front, two at the rear cover. Now it's time to install the oil pan and torque the 6-mm bolts going into the front and rear covers to 89 in-lbs. This will allow the covers to pivot around the seal surfaces to mate flush with the oil pan. The twelve 8-mm fasteners around the oil pan are then final torqued to 18 ft-lbs in a radial pattern.

While this process might sound tricky, after you do it once, you'll marvel at how straight-forward it is to assemble these components.

First, a 3/8-inch-diameter glob of sealer needs to be applied at the four corners of the engine where the mating surface of the cover plate, oil pan, and engine block meet. In this case, you can see how the sealer has oozed out from this seal surface of the oil pan and engine block. The cover will be installed into this sealer glob and the leak path will be completely sealed. In a radial pattern torque the cover fasteners to 18 ft-lbs.

The front and rear cover installation process involves the only application of liquid sealer required on the Gen III V-8 and some finesse to get everything sealed up and positioned correctly.

Then, final torque the snugged down oil pan bolts to 18 ft-lbs in a radial pattern from the center bolts.

2. The rockers are easy to install as they are mounted to a single tie bar per head that holds all the rockers. The entire rocker system can be slid onto the head and bolted on with eight 8-mm diameter, 8-mm hex-head bolts per head that are torqued to 22 ft-lbs. The rockers should be lubed up fully with 30-weight oil, but especially on the ends where the rockers touch the pushrods and valves. The Gen III V8 valvetrain preload is non-adjustable, so if a change has been made to the deck height, camshaft base circle, or other valvetrain geometry altering changes, the valvetrain will need to be adjusted to make sure the proper preload exists on the hydraulic lifters. Many aftermarket companies are now offering adjustable rockers as a solution. But a simple way to attain the correct preload is through installing different length pushrods. The valvetrain preload is checked by spinning the pushrod in your fingers while tightening down the rocker tie bar bolts. The factory preload has the pushrod becoming difficult to spin in your fingers about 1.5 turns of the 8 mm bolts before the tie bar seats to the stands. W2W recommends using a little more than a 1/2 turn of valvetrain preload with the engine hot. This prevents the common thrashing valvetrain noise at low rpm on performance LS1 engines. Getting the valvetrain geometry and preload correctly adjusted with pushrod length is a big deal. So spend the time to get it right.

3. You should check the valvetrain geometry with the top end bolted together. The '01 and earlier LS1 and LS6 have the same 7.400-inch pushrod lengths from the factory. W2W often uses different length pushrods because of head milling and their desire to run a lighter lifter preload than was recommended by the factory (to release some hidden power). Their most common length pushrod ends up being a Smith Brothers 7.325-inch pushrod for the '02 and later LS6 cam. With a ported oil pump body and increased oil pressure pop-off spring pushing more oil through the engine, W2W recommends setting a 0.035-inch opening in the Smith Brothers pushrops to control oil flow to the top of the engine.

INSTALLING AND TORQUING THE CYLINDER HEAD

1. The CNC-ported cylinder heads are installed using a stock-type Cometic sandwich gasket that has three thin pieces of stainless covered by a sealing material. Depending on the compression ratio they need to achieve, W2W uses everything from the stock 0.057-inch-thick stock gasket, down to a 0.040-inch-thick gasket to get the compression ratio up to 12:1 on the race engines they build. W2W likes to use the Cometic gasket, as it has proven to be extremely durable under severe conditions.

2. As in the case of the other critical fasteners, apply grease under heads of the cylinder-head fasteners.

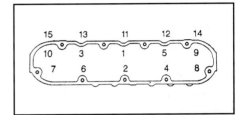

3. To begin, snug the head bolts numbered 1-10 in the illustration above to 22 ft-lbs.

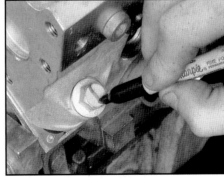

4. Next, draw a vertical line on the top of each head bolt with a Sharpie permanent felt marker. This is used as a reference when going through the torque angle tightening sequence — in case you get mixed up as to which ones you've already done.

DYNO RESULTS		
RPM	**Torque**	**Hp**
3,500	380	253
3,600	384	263
3,700	391	275
3,800	400	289
3,900	408	303
4,000	413	314
4,100	418	326
4,200	424	339
4,300	431	353
4,400	438	367
4,500	444	380
4,600	448	392
4,700	451	404
4,800	453	414
4,900	454	424
5,000	**455**	433
5,100	**455**	441
5,200	453	449
5,300	452	456
5,400	451	464
5,500	449	471
5,600	448	478
5,700	445	483
5,800	441	487
5,900	436	490
6,000	431	492
6,100	426	494
6,200	420	496
6,300	413	496
6,400	408	**497**
6,500	401	**497**
6,600	394	496
6,700	389	**497**
6,800	382	495

5. As with the other important fasteners on these engines, head bolts 1-10 are torque angled first to 76 degrees. Then, head bolts 1-8 are torque angled 76 degrees more. For head bolts 9 and 10, add 38 degrees of torque angle. Next, torque bolts 11-15 to 22 ft-lbs in the order shown above. From there, torque down the five 8-mm bolts at the top of the head to 18 ft-lbs.

Then install the steam vent crossovers at the front of the block the steam hole blockoffs at the rear of the block. Use this diagram to torque the 10 intake manifold bolts to 44 in-lbs on the first pass, then to 89 in-lbs in the final sequence (see page 98 for torquing illustration). Also, install the throttle body and MAF sensor on the front of the intake.

The engine tested here used the aftermarket components shown in this chapter, but engines with stock short-blocks have made similar power. The key components to make this power include the GMPP CNC-ported cylinder heads (which yield a 10.5:1 compression ratio), the GMPP Showroom Stock camshaft or similar aftermarket cam (less than 0.600 inch lift), 1-3/4- inch primary long-tube headers, 38-lb/hr injectors, F.A.S.T. controller, and open-element air cleaner. Increasing the compression to 12:1 would increase the horsepower curve about 20 to 30 hp over the last 1/3 of the power curve, but you'd need to run 100 octane gas to prevent the engine from detonating itself to death.

GEN III VORTEC TRUCK ENGINE BUILDUPS

There are many fans of the iron-block 4.8-, 5.3-, and 6.0-liter Gen III V-8s that power many of the '99 and later full-size Chevy and GMC trucks. That fan base is drawn to the Gen III V-8 because of its thick powerband, impressive peak power numbers, and good fuel economy. Simply, the Gen III V-8 pushes these 5,000+ pound trucks pretty well in factory form, and with a few performance tweaks, can really make them move out. This chapter gives a few examples of performance modifications that can be made to the Gen III V-8s to create a scootin' truck or SUV. The installation of superchargers, factory performance cylinder heads, and turbocharger kits shown here will work on any of these three engine configurations, but as usual, you should know the bigger the displacement of the engine, the more power it should make overall.

For comments and dyno charts on bolt-on component modifications external to the engine, like air cleaner systems, cat-back exhausts, and similar changes, see Chapter 5.

SIMPLE SUPERCHARGER INSTALL

The first performance upgrade shown here, the MagnaCharger supercharger kit, is by far the simplest considering its ability to make power. MagnaCharger has created a low-profile intake manifold that allows them to place the Eaton supercharger on top of the engine and still fit under the hood. Installation requires just a little more than removing the plastic intake and replacing it with the MagnaCharger system.

The MagnaCharger kit is surprisingly complete and the instructions are shown in step-by-step, photography-supported detail. There are a few things not shown, like how to remove fuel injector clips and other details, but

Just to clarify this one last time, the 4.8-, 5.3-, and 6.0-liter Gen III Vortec engines in Chevrolet and GMC full-size trucks and SUVs are of a common architecture to the LS1 engines in the Corvette, Camaro, Firebird, and GTO. This means practically all the parts that bolt on the Gen III V-8-powered performance cars will bolt on a Gen III Vortec truck engine.

Full-size GM trucks and SUVs are very popular because of their thoughtful design and rugged capabilities. The Gen III V-8 in the 1999 and later trucks is easy to modify for more power using either aftermarket components or GM performance parts. Both can provide increases in power without any degradation in reliability, and some provide an increase in mileage.

lucky for you, those steps are detailed here and in Chapter 4 in the full-size truck section. A dyno test was performed to quantify the power increase and the results are shown.

Product Comments

The main reason that a supercharger is such a great way to increase power in the truck Gen III V-8 is the fuel these engines were built to run. Since most consumers for these trucks are concerned with fuel costs, GM designed the Gen III

The most popular and powerful change you can make to a Gen III V-8 truck today is to add a supercharger kit like this MagnaCharger system. For about $4,800, you can bolt on an additional 110 hp — an impressive $$/hp figure for any aftermarket system. But on top of that, these systems have proven to be very reliable over time.

The MagnaCharger kit comes with all the components required to install the supercharger and get the engine running with it — including the new calibration flashed into the PCM with a downloader pod. Plus, the whole setup is emissions legal.

V-8 truck engines to operate on regular 87-octane fuel by optimizing combustion-chamber pressure, fuel stratification, and detonation/knock detection. This means there is considerable room for more performance by tweaking the compression ratio, cam specs, and knock controls, if you accept running higher-octane fuel. To put it simply, boosting the inlet charge on the Gen IIIs with a crank-driven blower creates a thick powerband that is truly addictive — so you'll probably be accepting of the added cost of premium fuel.

The top choice by most enthusiasts for full-size trucks is the MagnaCharger. The common reasons for this are its ease of installation, durability, impressive power production, and limited impact on the mileage. As a general rule, most superchargers offer simple installation, impressive power production, and reasonable cost for the power you get in return. But one advantage the MagnaCharger has over other blowers is a bypass feature at low RPM so the engine can run essentially unboosted, freewheeling the blower. This helps to improve the mileage and is transparent to the driver of the vehicle.

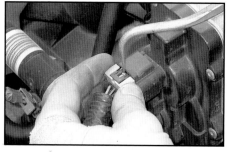

While the MagnaCharger instructions are very intricate, here are some details that will make the job easier yet. The electronic throttle control (ETC) has an electrical plug that is a little tricky to remove. Many folks destroy this connector trying to get it off because they did not know the gray clip should be removed first, then the conenctor can be removed. First, place the tip of a radiator hook tool under the clip and pull with your fingers (as shown) to remove the clip. If you don't have a radiator hook tool, go buy one, because you practically need one to get the Gen III connectors off.

Installation Notes

The Magnuson supercharger system shown here is being installed on a Hummer H2 LQ4 6.0-liter V-8. The LQ4 is ideal for supercharging because of its 9.41:1 compression ratio and 6-liter size. The hi-po LQ9 has 10:1 compression, which doesn't allow for as much boost and timing, so the improvement isn't as impressive. The 4.8- and 5.3-liter engines all have 9.5:1 compression, so they make good power under boost — they just don't have the same displace-

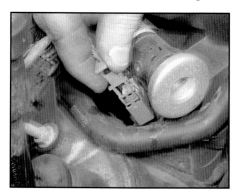

The Gen III powertrain was designed to simplify manufacturing and improve overall quality, so most parts only go on one way and are difficult to install partially — which is good for quality, but can make it interesting to take things apart. One good example of this is the truck fuel-injector connectors. They have a secondary clip that ensures they are locked on the injector. To remove them, this clip needs to be pulled up out of the connector body using the radiator hook tool.

With the secondary clip removed, you can depress the main locking tab on the injector connector (under thumb) and remove it from the injector.

To remove the Air Injection Reaction (AIR) system tube (what many would call the EGR) on the intake manifold behind the throttle body, you'll need to depress the gray sliding tab into the connector body and wiggle the connector to the side of the mounting tube while lightly pulling on the AIR tube. Once it's off, look at how the offset clip moves over when you squeeze it to release the tube from the intake.

Probably the most frustrating part of removing the intake manifold is removing the vacuum tubes, fuel-injector electrical connectors, and other wires and hoses from the back of the intake. The H2 is like the cars in that the windshield hangs over the engine slightly, but the other full-size trucks do not intrude on the engine bay — but even so, the space around these components is tight! Vacuum the top of the engine to remove the debris, and then carefully remove the intake by prying up on it and pulling it out of the engine bay.

ment as the LQ4.

The supercharger/intake combo bolts on just like the stock intake, and the front drive installs quickly. Probably the only thing that is not intuitive in the installation is how to get the fuel injector wiring and a few other sensors and connectors released — those steps are shown here and in Chapter 4. Before removing the intake manifold, vacuum the top of the engine with a powerful vacuum to remove any dirt and debris that would otherwise fall in to the exposed intake ports of the engine.

Actually, as a testimony to the engineering work that went into the MagnaCharger system, getting the stock wiring reinstalled and wiring up the added Magnuson components takes longer than the mechanical installation work — that's how simple it is to install the hard parts.

POWER PRODUCTION

The supercharger comes with a 3.3-inch-diameter pulley from Magnuson, but there are a plethora of pulley diameters available. Going to a smaller pulley spins the blower more and increases the amount of air entering the engine at any given time. Usually, if you do this you're going to need some calibration work done beyond the calibration that

With the intake removed, carefully scrape off the mounting surface of the intake, using a vacuum to suck away any debris before it can fall into the intake. Wipe this surface down with solvent, allow it to dry, and cover it with tape until just before the supercharger/intake manifold combo is installed.

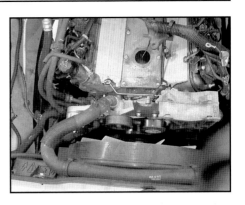

The MagnaCharger supercharger pulley drive is very simple to install. It uses the factory front engine accessory drive (FEAD) but adds a longer belt and a pulley.

Pull the protective tape off the intake ports just before you install the supercharger and intake manifold combo. Always make sure nothing falls down into these ports as it will cause terrible damage to the engine.

The final installation of the MagnaCharger supercharger looks almost like it could have come from the factory. It uses the factory air cleaner box, front drive, and wiring harness. The engine will require premium fuel since the increased inlet pressure ups the dynamic compression ratio.

MagnaCharger provides. This points out what might be considered the negative to the MagnaCharger system—it is not intended for big power engine combos. This means if you want more than 10 psi whistling in to the intake, or anywhere close to this, the MagnaCharger system really isn't the system for you. This system is intended to operate on a stock engine with boost pressures less than 5 psi. But, after looking at the dyno figures, you're probably wondering why anyone would want to spin this blower harder since it is already making over 500 ft-lb of torque and 500 hp!

LS6 PARTS FOR POWER

The commonality of the Gen III architecture really is shown right here. Adding certain components originally developed for the special performance LS6 engine in the Z06 Corvette to any Vortec truck engine can provide up to 40 more horsepower with no other mechanical modifications.

What's impressive about this is that it's using all components manufactured

Hot Rod Hummer

Starting with a 6.0-liter Gen III engine short block, the list of additions required to make an honest 550 hp and 600 ft-lb of torque with a MagnaCharger is relatively short. This engine was designed to make power all day long without any need for special care or components. The engine will need to run on premium fuel and the whole setup cost $13,000+ to build based on this parts list.

Parts list:
Magnuson roots-style supercharger and intake
  w/2.75-inch diameter pulley
Forged, dished aftermarket aluminum pistons
  (W2W PN 6.0SC)
(installed to attain a 9:1 static compression ratio)
Headers (1-3/4 or 1-7/8-inch primaries)
6.0-liter mass-air sensor with W2W upgrade kit
CNC LQ9 truck cylinder heads (for the 8 cc larger chamber vs. the LS6 head)
Nitrided stock crank (for insurance)
W2W camshaft
Comp Cams valvesprings and pushrods
38-lb/hr Delphi marine fuel injectors
Oil pump pressure and flow upgrade
Stock controller with LS1-Edit calibration
  upgrade

Labor:
Remove and reinstall engine from vehicle
Complete tear down
Hone cylinders for forged aluminum pistons
Fabricate long-tube header exhaust system
Modify oil pump for increased flow/pressure
Build engine with new component set
Upgrade PCM with new calibration

SUPERCHARGER DYNO

	Baseline '01 LQ4 6.0-liter Stock Engine		Engine Magna-Charger	
RPM	Trq	HP	Trq	HP
3,000	356	207	492	281
3,100	359	212	496	293
3,200	361	220	499	305
3,300	363	228	504	316
3,400	365	237	506	327
3,500	369	246	507	338
3,600	370	254	508	348
3,700	**373**	263	508	359
3,800	**373**	270	508	368
3,900	**373**	277	509	378
4,000	372	284	**511**	389
4,100	372	290	**511**	399
4,200	372	297	510	408
4,300	371	304	510	418
4,400	371	311	510	427
4,500	371	318	508	435
4,600	369	323	505	443
4,700	366	328	504	451
4,800	362	331	501	458
4,900	358	334	498	465
5,000	352	336	495	471
5,100	347	**337**	491	477
5,200	339	335	488	484
5,300	332	334	486	491
5,400	324	332	485	498
5,500	317	330	479	502
5,600	309	329	474	505
5,700	303	329	468	508
5,800	296	327	462	510
5,900	—	—	456	512
6,000	—	—	449	513
6,100	—	—	443	**515**
6,200	—	—	436	514
6,300	—	—	428	513

	Baseline 6.0-liter Stock Engine		Modified 6.0-liter with Aftermarket Components	
RPM	Trq	HP	Trq	HP
2,500			561	267
2,600			565	280
2,700			571	294
2,800			576	307
2,900			581	321
3,000	356	207	585	334
3,100	359	212	589	348
3,200	361	220	593	361
3,300	363	228	597	375
3,400	365	237	601	389
3,500	369	246	602	401
3,600	370	254	603	413
3,700	**373**	263	602	424
3,800	**373**	270	600	434
3,900	**373**	277	600	446
4,000	372	284	601	458
4,100	372	290	**604**	471
4,200	372	297	601	481
4,300	371	304	599	491
4,400	371	311	596	500
4,500	371	318	595	510
4,600	369	323	591	518
4,700	366	328	585	524
4,800	362	331	581	531
4,900	358	334	576	538
5,000	352	336	569	541
5,100	347	**337**	560	544
5,200	339	335	552	547
5,300	332	334	545	550
5,400	324	332	537	552
5,500	317	330	528	**553**
5,600	309	329	518	552
5,700	303	329	506	549
5,800	296	327	497	549
5,900	—	—	485	545
6,000	—	—	475	543

A great way to increase the power output of your Vortec Gen III V-8 with OEM-quality GM products is to install the '02 and later LS6 camshaft and cylinder heads.

If you are looking for used LS6 heads, the easiest way to identify them by a visual inspection is by the exhaust ports. The stock LS1 heads have oval exhaust ports, while the LS6 heads have "D"-shaped port exits. The head on the right with the "triangle" casting mark is more desireable because it is the semi-permanent mold casting — these consistently make 5-7 horsepower more than the sand cast head at the left.

by GM. They have GM part numbers. They all bolt on to the 4.8-, 5.3-, and 6.0-liter engines with no modifications to the basic architecture (which makes sense, as the architecture is common). Yet, they provide a real performance improvement. Now *there* are some good reasons for checking out this plan of action.

ON THE 6.0-LITER

The LQ4 and LQ9 aluminum cylinder heads have 72-cc combustion chambers, while the LS6 combustion chambers are 64 cc. The 8-cc decrease in chamber volume results in an increase in mechanical compression ratio of about 1 full point (from 10:1 to 11:1). Usually,

increasing the compression one point with a performance engine would result in detonation that would damage the engine if it ran on anything but premium fuel. But again, almost all of the Gen III V-8 truck engines were originally designed to operate with regular 87-octane gasoline; as far as I know, only the hi-po 345-hp LQ9 was designed for premium. So, on most truck engines, the new compression ratio can be accommodated by using premium 92-octane gasoline. For some extra power, you can also install the LS6 camshaft. This cam, with its extra duration, will make more high-RPM power *and* bleed off some of the static compression at low RPM, giving you a little extra cushion against detonation.

INSTALLATION NOTES

Unlike the cars, the Gen III V-8 is not mounted halfway under the windshield on the full-size trucks. This means you could make the cam and head swap in the trucks without being a contortionist. To make the job easier, it's a good idea to remove the hood. Also, the radiator will need to be removed, along with the grille. Then you'll be able to slide the cam forward enough to remove it from the engine. The grille is straightforward enough you can figure it out as you go, but the hood and some other component removal procedures are covered in Chapter 4.

Camshaft Installation

The cam swap is actually a neat process on the Gen III V-8. If you aren't swapping the heads, the cam can be changed without removing them, the valley plate, or the intake manifold. The swap can be performed this way because the lifters ride in plastic retainers that will hold them up at the top of their lift for a short amount of time if the pushrods have been removed. This makes swapping cams on the Gen III a really fast process.

First, spin the engine over until the number-1 cylinder is at top dead center (TDC). This is done to line up the timing gear 'dots' before tearing the engine apart if you are going to make this swap

PRODUCT COMMENTS	
'02 LS6 Parts To Add for More Vortec Truck Engine Power	**GM Part Numbers**
'02 LS6 Head	
Casting	12564243
Machined	12564824
Assembly	38958622
Head bolts 2 kits required for each engine	12498545
Valves, LS6	
intake, hollow	12565311
exhaust, sodium/ potassium filled	12565312
Valvesprings, LS6	12565313
Camshaft, LS6	12565308
Pushrods	
stock	LS1/LQ pushrods are 7.400 inch with the smaller base circle '02 LS6 cam, you'll need to install longer, more robust pushrods (which will depend on the cam and how much the cylinder heads are milled)

without pulling the heads. This helps you avoid having to turn the engine over in minute increments with compression in all the cylinders to find TDC when reinstalling the cam. Then, simply loosen the rockers, pull out the pushrods, spin the cam 360 degrees, remove the bolts holding the upper timing gear and cam retention plate in place, and pull out the cam.

No matter what cam you are swapping and how knowledgeable your source of valve-to-piston clearance info is, you should always check it yourself just to be sure. Valve/piston contact is a catastrophe that'll require considerable work and money to replace bent/broken valves, bashed up cylinder heads, broken pistons, and sometimes a broken engine block if you're really lucky.

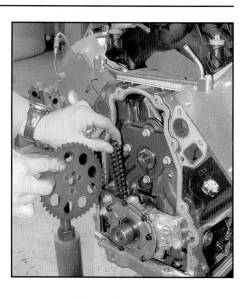

1. If you are just swapping the cam, then skip unbolting the intake and draining the coolant (shown in the next few captions), but do remove the coil packs, valve covers, and rocker bolts. Pull the pushrods. It's a good idea to replace the stock 8-mm pushrods with 0.080-inch wall thickness chrome-moly pushrods whenever you upgrade the camshaft.

4. To get the heads off but limit your work, unbolt the intake and prop it up on 2 x 4-inch wood blocks — that way you'll only need to unhook a few electrical connectors like the coil wiring and some hoses.

7. Next you'll need to remove the upper timing gear from the cam and set the chain off to the side.

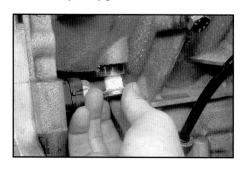

2. It's important that you drain the coolant out of the top of the Gen III V-8 before pulling the heads or you'll dump coolant all over the deck surface and into the cylinder bores. Getting coolant in the blind head-bolt holes and cylinder bores can lead to many tragic problems — like cracked blocks and hydraulic'd pistons — so do yourself a favor and drain the top of the engine before pulling the heads.

5. To access the camshaft, you'll have to remove the balancer. The crank is threaded for a balancer bolt, so W2W has created this spacer for the balancer puller bolt to seat against to protect the threads. Then remove the water pump. When reinstalling the harmonic balancer, torque it to 37 ft-lbs (50 N-m), and then another 140 degrees (which will be tough to do!).

8. Rotate the camshaft 360 degrees to nest the lifters up into their plastic retainers. This allows the cam to be removed without having to pull the lifters out of the engine.

3. If you're swapping heads, remove all the fasteners (10 head bolts and 5 valley bolts at the top of each head) and pull the heads off the engine. (See next caption.)

6. Remove the front engine cover by unbolting all eight of the 8-mm-diameter, 10-mm hex-head bolts in the front of the cover and the two oil pan mounting bolts coming up from underneath.

9. Remove the four 8-mm-diameter, 10-mm hex-head cam plate bolts (these are shorter than all the other 8-mm bolts) and the retainer plate to pull the stock camshaft out.

10. When installing, lube up the LS6 cam with engine oil and slide the cam into the engine. A long screwdriver is being used here for leverage, but anything that will fit up inside the gun-drilled cam will help you get it past the bearings without damaging them.

11. If you're swapping heads, you'll need to install them with new head bolts, as the GM head bolts are for one-time use only. The head bolts are of a torque angle design, which means they're taken to their yield point to provide a common level of clamping force. GM did this to simplify the assembly process in the plant, but it also makes building a Gen III relatively easy for you. Follow the torquing sequence called out in Chapter 7 when it comes time to install your new heads.

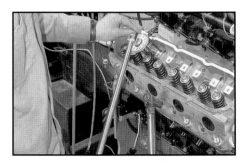

12. A torque wrench and a breaker bar with the torque angle socket on it are shown here. Follow the installation process described in Chapter 7 for the amount of torque to apply to the head bolts and the ensuing torque-angle sequence to achieve the desired clamping load.

13. Reinstall the pushrods with a light dab of extreme-pressure assembly lube on each end of the pushrods, bolt the rockers back into place and select pushrods to achieve a valve lash of 1/2 turn (see Chapter 9 for more detail on this), and reinstall the valve covers and coil packs.

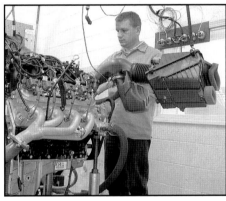

14. All the 6.0-liter dyno testing was performed with shorty headers flowing into a substitute exhaust system, a stock inlet air cleaner system, and premium pump gas.

Comparing 5.3 and LS6 Cylinder Heads

If you're going to swap LS6 heads on your 5.3-liter Vortec truck engine, it will help to know the specs. One figure to pay attention to is the coil bind on the '01 LS6 — this could trip up some folks and it needs to be measured before installing the heads. Also, the increased combustion chamber volume means you should either have the heads milled, use a thinner head gasket, or change the pistons to get the compression back up. Otherwise, this is a great way to pick up some power.

	LS6	LW4
Coil bind	1.140 in ('01)	1.255 in
	1.225 in ('02-'04)	
Valvespring installed height	1.805 in	1.805 in
Intake valve diameter	2.000 in	1.900 in
Exhaust valve diameter	1.550 in	1.550 in
Combustion chamber vol	65.6 cc	61 cc
Valvespring seat pressure	100 lb/in	91 lb/in
Valvespring open pressure	271 lb/in	235 lb/in
Exhaust port shape	"D" shaped	oval shape

Swapping in a 6.0-Liter

If you have a 5.3- or 4.8-liter Gen III-equipped truck or SUV and desire more power, swapping in a 6.0-liter Gen III could be the solution. Externally, the 4.8-, 5.3-, and 6.0-liter engines look almost exactly the same, so the external components should bolt on with little or no modifications required.

Regarding the controls to run the engine, some hot-rodders have installed 6.0-liter engines in 5.3-liter vehicles, hooked up the original 5.3-liter electronics, turned the key, and driven the vehicle with no change to the calibration. This won't always work, so it's recommended you consult one of the many calibration companies, like The Turbo Shop, DiabloSport, HyperTech, LS1-Edit, and others, to make sure the fuel, spark, transmission controls, and other key parameters are managing the new engine properly. But, as far as engine swaps go, this might be the easiest on the planet.

To check valve-to-piston clearance properly, refer to the process detailed in Chapter 6. If the clearance between the valves and pistons is less than 0.160 inch, you may have to cut reliefs in the pistons. Another possible solution is to increase the head gasket thickness (probably not that great of an idea, as it will increase combustion chamber volume and decrease combustion ratio, which will reduce power). Or you could change the advance or retard of the camshaft to move maximum valve lift (which will also affect power), or change the cam altogether.

If you swap the '02 LS6 cam into a Vortec engine and put in a longer, stronger pushrod to correct for the smaller base circle on the '02 LS6 cam and get back to good valvetrain geometry, there should be no problems. Even with that said, though, it's a good idea to check everything to make sure there are no valve-to-piston clearances, valvetrain wear, or other issues that might ruin a good running engine.

POWER PRODUCTION

Well, what can you say other than all hail Jim Hicks? He is the GM engineer that led the team that created the LS6 cam. To say they are fantastic would be an understatement. It seems whatever Gen III V-8 engine this cam is slid in, about 40 hp comes barreling out. Then, add in some freer breathing equipment on the inlet and exhaust side, and maybe some increased compression and whoa, at least another 10 or 15 hp rolls out. In case you don't know, 50 hp can be felt in the seat of your pants and it feels good.

ON THE 5.3-LITER

The 5.3-liter Gen III Vortec V-8 is probably the most common Gen III engine sold by GM (having been built in a 2:1 ratio to any other Gen III V-8), we have provided a full host of dyno tests adding various components to the base engine. You'll probably notice there is not a dyno test with LS6 heads bolted to the base 5.3-liter engine. Well, this test was run, but since the engine *lost* power, it wasn't included in the rundown.

The reason the engine lost power can probably be traced to the change in compression ratio, as the 5.3-liter heads have 61.1-cc combustion chambers and the LS6 heads have 64-cc chambers. While this might not seem like a lot, it's enough to eliminate the potential power increase from the larger ports and improved flow of the LS6 heads. Milling the deck surface on the heads, or using the milled GMPP CNC-ported LS6 heads, would probably show a gain, but due to time constraints, that test was not run.

Just looking at how well the LS6 cam did in the 5.3- and 6.0-liter should be enough for most enthusiasts. On both engines, while peak power was slightly raised in the powerband, each engine made about 40 more horsepower

6.0-LITER/LS6 DYNO

The baseline for this test was performed with a 6.0-liter engine running shorty headers, a stock air cleaner housing and tube, with the water pump, and no alternator or power steering. Test 2 adds LS6 heads to the baseline engine. Test 3 adds the LS6 heads and cam to the baseline engine. And finally, Test 4 adds CNC-ported LS6 heads and the LS6 cam to the baseline engine. All tests were done using 94-octane street gas, and the compression ratios for the engines are listed at the top of the dyno chart.

	Baseline 9.25:1		Test 2 9.915:1		Test 3 9.915:1		Test 4 10.362:1	
	Trq	HP	Trq	HP	Trq	HP	Trq	HP
3,000	356	207	374	214	354	203	353	202
3,100	359	212	377	222	357	211	355	210
3,200	361	220	378	231	360	219	358	218
3,300	363	228	380	239	363	228	361	227
3,400	365	237	383	248	368	238	367	237
3,500	369	246	386	247	372	248	372	248
3,600	370	254	390	267	378	259	380	261
3,700	**373**	263	393	277	383	270	386	272
3,800	**373**	270	395	286	386	279	389	282
3,900	**373**	277	**396**	294	388	289	390	289
4,000	372	284	395	301	390	297	390	297
4,100	372	290	394	307	390	305	393	307
4,200	372	297	393	314	392	313	397	317
4,300	371	304	393	322	394	323	401	328
4,400	371	311	391	327	395	331	403	338
4,500	371	318	390	334	396	339	406	348
4,600	369	323	389	340	**398**	348	**407**	357
4,700	366	328	387	346	**398**	356	**407**	364
4,800	362	331	382	349	396	362	405	370
4,900	358	334	377	352	395	368	403	376
5,000	352	336	372	354	390	372	400	381
5,100	347	**337**	366	**355**	386	375	397	385
5,200	339	335	359	**355**	382	378	393	389
5,300	332	334	351	**355**	376	380	389	393
5,400	324	332	344	353	372	382	385	395
5,500	317	330	337	353	367	384	380	398
5,600	309	329	328	349	361	385	373	399
5,700	303	329	319	347	356	386	369	**401**
5,800	296	327	312	344	352	**389**	360	398
5,900							354	397
6,000							347	396
6,100							339	394
6,200							331	390

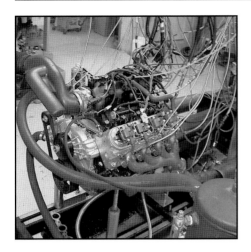

The 5.3-liter testing was performed on an engine out of an '01 SUV. The stock air cleaner, intake tube, and full exhaust were bolted up to the engine on the dyno.

The big advantage of adding 50 horsepower to the 5.3-liter Gen III is that it can be accomplished with just the LS6 cam and freer-flowing, bolt-on intake and exhaust systems. To install the cam, you'll just need to pull the valve covers, loosen the rockers, and disassemble the front of the engine as previously shown on the 6.0-liter engine. This could be the easiest 50-hp bolt-on sequence in hot-rod history.

just by swapping in the Z06 cam! Add in a few aftermarket components if you wish and the power can be raised another 10 to 20 hp. Not bad for a day's work.

TURBO!

The word alone sounds sexy. Up until recently, there haven't been any turbo kits for the truck Gen III V-8 engines. But now Wheel to Wheel

5.3-LITER/LS6 DYNO

The baseline for this test was performed with a 5.3-liter engine with cast-iron manifolds, full exhaust with factory catalytic converters, stock air-cleaner housing and tube, and partial FEAD (no alternator or power steering). Test 2 adds the LS6 camshaft to the baseline engine. Test 3 adds the LS6 cam, a cat-back exhaust, and an open-element air cleaner. Test 4 four adds 4 degrees of ignition advance to the engine in Test 3. All engines are tested with 94-octane street gas.

	Baseline		Test 2		Test 3		Test 4	
	Trq	HP	Trq	HP	Trq	HP	Trq	HP
2,500	308	146	287	137	291	139	296	141
2,600	308	152	291	144	294	146	297	147
2,700	308	158	294	151	296	152	299	154
2,800	308	164	295	157	298	159	299	159
2,900	310	171	297	164	299	165	300	166
3,000	311	178	298	170	301	172	303	173
3,100	311	184	299	177	303	179	305	180
3,200	313	191	302	184	304	185	306	187
3,300	313	197	303	190	306	192	307	193
3,400	314	203	305	197	309	200	309	200
3,500	316	211	309	206	312	208	313	209
3,600	318	218	313	215	316	217	317	217
3,700	320	225	318	224	320	226	321	226
3,800	322	233	321	232	324	235	326	236
3,900	323	240	324	240	328	243	329	244
4,000	**324**	247	324	247	328	250	331	252
4,100	323	252	325	253	329	257	333	260
4,200	322	257	326	261	332	266	334	267
4,300	322	264	328	268	334	273	336	275
4,400	321	269	330	276	337	282	339	284
4,500	319	273	331	284	338	290	340	291
4,600	317	278	333	292	341	299	343	300
4,700	316	283	**335**	300	**343**	307	343	307
4,800	313	286	**335**	306	**343**	314	**346**	316
4,900	310	289	334	312	342	319	344	321
5,000	306	292	333	317	341	324	344	327
5,100	302	**293**	330	320	338	328	342	332
5,200	296	**293**	325	322	333	330	339	335
5,300	290	**293**	321	324	330	334	335	338
5,400	284	292	317	326	328	337	332	341
5,500	278	292	314	329	325	340	328	344
5,600			309	329	319	340	323	345
5,700			305	331	314	340	320	347
5,800			300	**332**	309	341	317	350
5,900			295	331	306	**344**	313	351
6,000			290	**332**	301	**344**	308	**352**
6,100			284	330	295	343	301	350
6,200			279	330	290	342	297	350

Powertrain (W2W) offers a turbo kit designed to bolt on to a stock 4.8-, 5.3-, or 6.0-liter Gen III V-8 engine and help it make considerably more power than GM ever imagined.

After reading any of the previous chapters in this book, you know that making power in the 600 horsepower range is asking a lot of the stock short block. While this is true, turbos in general are much more "kind" to internal combustion components than high compression, naturally aspirated combinations, or power adders like superchargers or nitrous oxide. This is because most turbo applications are very linear in their increase and decrease in cylinder pressure, which means there are few pressure or temperature spikes during engine operation that might lead to detonation of pre-ignition that could damage a piston or other parts. Also, with electronic controls on the fuel and especially the spark advance, turbo systems today can be monitored very closely to make sure the engine doesn't run lean or detonate the pistons into submission.

The W2W kit comes with all the tubing, turbo, intercooler, calibration, and other necessary components.

PRODUCT COMMENTS

Usually, turbo systems have a very high cost because of the tubing, intercooler, and other ancillary components needed to create the turbo system. In this case, W2W uses the stock exhaust manifolds but flips them 180 degrees so the outlets are pointing up. This eliminates one of the most expensive components on a turbo system — the tube headers. W2W creates all the tubing required to hook up the turbo to the exhaust and intercooler and then to the inlet, which eliminates the second most expensive component set on a turbo system — the custom headers.

The Garrett turbo used here has a 67-mm inlet to match the size of the engine. A set of Delphi 42-lb/hr injectors are swapped into the intake manifold to provide increased fuel flow to the more powerful turbocharged engine.

W2W recommends replacing the exhaust system with a less restrictive one so there will be less backpressure to prohibit the turbo from spooling up. The

The W2W turbo kit is straightforward to install. The cast-iron exhaust manifolds are unbolted from the engine and flipped 180 degrees to position the outlets upwards and towards the front of the vehicle. The W2W tubing is then used to connect the turbo, intercooler, and inlet tract together. The total installation time is less than a day.

This photo shows the initial dyno testing of the Wheel to Wheel Powertrain single turbo upgrade for the Vortec Gen III V-8 truck and SUV engines. With electronic controls, this turbo package can make impressive power with stock components.

stock catalytic converters are one of the real problems. They'll melt into one solid glob if you try to run them with this turbo motor. This might sound comical, but the resulting infinite backpressure can cause some grim damage to the engine and turbo components. Aftermarket high-flow catalysts are required.

INSTALLATION NOTES

The kit bolts on without any changes required to the engine itself. W2W provides all the tubing and mounting components, and the kit uses the stock exhaust manifolds. Calibration work will be required to alter the fuel and spark tables, and more importantly, the transmission controls, to handle the newly found power. If you vary from the W2W kit, you'll need some specialized calibration work, as there is considerable detail in getting this type of system to work smoothly and reliably.

POWER PRODUCTION

W2W built a few early versions of this kit with forged cranks, rods, and pistons of stock dimensions in 6.0-liter blocks to determine what kind of power the engine could take. As you can see by the dyno chart, this turbo package can make almost 900 hp without working too hard. Working backwards towards a stock engine combination, W2W was able to determine they could safely make over 600 hp on an otherwise stock 6.0-liter LQ4.

This is with stock pistons, stock rods, stock heads, and other stock components. This points out one of the impressive aspects of turbo systems. Just cranking up the boost can provide impressive returns on power — you just need to have internal components that can handle the increased boost. A stock 2004 4.8-liter Gen III V-8 makes peak power of 290 ft-lbs of torque at 4,000 rpm and 285 hp at 5,600 rpm, so you can see the turbo motor is making almost double those numbers without a single change to the engine. but the fuse is much shroter on the internal components at those power levels.

TURBO DYNO

The durability of this kind of project isn't 100,000 miles, but the owner of this truck wanted to test the limits of the vehicle. The first engine is a stock 6.0-liter engine. The second engine is a 6.0-liter '02 LQ4 equipped with a W2W turbocharger system, a Lunati crank, Oliver rods, and CE pistons to handle the rather excessive 19 psi of maximum boost from the single turbo. It's equipped with 38-lb/hr injectors and has the fuel pressure set at 80 psi on an adjustable fuel regulator. The exhaust consists of stock exhaust manifolds running pressure up to the turbo through a W2W tubing kit. the dyno test starts at 3,500 rpm on this engine because the dyno struggled to hold the engine below that rpm.

The 4.8-liter turbo engine in the third test is bone-stock except for the 42-lb/hr injectors and fuel pressure regulator to get the pressure up to 80 psi. The W2W turbo is set for 8 psi of maximum boost.

RPM	Baseline 6.0-liter Stock Engine		Modified 6.0-liter W2W Turbo Kit		Stock 4.8-liter w/W2W Turbo	
	Trq	HP	Trq	HP	Trq	HP
2,500					493	235
2,600					498	246
2,700					501	258
2,800					505	269
2,900					509	281
3,000	356	207			514	294
3,100	359	212			521	308
3,200	361	220			528	322
3,300	363	228			535	336
3,400	365	237			542	351
3,500	369	246	888	592	552	368
3,600	370	254	893	612	563	386
3,700	**373**	263	**897**	632	572	403
3,800	**373**	270	894	647	582	421
3,900	**373**	277	894	664	590	438
4,000	372	284	884	673	597	456
4,100	372	290	880	687	600	481
4,200	372	297	875	699	602	493
4,300	371	304	867	710	602	506
4,400	371	311	860	721	**603**	516
4,500	371	318	850	728	602	516
4,600	369	323	840	736	598	524
4,700	366	328	827	740	592	530
4,800	362	331	812	742	584	534
4,900	358	334	798	744	575	536
5,000	352	336	782	744	566	539
5,100	347	**337**	768	**746**	558	**542**
5,200	339	335	748	741	548	**542**
5,300	332	334	728	735	536	541
5,400	324	332	703	722	525	540
5,500	317	330	672	704	513	537

1,200-HORSEPOWER, 387-CUBIC-INCH C5R POWER

Throughout this book, we've focused on using simple parts and straightforward buildups, but this chapter will show what it takes to build a highly custom, special-use engine. With this engine buildup, you'll learn many processes to get the multiple systems of a one-off engine working in concert. An engine like this requires considerable time, skills, and money to put together, so not everyone should attempt it, but learning what these steps look like will help you understand more about Gen III V-8 engine buildups.

In case you should ever feel the need to slide behind the wheel of a car powered by a 1,200 hp, centrifugally supercharged Gen III V-8, you're about to learn what it would take. The only detail you'll need to figure out for yourself after reading this chapter is how to pony up a fair amount of resources (we mean money!) to make it a reality.

With that said, let's assume for a minute that you want the only 427-ci (7.0-liter) C5 Corvette on your block, or maybe your Camaro/Firebird just doesn't have the *scary* power that you just must have. If this is true, and if you have plenty of money to spend, then the engine being built in this chapter is for you. It is a 1,200-hp, hard-core street/strip Gen III-based V-8 engine that will propel a car with 10.5-inch-wide tires to mid-8-second 1/4-mile passes at over 160 mph. If that doesn't mean much to you, how about mid-3-second 0-60 mph times and mid-5-second 0-100 mph times! Just imagine being shot out of a cannon.

While you might not be building a supercharged C5R engine, if you want a big cube and/or 700+ hp engine, the long block being built here is what you are looking for. Now, for more single usage vehicles, you could have a machine shop bore out the stock cast-in cylinder liners on a stock Gen III V-8 block and glue cylinder liners into the remaining holes (like those from Darton). But, if you want something that has been engineered by GM to reliably operate while making obscene power, the engine being built here is for you.

This specialized power does come at a price, though. The aluminum GM Performance Parts C5R engine block alone costs $6,500 and still needs machine

work before it is useable (we are told by machine shops that to have your stock block sleeved with Darton sleeves will

The component list for this engine is race-inspired, expensive, and requires considerable knowledge to maximize the power production — but this engine can make sick power all day long when it's done. Just to give you an idea of the type of components shown here, the C5R Corvette racing engine block lists for $6,500 from your local GM Performance Parts dealer — and then you need to do a bunch of machine work to make things fit! The heads here look like regular Gen III aluminum heads, but they're the special 12-degree (instead of 15-degree) valve angle C5R cylinder heads, also available from GMPP, which require a fabricated intake manifold and other one-off pieces. The mallory distributor and MSD 7AL ignition system are completely custom, as is the oiling system.

run you at least $2,400). The aluminum C5R cylinder heads are CNC-ported and cost $4,000 a pair. The Lunati forged crankshaft will run you about $2,500, the custom billet steel Oliver rods about $1,100, and the specially machined and coated forged-aluminum JE pistons are

Clean the Parts

Cleaning the parts as thoroughly as possible is very important, especially for a high-horsepower engine build. W2W, like many pro shops, has a special steam cleaner for the engine parts, and they use it constantly. They believe you can never get one of these engines clean enough. They clean everything when it first shows up and between just about every step of the way after that. They've found that the production engines clean up very quickly, but the C5R engine components that have never run a moment in anger, have a lot of stuff that comes out of them throughout the cleanings.

The best way to clean an intricate part like the LS6 intake manifold is with a high pressure parts steam cleaner. These have replaced the toxic hot tank cleaners used years ago and are much better at getting parts clean.

about $1,000 a set. The F1 ProCharger centrifugal blower will set you back about $3,000. And this is just the basics.

The machine work and general massaging to get these one-off components to work in concert to make the 1,200 hp will probably cost you at least as much as the parts. The machine work includes modifying the engine block to accept massive, custom 1/2-inch head studs, cutting off the stock oil pump mounting bosses, clearancing the bottom of the cylinders so the heavy-duty rods can swing through, and more. You'll need to get all the bearing diameters set up with the proper tolerances, set the minimum valve-to-piston clearance without sacrificing any performance, tune up the oiling system, build a custom ignition system, and more.

The one advantage you have in front of you is that every little detail it takes to build this engine is thoroughly photographed and explained here. The exact component set and process, down to tips like tolerances and assembly lube, is shown for anyone to duplicate, improve on, and enjoy.

THE BUILDERS

The head engine builder at Wheel to Wheel Powertrain (W2W), Kurt Urban,

personally assembled this engine. Up until this point, 1,200 hp is the most power W2W has made with the Gen III V-8 architecture. The engine is being built to power an F-body street/strip car. Previously, this car has completed the 1/4-mile in just under 9.55 seconds @ 145 mph with a stock-block Gen III V-8, making it the fastest supercharged Gen III-powered vehicle known at the moment.

THE ENGINE

There are a few ways to build 1,000+ hp street/strip engines. W2W has built both supercharged and turbocharged stock-block Gen III V-8s that have made over 700 hp, so they had an idea what it would take to make 1,000 hp. While a turbo engine would be easier on parts, the previous engine in this car was a supercharged engine, so it was decided a more powerful supercharged engine would be easier to integrate into the existing set-up of the car.

The one impressive thing about a supercharged engine is the monstrously deep powerband they provide. Now, a supercharger does consume a fair amount of crankshaft power to spin it, but the immediate power production is the payoff versus a turbo. For example,

Clean Tools!

W2W makes a point about the cleanliness of the tools used to assemble an engine. Make sure they are clean before using them to assemble your engine! Probably one of the biggest culprits to introducing dirt, grit, metal shavings, and other engine-damaging substances into a newly assembled engine are the sockets. Urban routinely flushes his sockets in the solvent tank and forbids their usage for anything but engine assembly. Any gunk on sockets will be left in the engine and possibly lead to an early failure.

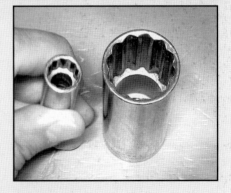

Keeping the engine assembly tools clean is key. Sockets are the worst enemy, but other tools, like scrapers, ratchet wrenches, torque wrenches, and pry bars also need to be completely clean to avoid introducing potentially destructive materials into the engine.

based on W2W's testing, the F1 supercharger boosting this engine requires about 200 horsepower to make about 1,200 hp at the flywheel. So really, the engine is producing 1,400 hp at the crank, but who's counting, right?

As you'll see, the ignition system, intake manifold, front accessory drive system, blower drive, and fuel system on this engine are completely custom built and required some dyno time and engineering to get right. The ignition fires off an MSD 7AL called to action by a belt-driven mallory distributor that runs off the camshaft. The offset-belt-drive distributor mount is a custom piece machined up by W2W (and now available from W2W). It is offset to allow room for the massive 90-mm throttle body that is bolted to the inlet of the fully fabricated W2W intake manifold. The drive pulley on the camshaft is available from Jesel.

The intake is built for a big throttle body and massive 160-lb/hr fuel injectors with a chamber volume and ports big enough to flow air for 1,000+ hp. W2W had the aluminum intake polished by ace polisher Gary Lentz to give the engine some sparkle.

The front accessory drive is a packaging masterpiece. Faced with having to package the supercharged engine into the engine bay of a late-model F-body, W2W turned to their fabrication team to figure it all out. W2W designed the blower mount, and machined it out of billet aluminum plate. The blower needed to be mounted low and tucked close to the engine on the driver side to allow enough room for the supercharger air inlet behind the radiator. Also, since the blower will require a lot of power to spin, the mount needed to be extra sturdy. The main mounting plate is whittled from 5/8-inch-thick billet 6061 aluminum.

While it's not mounted to the engine, part of the reason for the engine's power production is the W2W fabricated, Sparco-core air-to-water intercooler, which has an advertised flow of up to 1,800 hp of air at 1 psi drop (which is an extremely high efficiency rating). In the car, the intercooler is mounted in the passenger backseat area, and connected to the engine via a

looooonnnnggg 4-inch-diameter aluminum tube snaked from the blower back to the intercooler and back up into the engine intake along the trans tunnel. On the dyno, the intercooler was placed next to the engine with special tubing built just for the dyno testing.

HOW TO BUILD 1,200-HORSEPOWER ENGINES

W2W pointed out that the crank, rods, pistons, valves, and other moving parts in the engine are overbuilt as compared to a naturally aspirated (NA) or

What is a C5R?

General Motors usually introduces new performance engines in the Chevrolet Corvette, which is why the Gen III V-8 first appeared in the '97 C5 Corvette as the LS1. The Corvette is also a proven winner on the racetrack with components designed by the Engineering team in the GM Racing Division and outside race shops. The C5R engine block and cylinder heads are products of the GM Corvette road-racing program—the C5 standing for the generation of Corvette they are intended for and the "R" for racing.

The C5R engine block is designed for 4.125-inch bore diameter and runs a crankshaft with a 4.000-inch stroke. This creates an engine of about 7.0 liters, or 427 cubic inches, which was what the road racing rules allowed the Corvette team to run.

The C5R engine block was designed specifically for road racing, which means it was built with the idea it would have a dry-sump oiling system to maintain a constant flow of oil. But it is also set up to run on the production wet-sump oiling system. Besides their complexity, the dry-sump oiling systems are very expensive. They use externally mounted, multi-stage oil pumps to extract as much freestanding oil from the engine as possible. This means any oil not contributing to lubrication or cooling of the engine at that moment is sucked away

(continued on next page)

The GM Performance Parts C5R block on the left is truly a piece of artwork. The block is cast of 356 T6 aluminum and machined to exacting standards for GMPP. The C5R Gen III V-8 block has some critical differences from the production block on the right. Some of the bigger differences include it not having the side windows between the mains in the crankcase, since it's intended to be oiled by a dry-sump system. As a note, the LS6 block is made of 318 T5 aluminum, which has a little less ultimate strength than the 356 T6.

The LS6 liners (left) are cast in place, while the C5R liners (right) are pressed in. The bore diameters are different also — 3.898 inches for the LS6 and 4.125 inches for the C5R.

What is a C5R? (continued)

(continued from previous page)

from the internals of the engine to minimize parasitic power loss. This power loss usually comes from things like the oil roping around the crankshaft.

The dry-sump system also has the added benefit of pulling a vacuum on the crankcase — which is good for a naturally aspirated engine, but really good for a massively supercharged engine. This is because the vacuum in the crankcase prevents blowby, the small amounts of the pressurized air/fuel mixture coming into the engine that gets by the piston rings, from building up in the crankcase and causing an explosion.

This may sound a little dramatic, but it's a situation that could occur without the vacuum.

The bottom lip of the C5R pressed-in liners will most likely need to be notched if you use more than a 3.622-inch stroke or big lunky rods. The displacement of this blown engine was kept at 387 cubic inches to keep a low numerical compression ratio. This engine has the expected 3.622-inch stroke, but where most road race engines would have lightweight rods, this engine has rather heavy-duty rods to handle the added forces of spinning a crank-driven supercharger.

The vacuum also helps allow the engine internals to spin more freely, as it minimizes the vaporized oil that usually hangs in the crankcase.

The C5R block comes with billet steel main caps and dowels to lock the caps in place to handle extreme power. The stock block wedges its powdered-steel mains in place between the block surfaces (top). For street-type power (under 650 hp), the production system seems to work just fine, but making big power requires doweled-mains (bottom).

On the exhaust port side, the C5R heads look similar to the factory LS6 Gen III V-8 heads (bottom), but the C5R heads have benefited from some considerable tweaks to extract maximum horsepower.

The C5R cylinder heads at first look like prettied-up Gen III cylinder heads, but they're much more than that. The GM Racing team developed cylinder heads based on the Gen III design, but with a few major changes, the biggest being a 12-degree valve angle, from the production 15 degrees, for a straighter intake port shot. They also changed the "cathedral" intake ports to rectangular ports, offset the valvetrain to clear the now wider ports, and set the valve centers at a tighter spacing to take better advantage of the big valve diameters and big bores.

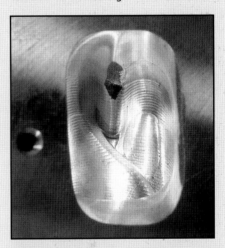

The intake ports on the C5R heads are rectangular (top), instead of the factory cathedral ports (bottom). This is accomplished by offsetting the ports, which requires offset lifters and rockers to move the pushrods out of the way.

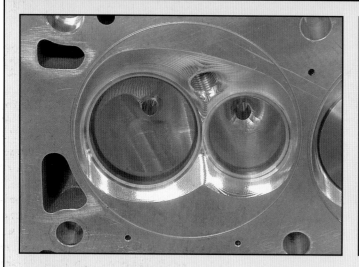

The C5R combustion chamber is smaller, at 42 cc (left), while the factory LS6 chambers are 64 cc (right). The valve sizes in the C5R are larger (2.15/1.60 inch) than the LS6 valves (2.00/1.50 inch). The bore size is bigger on the C5R block, which reduces valve shrouding and obviously allows for engines with larger displacements. The groove around the combustion chamber is for a steel O-ring used to seal the head to the block under the severe combustion pressure of a boosted engine. This engine could be used in a regular driver hot rod, but it would drink a small amount of coolant — common on engines with copper head gaskets.

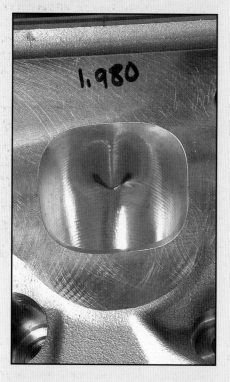

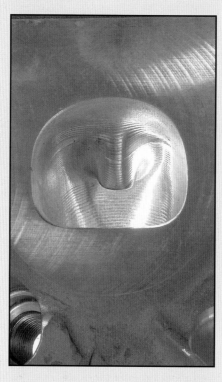

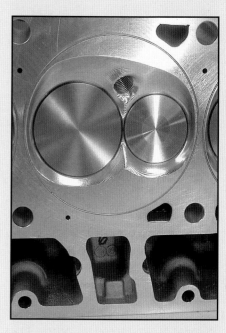

The fully CNC-machined C5R chamber really shows how the 12-degree valve angle allows a more shallow combustion chamber, which puts the bigger intake valves more directionally into the cylinder bore.

The C5R exhaust ports (left) are very similar to production Gen III V-8 exhaust ports (right), but the C5R has a smaller valveguide protrusion and is a rectangular port (the production LS6 exhaust is "D" shaped, as shown). Both flow very well.

turbo engine. This is because the super-charger puts a lot of strain on all the components. The crank/rod/piston combination is heavy enough that it requires about 160 grams of mallory to balance the crank — much more than what they would have to put in the crank of a NA engine. Mallory is a heavy metal inserted into different parts of the crankshaft to help balance the rotating assembly.

The oil control on an engine like this is critical to it surviving the abuse, so W2W chose to build a dry-sump oiling system with a Dailey Engineering 5-stage belt-driven oil pump to protect it. The dry sump also helps to pull a vacuum on the crankcase, helping to prevent the combustion blowby passing by the piston rings from building up in the crankcase and causing an explosion. While this might sound extreme, with enough fuel and air being pushed in to this engine to make over 1,000 hp, things like this can happen without vacuum in the oil pan.

Also, you'll see the experience W2W has with this race-inspired block. A good example is them knowing the lifters need to be "clocked," so the restrictor in one side of the lifter body is located on the main oil galley side — which runs through the lifter bores and routes pressurized oil throughout the engine. The lifters are a good example of the minefield these blocks present. As you'll see in the photos, the lifter oil feed hole is at different heights on each side of the lifter. Put the lifter in the engine block 180 degrees opposite of the proper way and boom, you've got no oil pressure when the engine is fired up because its pouring through the galleys at breakneck speed. And as an added bonus, you'll drown the top of the engine because oil is going up the pushrod just as fast.

As a final step in oil control, once on the dyno, W2W discovered there was an excess of oil ending up in the top of the engine. The oil was pooling in the valve covers and being pumped past the valvestem seals. To fix this, restrictors were added to one end of the pushrods to reduce the opening by 50 percent. W2W presses a small roll pin into the opening

with Loctite on it to hold it in place (A photo shows this being performed on the 500+ hp engine in Chapter 7).

This engine is not meant to drive across the country, but it will survive some Saturday-night cruising. As you'll see, the front drive was originally built with a chain driving the super-charger. W2W felt that was necessary for this size blower based on their experience and after consulting with some Fastest Street Car competitors using a similar blower. What they found was the chain was too short to dissipate the heat generated in driving the blower and would quickly seize up. A belt system was created to complete the dyno testing and quarter-mile passes and has been very durable.

PREPPING A C5R RACE BLOCK

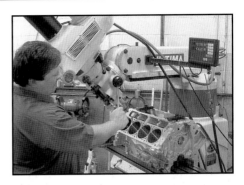

1. Even though the C5Rs are meticulously machined, W2W recommends always measuring the bore size, deck height, main bearing diameters, and other critical dimensions of any block instead of assuming the tolerances are okay. Writing these dimensions down in an engine log keeps all the critical info in one place and minimizes tolerance problems as the build progresses.

2. With the ProCharger F1R centrifugal-supercharger whistling a 21-psi wind into the intake, even the mighty C5R Gen III V-8 engine block is stressed to its limit to hold the cylinder heads down tight. Because of this, W2W prefers to convert the block from the original 11-mm head studs to 1/2-inch head studs. (Note: the top 5 head-bolt holes on the C5R are 5/16-18 thread, so you don't need to change these threads when going to 1/2-inch head studs.) The 1/2-inch studs are a custom design that W2W has ARP create for them to install in the C5R block. W2W positions the C5R engine block on a Bridgeport mill so the deck surface is perpendicular to the drill. Then, they drill the holes out and thread them with a 1/2-13 tap. The threads are drilled out about 1 inch down to mimic the factory setup. The mill guides the tap into the drilled-out holes on the block to maximize the chances of the studs being perpendicular to the deck face.

3. Here are the original 11-mm C5R studs (left) and the W2W 1/2-inch (right) to show the difference in size. Remember, the holes in the heads will need to be drilled out to accept these bigger studs. W2W says this work is required if you want to keep the head from lifting off the block while making more than 800 hp – and it works on either the stock short block or the C5R block.

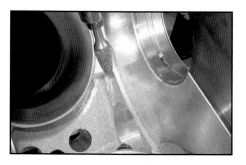

4. This engine will use a Gen III V-8-specific Jesel belt drive to spin the camshaft. While the Jesel drive is designed for the C5R, there's still a considerable amount of machining required to install it. Jesel provides a paper template to determine what areas require machining. Since W2W does this work often, they created a 1/4-inch aluminum plate template to use as a guide for the machining. To get the Jesel base plate to bolt to the block, you need to machine-off the stock oil pump mounting bosses (see shaded area on block) and make a few other modifications.

6. Prepping the cylinder bores is a major step in building this engine. To do this, W2W has created a torque plate to work with 1/2-inch studs and a 4.155-inch bore, which you'll need for honing the bores. Every engine builder has their own combination of grinding stones and speeds to get the surface prepped properly for each specific piston and ring combination, so find a reputable shop and let them do their thing.

8. An engine block casting that has never been used should be thoroughly inspected for remaining sand or rough metal areas. This is especially important for the crankcase, where oil will be whipped around at high forces. W2W does this inspection, then removes the sand and smoothes the rough areas with a metal bit first, then with an 80-grit sandpaper "tootsie roll" on a die grinder. Once this is done, the engine block needs to be thoroughly cleaned, which includes removing the factory-installed cam bearings.

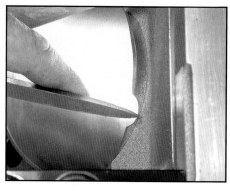

5. When you use the Jesel base plate, it exposes the pressurized main oil galley opening on the driver-side of the engine block, so you'll have to plug it. This opening in the main galley would normally be covered by the stock front cover, which isn't being used on this engine, so plugging it won't affect the oil flow. Oil will instead come from an external multi-stage dry-sump oil pump.

7. Since this block has had a lot of machining done to it and hasn't been run, now is a good time to inspect it for metal burrs on the edges of any machined surfaces. A good example is where the cylinder liners were trimmed. The sharp edge left over was removed with an edge-cutting stone or file. This is a good idea as these sharp lips have a tendency to fall off once the engine gets going and could get lodged in a bearing surface or gear, causing a failure.

9. With the block machined and cleaned, W2W sets the ring gaps on the top and second rings (see page 105 for details). The rings being used on this engine are Speed Pro's heat-treated, ductile-iron Hell Fire rings. These rings are designed for pressurized applications. W2W likes to set ring gaps using the following equation: 0.004 to 0.006-inch per inch of bore diameter. With that in mind, the gaps were set at 0.024 inch, which is on the high side, to account for the abuse encountered in a supercharged engine. As an aside, if this was a nitrous engine, the ring gaps would have been set at 0.028 inch to take into account the severe thermal and pressure shock that occurs when the nitrous hits. The block is cleaned again after all ring gaps are set to remove any metal shavings.

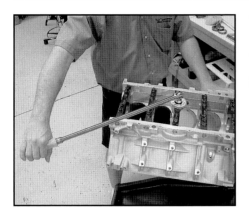

10. *The dimensions for the main and rod bearings are then rechecked. To do this, install the main bearings in the main caps and bolt them into the block with the torque/torque-angle process. The main, rod, and head fasteners are all initially torqued, then turned a pre-determined angle to provide a torque-angle clamping load. These values are different from the stock Gen III V-8 figures, as the block, mains, rods, heads, and fasteners are all different from the stock Gen III V-8.*

12. *The crank journals need to have 0.0025 inch of clearance. This tolerance is measured with the bore gauge feelers in the twelve-to-six and three-to-nine o'clock positions on the inside crank journal bearing of the torqued-down caps. Sometimes the inside diameter (ID) is measured in the 10:30 to 4:30 and the 2:30 to 8:30 positions as a check to the initial measurements. The 0.0025-inch tolerance is attained by putting together combinations of bearing shells.*

As a note, W2W usually builds their engines with a main bearing clearance of 0.002 inch in aluminum blocks, but since this is a big-power engine with a dry-sump oiling system, they are opening the tolerance up a little. To give you an idea of how sensitive this area is, W2W says they would not build anything with 0.003-inch clearance, as it would have an oil pressure of 80 psi at startup, but once the oil got up to 180 degrees and higher, the pressure would drop to 20 psi.

14. *The amount of heavy mallory added to the counterweights in this Lunati crank is substantial, to balance the heavy-duty rotating/reciprocating components used to handle the 1,400+ hp crank power — the blower eats about 200 hp and the dyno showed 1,200 hp — that's 1400 hp at the crank!*

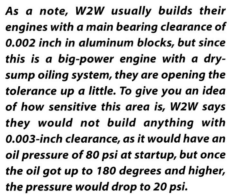

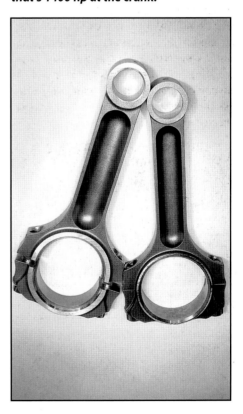

11. *The C5R block torque/torque-to-yield scheme is different from the factory engines. In fact, based on their experience, W2W has developed their own scheme to perform the torque-angle process. First, all the fasteners are lightly covered with #3 lube on the threads and washer heads (this lube comes in the C5R block packaging). Then, the crank main studs are torqued to 100 in-lbs. The inner and outer fasteners are then torqued to 20 ft-lbs. With the torque-angle socket, the inners are then turned 80 degrees, and the outers 60 degrees. The side bolts are then torqued to 20 ft-lbs.*

13. *The Lunati forged crank was washed before beginning the assembly process (to remove the shipping Cosmoline), then wiped with engine oil before being installed.*

15. *Here is a great comparison shot of a stock Gen III V-8 connecting rod on the right of the Oliver billet steel rod. With the difference in size, it's easy to see why there is so much mallory in the crank.*

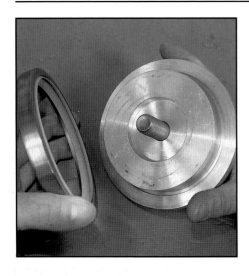

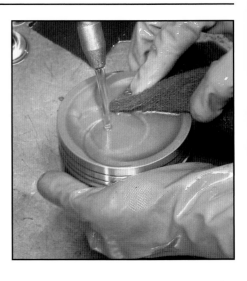

16. *The covers that bolt on the front and rear of the Gen III V-8 block have a dual lip seal to prevent oil leaks. For boosted Gen III V-8s, this factory seal needs to be replaced with a TKO high-performance seal. W2W built this special tool to remove and replace this seal. Installing these covers also requires a lip-setting tool to get the seal seated properly on the crank surface.*

18. *W2W has JE Pistons machine valve reliefs in the pistons based on their experience building these engines. Once the piston-to-valve clearances were checked, W2W deburred all the edges on the piston using a 180-grit tootsie roll sandpaper attachment on a die grinder. As a final touch, DART coated the top of the pistons with heat-reflecting material and the sides with moly-based material to minimize wear.*

3. *The piston dish faces also get the Scotchbrite treatment, especially in the valve relief area.*

CLEANING PARTS FOR FINAL INSTALL

1. *Cleaning all the parts is critical to building an engine that will last. W2W has a solvent tank that is only used to clean parts for the engine assembly area. To start the cleaning process, W2W uses wire brushes of every diameter and length you can imagine to clear out the passages.*

17. *The rod bearing clearances are attained by measuring each crank rod journal and the ID of the appropriate connecting rod in the multiple positions as on the crank main bearing setup (twelve-to-six and three-to-nine o'clock). For more on this, see page 106. Again, using various bearing shell combos helps to get the proper clearance. Once these numbers have been determined, the engine is tightly "bagged" with a plastic bag, to prevent dust and dirt from adhering to the inside of the engine.*

2. *W2W uses Scotchbrite to lightly scrub all the piston thrust faces and brushes to clean out the ring lands and holes. The gloves are for anyone who has a brain and wants to keep it — especially if you're washing parts in a tank all day.*

4. *After being thoroughly soaked, brushed, and scrubbed, each component should be blown off with pressurized air that has a water separator and filter in the system — this avoids spraying the part with water vapor that will invariably have micro-sized rust particles in it.*

PISTON AND ROD ASSEMBLY

1. After cleaning the parts, place them in a clean area in preparation for assembly. It's important for the assembly area to be surgically clean — notice the unsoiled white butcher paper on the countertops. Here, the rods and pistons are assembled together. The first step is to install the double spiral locks in one side of the piston. Then, the piston pin bores, rod bore, and pin are lightly coated with engine oil or assembly lube before being slid together. Most pistons need to be clocked on the rod, as they are built to handle forces in a certain orientation, and the valve reliefs need to mate with the valves they are meant to clear. If you are unclear on this, check it with the piston manufacturer.

3. It's important that after you assemble the rods and pistons, the rings are installed on the pistons and the entire combo is immediately installed in the engine. Why? Because these components have lube on them and this oil attracts dirt and crud and you don't want any of this in the engine — especially not in the piston/bore/crank/oiling-system areas.

5. W2W uses ring spreaders to install the top and second rings. Many believe winding rings onto the piston ring land introduces a twist on the ring, which negatively impacts the ring's ability to seal the combustion pressure. The rings will be stressed to hold the supercharger's boost, so they're installed with the spreader, just to be sure.

6. W2W believes the way you set up the oil rings is critical to achieving good oil control. They don't use the small red spacer on the spreader portion of the oil ring for fear of it ending up somewhere else in the engine. Instead, they carefully position the spreader so it isn't overlapping, and install the piston.

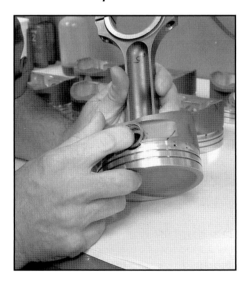

4. Before installing the pistons, W2W wipes the face of the top and second rings with a light coat of 30-weight oil dripped on the fingers. They then wipe the rings with a non-linting towel before installation. Using a light brush, the oil ring lands are lightly covered with 30-weight oil, and then wiped with a non-linting towel to remove any excess oil. You need to remove the excess oil to prevent it from "cooking" into the ring lands upon startup, which could prevent the rings from sealing properly.

2. The last step to assembling the rod/piston combo is to install the final two spiral locks in the piston. For more details on the piston/rod assembly process, see the buildup in Chapter 7 (see page 108).

7. The rings are clocked on the pistons for startup using the GM Power Book recommendations. This puts the rings in the best location during startup to insure proper ring seating in the ring lands and on the bore surface.

8. Wipe a light coat of 30-weight oil on the thrust faces of the pistons just before they're installed.

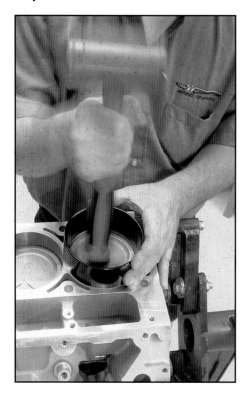

9. Don't forget to apply two drops of engine oil to each bore and wipe it evenly across the entire bore before you install the rods and pistons. Give the rod bearings a thick coat of Pro Blend assembly lube before you carefully lower them down into the bore.

10. W2W follows the Oliver-spec torquing procedure for the rods to torque/torque-to-yield them. The process is similar to that for the production rods. First, the rod bolts are torqued to a relatively low 30 ft-lbs. Then, a vertical line is drawn on the rod bolts with a Sharpie pen — do this so you don't forget which ones you torqued already. Use the torque-angle socket to add 40 degrees of rotation to the rod bolts. Note the factory crank sensor wheel on the crank. This was removed after a few mock-up sessions revealed that it was in the way. The OE trigger wheel crashes when a a 6-1/8-inch rod and 4-inch stroke are used. On big-inch, big-hp engines, the trigger wheel also limits the amount of mallory that can be put in the crank to balance the rotating/reciprocating assembly.

INSTALLING THE CAM

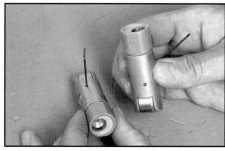

1. Lube the cam up with engine oil and install it (for cam installation tips, see pages 93-94). The next step is to soak the Jesel solid roller lifters in engine oil before you install them. The tip here is to make sure the lifter is installed with the open oil feed hole exposed to the main oil galley. The Jesel lifters have two holes 180 degrees apart: one that is open and another that is blocked off. The way to make sure you are installing the lifter correctly is to plunge a small Allen wrench in there to make sure you have the open hole in the right spot.

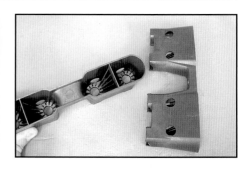

2. The result of the offset of the Jesel lifters, which makes room for the C5R intake ports, can be seen here. The factory Gen III V-8 plastic lifter carriers are used, but the pushrod holes need to be ground on to open them up to an oblong shape so the Smith Brothers 3/8-inch pushrod can seat in the offset lifter bucket.

DEGREEING THE CAM

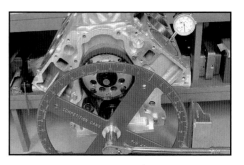

1. This photo shows the degree wheel zeroed to top dead center (TDC) on the number-1 piston, but you always want to check this before going on to the next step of checking the specs on the camshaft.

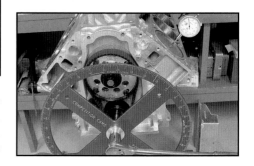

2. To check the degree wheel location to the piston location, rotate the crank 360 degrees to get the piston to 0.050 inch before TDC on the number-1 piston, as shown. Note that the degree wheel is showing 12 degrees approaching TDC. The 0.050-inch value is used to ensure the tolerances in the components don't affect the readings.

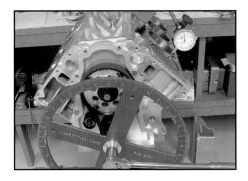

3. Then, rotate the crank 360 degrees the other way to get the piston back to 0.050 inch BTDC on the other side. Note that the degree wheel reads 12 degrees on the other side of TDC. This is a good check to make sure you have the degree wheel zeroed to piston TDC.

4. With a solid roller lifter and pushrod in the block on the intake cam lobe, rotate the crank until the dial indicator reads full lift. Set the dial indicator to read zero.

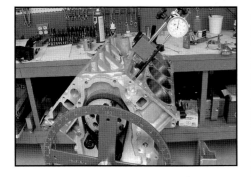

5. Go to 0.050-inch lift on each side of the cam lobe, rotating up to the location by turning the crank in both directions. Record the numbers off the degree wheel. In this case, the degree wheel is reading 154 degrees. When the crank was rotated the other way, the degree wheel read 66 degrees. Add the two figures together, 154 to 66 degrees to get 220. Then, divide that figure by 2 to end up with 110 degrees.

6. While it doesn't need to be done, the crank is rotated back to 110 degrees on the degree wheel to show the intake lobe center of 110 degrees. Now you can read the cam card to determine whether the cam is set properly in relation to the crank location. In our case, if the cam wasn't located properly, we could use the Jesel belt drive for exacting adjustment.

BUILDING THE HEADS

1. Once the heads were checked to make sure they were within spec, the valves were installed. To do this, the valve stems were coated with Pro Blend assembly lube and then slid into the valve guides.

2. Next, the valvespring seats, valvestem seals, and Jesel rocker stands are installed. The seats are provided with the heads, but W2W had to purchase the TKO seals. The Jesel rocker mount required the cylinder head bosses be machined down about 0.130 inches so they'd end up at the proper geometry. Notice the O-ring in the groove in the head — this is only on the C5R head, as the stock head has the O-ring groove in its valve cover.

3. Since this engine is going to run above 20 psi of boost, we're using a coated copper gasket with a steel o-ring in the deck surface. Copper gaskets are for full-out engine combinations because they don't have as much give as composite gaskets, but the clear coating does improve their sealing capability over older uncoated copper gaskets.

4. The C5R cylinder heads have a valve angle of 12 degrees (vs. the factory 15 degrees) and offset intake ports. Because of this, the intake flange is different from the production Gen III V-8 heads (so the stock intake won't bolt up), and the rockers are different. You'll also need some special pistons, but the exhaust flange is unchanged. The C5R head fasteners are torqued to 105 ft-lbs, which is much more than the factory head fasteners.

6. This is what the valvestem should look like when the valvetrain geometry is correct. Many believe the best way to set the proper valvetrain geometry is to purchase valves that have the proper stem length.

9. Another racing-type feature of the C5R heads is their ability to accept 1.650-inch-diameter valvesprings with only slight machining to open up the seat — even without changing the seat depth. To minimize valvetrain weight, this engine is getting Del West titanium locks and retainers.

FINISHING IT OFF

7. To avoid valvespring coil bind, it's a good idea to check the required valvespring height. You can do this with a valvespring height checker, shown, or a micrometer.

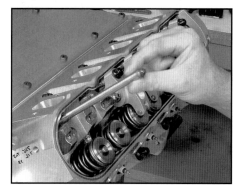

5. The Jesel rocker system comes with a geometry-checking rocker, shown here, that measures the height required for the rocker stand. Often, the rocker stand will need to be shimmed up using the Jesel-supplied shims. One way to quickly determine the necessary shim pack is to stack up shims on the rocker until they match the distance that the valvestem protrudes past the rocker face.

8. W2W used Smith Brothers' 8.350-inch pushrods here. Notice how the pushrod has number-3 assembly lube on the tips (it comes with the GMPP C5R block). The camshaft comes from Cam Motion and features 257/270-degrees duration at 0.050 inches lift, and 0.726/0.713 inches of max lift on 114-degree lobe centers.

1. This clean setup is the result of the early machining work. The Jesel belt drive is fully installed, the distributor drive pulley is on the camshaft, and a belt connects the Jesel/Mallory distributor on the offset mount (built by W2W). Since the intake inlet is at the front of the engine on this intake, W2W had to build a special offset plate to work with the special offset intake inlet that places the throttle body off to the passenger side of the engine.

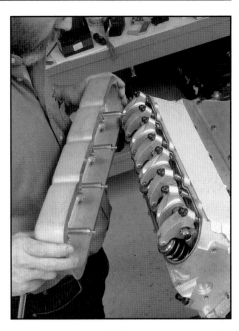

2. The water pump on this engine is a high-flow Meziere electric unit. Notice the shallow cast-aluminum ARE oil pan with the three scavenge-stage pickups (lower left). The four-stage, dry-sump oiling system is used to keep oil off the crank (which would rob horsepower), but also to pull a vacuum in the crankcase to prevent a blowby explosion — which is not uncommon on high-boost engines.

4. The W2W aluminum intake manifold was polished to a mirror finish by Gary Lentz and bolted to the cylinder heads. The intake is O-ringed, so no gasket or sealer is necessary.

6. The deep C5R valve covers are different from the shallow factory valve covers in that they have these four unequal-length stands inside them and an O-ring on the valve cover. The production Gen III V-8 heads have the O-ring seat and O-ring in the head, not in the valve cover. The C5R covers have no provision for the factory coil mounts, but they aren't needed anyway. The Jesel valvetrain is fully custom, with offset rockers to negotiate the pushrods around the oversize ports and large valvesprings.

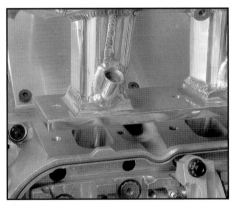

3. This engine won't be running the production engine controller, so the factory knock sensors aren't required. Also, the knock sensors struggle to seal the crankcase on boosted engines, so W2W installed one of their billet valley covers. The bolts need to be torqued to 89 in-lbs at first, and then torqued to 18 ft-lbs in a radial pattern.

5. There are two bolts in the intake manifold/head for each port. W2W has used all the intake bolts before, but found that they really aren't needed. The bolt that's under the short side of the port is very difficult to get in and out anyway — so it's one bolt per port. Notice the injector seat placement and angle — injector placement is one of the reasons this engine makes the power it does. Next, the BBK 90-mm throttle valve was installed on the intake. There will not be a MAF installed, as this engine will run in speed-density mode on a F.A.S.T. aftermarket controller.

7. The job of installing this engine under the hood of a Camaro/Firebird is always a challenge for W2W's fabrication crew. There is little room for a 1,200-hp huffed C5R and its intercooler, so on this car the intercooler is in the back seat. The tubing runs through the firewall and into the interior. It looks impressive and took a long time to create, but even more important — it all works and makes tons of horsepower.

Belt vs. Chain Drives for Centrifugal Superchargers

The supercharger on this engine started with a chain drive, and was then converted to a belt drive. The chain was thought to be the solution because there are very few belts that can handle the 200+ hp required to spin the 9.75-inch impellor sucking air through an inlet diameter of 4 inches on the ProCharger F1R supercharger.

This isn't the first time a chain has been used to drive a supercharger. When Roots-type superchargers first came on the scene in the 1950s and 1960s, some were chain driven. A few spectacular failures led to them being written out of most rulebooks, but they are finding a new life in centrifugally supercharged, Fastest Street Car drag racecars.

The chains are essentially motorcycle chains, but there is more to the story that just buying a chain and slapping it on your engine. The drive system you see on this vehicle was custom built by W2W for this C5R buildup. They have many hours in building the mounting plate, the chain-tensioning system, and developing an oiling system. The oiler is needed because the chain is being stressed to its limits on every run. After each run, oil will be applied to the chain so it can soak in before its next pass.

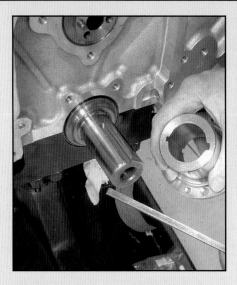

The Lunati crank was keyed all the way to the end of its nose, unlike the production crank, which is keyed only for the oil pump drive spud, not the harmonic balancer. A second keyway, 1/4-inch wide, was cut in 180 degrees out of phase from the factory 3/16-inch key. Two keyways were needed because the harmonic balancer will be called on to spin the supercharger, so it needs to be able to handle 200 hp of force without problems.

The chains usually only last about six pulls on the dyno before stiffening up and needing to be replaced. Many of the drag racers running chains take them off between runs to flip them over. Doing this lengthens the amount of time the chain will last.

If you do end up using a chain and want to know when to replace it, just monitor the stiffness of the links. They should be free of binding. Once it takes two hands to work the links back and forth, the chain should be replaced.

So why did the chain not work in this situation? W2W thinks the chain was too short to dissipate the heat generated from driving the blower. As a fix, a Gates 50-mm-wide blower belt with 8-mm-deep teeth has been fitted up with custom-made W2W pulleys to comprise the drive system. It seems to be handling the

W2W initially tried to drive the supercharger with a motorcycle chain — but the chain wouldn't live. The 5/8-inch aluminum plate with 1 x 2-inch aluminum stands was still used, but with a 2-inch-wide cog belt.

power. The belt is looking very good after a few runs, so W2W feels the belt will go many miles before needing to be replaced.

The drive system follies are a great example of the custom installation and finesse required when building a 1,000+ hp boosted engine — whether it is supercharged or turbocharged.

Since the supercharger is driven off the front of the crank, W2W wanted to shorten the front drive distance to keep the side forces to a minimum and strengthen the area. The factory front drive spud on the left is deeper to leave room for the A/C compressor pulley, which this vehicle isn't using. W2W created a new billet spud with about two inches less distance from the crank nose.

The belt was passed over in the beginning because W2W doubted it would survive, but it lasted longer than the chain ever did. The pulleys were initially from ProCharger. W2W cuts out the center of the pulleys and uses their own so they can package the system as they wish. W2W found the Gates belt will last for many runs, but they replace it when it starts to fray on the ends.

So How Did it Do?

As you'll see by the dyno chart, this engine made the power figure W2W was looking for. But nobody races dynos, so the car was stood up on its bumper a few times before the engine EFI calibration got sorted out. It was enough for this killer to lay down a viciously mid-track wheel-standing pass of 8.56 seconds at 156 mph. Anyone doubting the powerband of this engine was in awe at the ability of it to march after the driver had to lift mid track before getting the car straightened out. This performance puts this car on a level with only a few vehicles in the world.

The W2W team feels the car has an 8.50 at 163 mph pass in it if they can get the tune-up in harmony with the chassis. If that is accomplished, it will be, by far, the quickest streetable Gen III-powered vehicle in the world.

The engine was fired up with a W2W calibration and some soft pulls made without any boost to make sure that everything was working properly. The valve lash was set at a tight 0.025 inch. This is because W2W has seen the lash on an aluminum block/head engine grow as much as 0.015 inch from the cold lash settings. With 1.7:1 rockers like this engine has, that easily equals a total of 0.024 inch of hot lash. Once everything checked out, W2W hooked up the blower and made some power pulls, tuning on the cal and slowly inching up to the 1,200-hp range.

Why Build This Engine?

The person who requested this engine wants to own the fastest "street car" powered by a Gen III V-8 engine. The vehcile powered by this engine has gone mid-9s in the 1/4-mile, which used to be the record for a supercharged Gen III V-8, until someone else went faster. So, like any true hot-rodder would do, this customer placed an order for a more powerful, more durable Gen III V-8 to go even faster.

On paper, it quickly became apparent that to go faster, the goal for this engine needed to be at least 1,000 hp. The builders of this engine, Wheel to Wheel (W2W) Powertrain of Warren, Michigan, were confident they could achieve this power level. W2W has built several one-off C5R-based engines and has developed a knowledge base that makes them well suited to show how to do it correctly.

Just so there is no confusion, this 1,200-hp engine is not intended to be great in rush-hour traffic, though it probably could be driven like a regular car at any time. The purpose of this engine and the car it's going in is to run a quarter mile at a time. While the car will see limited street time, its main focus is superiority on the drag strip.

DYNO RESULTS

RPM	Torque	Hp
3,500	598	398
3,600	611	418
3,700	627	441
3,800	643	465
3,900	660	490
4,000	677	516
4,100	695	543
4,200	715	571
4,300	734	601
4,400	748	626
4,500	761	652
4,600	771	675
4,700	789	706
4,800	803	734
4,900	816	761
5,000	830	790
5,100	847	822
5,200	863	854
5,300	877	885
5,400	892	917
5,500	903	946
5,600	909	969
5,700	918	997
5,800	929	1,025
5,900	936	1,051
6,000	943	1,077
6,100	942	1,094
6,200	**946**	1,117
6,300	944	1,132
6,400	941	1,146
6,500	933	1,155
6,600	926	1,164
6,700	914	1,166
6,800	902	1,168
6,900	893	1,173
7,000	886	**1,181**

HOW TO CONTROL
THAT GEN III V-8

If you don't know how to "slew" a value in an EFI calibration — this chapter is for you. Here, you will be able to learn the basics of EFI and calibration, and how to take advantage of the advanced Gen III V-8 features like the built-in crank location sensor, cam sensor, and knock sensors. In fact, the Gen III V-8 engine, with its pushrod design *and* advanced sensors and controls, is perfectly suited to help bring the average automotive enthusiast into the next generation of modern hot-rod technology.

In this chapter, we'll discuss the operation, tuning, and debugging of both the GM factory EFI controller and aftermarket EFI controllers. You'll see as much of the basics as is possible to show you in one chapter. Actually tuning the EFI calibrations isn't *fully* documented here — that's a book unto itself, and even that might not be enough to get you doing full "cal work" — as the pros call it. If you need to know more about EFI tuning, one such book to check out is the CarTech® title, *Building and Tuning High-Performance Electronic Fuel Injection*, by EFI101 guru Ben Strader. There is still plenty to talk about though, like defining EFI controls, exploring the common tables and values in the calibration, and discussing the many mistakes and successes you may encounter when setting up and calibrating your EFI engine.

In general, the EFI and calibrating business is an ever-changing landscape of technology. The calibration process requires short, careful steps to achieve a good tune-up. Taking small steps is a great way to avoid taking big steps backwards, which usually leads to broken parts and money being spent. Installing EFI systems and getting them calibrated is rewarding though, and it's the future of performance vehicles. So read on to develop a foundation of info on this new high-performance world.

SLEWING

Slewing is the act of increasing or decreasing a specific value in one of the many lookup tables in the software program that controls an EFI system. Lookup tables are spreadsheets loaded with many values that the computer uses to determine the amount of fuel, spark, or one of the many other parameters to provide to the engine at a specific time to run it.

The EFI system works like this: the computer takes inputs from the many sensors that are on the engine and vehicle, then cross-references that data on the X and Y axis of lookup tables to find the correct amount of fuel or spark to apply at that specific moment. The computer applies the value located in the cell of the selected column and row, which usually represents an amount of voltage

for a moment in time to act upon the engine. The ability of the computer to search through the lookup tables multiple times per second and then make adjustments on the fly is one of the advantages of an EFI system.

The most important actions the EFI system carries out include opening the fuel injector at a predetermined moment in the crank's rotation for a specific amount of time, adjusting the spark advance, and engaging the idle air control (IAC) valve. The IAC is used to add more air to the engine as it is decelerating or warming up, like a high idle cam on carburetor linkage used to keep the

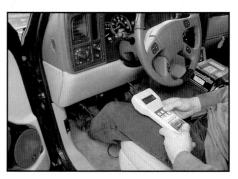

One of the more straightforward ways to make a change to the calibration on a Gen III-powered production vehicle is with a handheld calibration unit. This one, from Superchips, can make changes to the gear ratio, tire size, speed limiter, and other parameters in a Gen III controller.

engine from stalling.

As stated above, slewing means to tune the values in these tables. Calibrators will talk of slewing a specific value, an entire row, a large area of one of the tables, and sometimes an entire table. They'll say, "Slew that up 2 or 3," or, "I just slewed it a bunch as it was way too lean." In other words, a value of 25 slewed up 2 units would leave the value at 27.

The changes are usually driven by data the computer is reading from the engine sensors, like the engine temperature. As an example, if an engine is up to temperature, but the calibration is telling the IAC to stay open, the engine will idle fast. To make a change, the values that are controlling the IAC relative to that temperature are slewed to get it to close a little more. The value in this case would usually represent the pulses going to the IAC step motor that moves the small plunger up and down in the bore of the IAC. The "open" pulses sent to the step motor would open the plunger in the bore, increasing the air being bled into the engine. "Close" pulses would leave the plunger further down in the bore, shutting air off to the engine and reducing the idle speed.

The controller is doing this type of adjusting all over the engine to optimize its power output, efficiency (mpg), driveability, emissions, and other desired parameters.

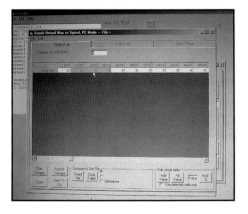

Changing the factory calibration on a Gen III V-8-powered vehicle with some of the aftermarket calibration tools, like LS1-Edit, is a complex, yet rewarding experience. It's best to begin with very minor adjustments when first getting started with these advanced calibration programs.

EFI COMPUTER CONTENTS

Port-injection EFI systems will usually consist of at least one electrically actuated fuel injector for each intake port, various sensors on the engine and vehicle, and a control module or computer. They'll also have an electric fuel pump, fuel rails to attach the fuel line to the fuel injectors, a fuel pressure regulator, a wiring harness to tie everything together, and a throttle valve at the inlet to the engine. A Gen III V-8-equipped vehicle comes from GM with all these components.

The EFI system serves a variety of performance masters. For most automotive enthusiasts, EFI is used to attain the best possible air/fuel ratio and spark advance for the engine to produce the most power while operating at the best efficiency. Enthusiasts also enjoy the pleasant "start on the key" capability of the EFI system vs. the carburetor's cold-start struggles. The EFI part-throttle control is also a welcome respite from the lean stumble often encountered with many carbureted cars.

For the OEMs like GM, they are looking for the best power and fuel economy with the lowest emissions, along with world-class driveability, durability, and NVH performance. It's also important to attain low emissions of nitrous oxides (NOx), carbon dioxide (CO), and hydrocarbons (HC), as required by the Environmental Protection Agency (EPA) and its associate in controlling air pollution in the United States — the California Air Resources Board (CARB). GM has an impressive, federally certified emissions lab at its proving grounds in Milford, Michigan, to meet these ever increasing requirements for production vehicles. Changing to an aftermarket calibration on a production EFI GM vehicle that is licensed to be driven on public roads is not considered legal, unless the calibration has an Executive Order, or EO, from the CARB.

Aftermarket companies can apply for and, if they meet specified requirements, attain an EO for specific calibrations and hardware packages. The EO allows the aftermarket components and calibration to be street legal. Calibra-

tions without an EO are for off road use only. This is done to control the amount of pollution being produced by road-going vehicles — whether they are stock production, or contain aftermarket components.

The computing power of the OEM and aftermarket controllers differs, but both are more than capable of creating smooth, powerful engines. The main differences are due to the complexity of the GM computer needed to control emissions, and more importantly, drive all the diagnostic codes. To give you an idea of the complexity, the calibration file in the GM controller is broken into eight large files for vehicles 1997 and up, each identified by a GM part number.

The programming inside the GM controller is larger because it needs to do much more than just control the engine operation. The GM controller contains OBD II, or onboard diagnostics version two, an EPA-mandated watchdog for the emission-controls on the vehicle. The GM computer is constantly logging values and adjusting the operation of the engine based on these values. This, along with a complex operating scheme, necessitates an abundance of computing power, which would explain the differences in capability of the GM and aftermarket controllers. In general, more computing power is good because it means better control of the engine is possible.

No matter whether you're using a handheld programmer or laptop-based software, they both connect to the vehicle through the multi-pin Assembly Line Diagnostic Link (ALDL) under the dashboard (also sometimes called the Data Link Connector - DLC). On the 'Vette, the port is located under the dashboard in the driver's foot well.

So why would you need to make a change to the calibration? Well, if you changed as many parts as the owner of this Z06 Corvette (heads, cam, air cleaner, headers, cat-back exhaust, flywheel, clutch, etc.), you'd definitely need a cal change! But, you'd probably benefit from calibration work if you just change an air cleaner inlet tube, too.

One good result of the OBD II system is very elaborate diagnostic software. This makes it easy for service shops to determine why a vehicle is not running correctly. They simply plug a reader into the diagnostic port and the vehicle will show them a numerical code that can tell them what's wrong.

Now, enthusiasts that change the engine parts and/or the factory calibration will occasionally experience an SES, or "service engine soon" light, illuminating on the dashboard of their GM vehicle. The SES will light up for a plethora of reasons, but often it's because the diagnostics software thinks a sensor reading is indicating that the pollution controls aren't working properly. This doesn't necessarily mean the engine is making more pollution than it did from the factory, but that the sensors and calibration think it's dirtier. This is why modifying the factory calibration is important to getting an engine to run properly with a component combination different from what it came with from the factory.

FUEL INJECTORS

Modern fuel injectors use an electrical current sent from the controller to stay open a short amount of time, usually a fraction of a second. The fuel injectors are all connected to a common fuel rail that contains pressurized fuel. When the injectors open, they allow pressurized fuel to spray into the intake port, mixing with the incoming air and entering the combustion chamber.

As an example, let's look at a stock LS1 fuel injector, which is rated to flow 26.4 pounds per hour (lbs/hr) of fuel at 58.0 psi (4 bar) of fuel pressure. The more you learn about EFI, the more you'll hear the lb/hr reference used often to denote the capability of an injector. The warning with this value is to know at what fuel pressure the lb/hr rating was measured at, as there are many different pressures used to rate fuel injector lb/hr flow. The two most common pressures are 43.5 psi (3 bar) and 58.0 (4 bar) psi.

Fuel injector capability is important to know because it needs to be matched with the power you intend to produce with your Gen III V-8. If you do change the fuel injectors, the fuel injector lb/hr calibration values will need to be changed so the computer will know the amount of fuel being let into the engine.

EFI Injector Usage Examples

Usage	Fuel Flow lb/hr @ 3 bar (4 bar) of fuel pressure	GM PN (unless stated otherwise)	Impedance (drivers)
Stock LS1			
'97-'98	24.7 (28.5)	12554271	high
'99-'00	22.3 (26.3)	12555894	high
Stock LS1/LS6			
'01-04	24.7 (28.5)	12561462	high
500-hp LS6	38 (43.9)	—	high
400-hp LQ4	28 (37.3)	—	high
650-hp LQ9	38 (43.9)	—	high
750-hp LS6	55 (73.3)	—	
1200-hp C5R	160 (213.3)	—	low

Note: The Siemens and MSD low-impedance drivers will not work with the OEM computer.
Note: 3 bar of fuel pressure is equal to 43.5 psi; 4 bar is equal to 58.0 psi.

Types of EFI system controls

Name	Common Usage	Sensors Being Used
Mass Airflow	Production Vehicles	Inlet air quantity, manifold air pressure (MAP) or vacuum, throttle position sensor (TPS), RPM, engine temp, inlet air temp, knock sensors, and O2 exhaust gas content (if it's a closed-loop system)
Speed-Density	Some prod. vehicles, racecars and hot rod	RPM, MAP, engine temp, TPS, knock sensors, and an O2 sensor (if closed loop)
Alpha-N	Racecars and hot rods	RPM, TPS, engine temp

MASS AIR, SPEED-DENSITY, AND ALPHA-N

Mass air, speed-density, and alpha-N are three different types of EFI systems. These names refer to the type of sensor reading used by the controller to operate the engine. Mass air is the most complex, with many sensors to allow the system to constantly adjust to changing ambient, engine, and application conditions. Speed density uses the engine RPM and manifold pressure to select air/fuel ratios and timing advance. Alpha-N is little more than an electronic carburetor using rpm to decide how much fuel to add. Each of these systems has varying capability and is used for a variety of applications. Most production vehicles use the mass air and speed-density systems for their ability to adjust to multiple situations. Alpha-N systems are commonly used in racing applications where the engine will mostly be running at WOT (wide open throttle), and idle quality and part-throttle response aren't really an issue.

The Gen III factory EFI is a mass-air system, so we'll spend some time here explaining it. The mass-air system uses many sensors to understand what fuel, spark, and other parameters to apply to the engine. The critical sensor that reads the incoming air volume is the mass airflow (MAF) sensor. The engine inlet air rushes through this sensor, which contains at least one exposed wire. To measure the air rushing through it, the MAF passes an electrical current through the exposed wire. The voltage conducted through the wire drops at a rate proportional to the amount of air passing by and cooling the wire. The resulting value sent from the sensor to the controller is then compared to values in a calibration table to determine the amount of the air the computer believes is entering the engine.

Other sensors used for mass-air systems include a manifold air pressure (MAP) sender that reads the vacuum in the intake manifold, if it's naturally aspirated. If the engine uses either a supercharger or turbocharger, the MAP will read positive pressure, too. Another sensor is needed to read the angle of the throttle blades, which obviously vary from closed to WOT. This sensor is called the throttle position sensor (TPS). Engine RPM also needs to be transmitted to the EFI controller. There are multiple ways to read RPM, but on past engines, it was usually off the ignition source, like the distributor. Obviously, the Gen III V-8 has no distributor, so it comes from the factory with an extremely accurate magneto-resistive-sensing crank trigger.

One of the most powerful sensors in an EFI system is the O2 sensor, because it's used to adjust the air/fuel ratio. Located in the collector pipe of the exhaust manifold, the O2 sensor reads how much oxygen is left in the exhaust gases. Through scientific research done years ago, it is known that the optimum air/fuel ratio for complete combustion is 14.7:1, or 14.7 air molecules to 1 fuel molecule. The more oxygen in the exhaust, the leaner the engine is running (above 14.7), and thus, the more fuel is needed. An EFI system that is automatically adjusting to the input of the O2 sensor is operating in closed-loop mode. An EFI system that is operating without the input from an O2 sensor is in open-loop mode. Advanced EFI systems will often operate in open loop when the engine is coming up to temperature and then switch to closed loop when everything is up to temp.

SEQUENTIAL, BANK FIRE, AND BATCH FIRE

Among the EFI systems listed above there is still more variety. The GM EFI system uses what is called a sequential-fire EFI system. The sequential system opens each fuel injector just before the intake valve opens. Bank-fire EFI systems open all the fuel injectors on each side of the engine at once and batch-fire EFI systems open all the fuel injectors to add fuel to each port all at once.

Sequential EFI requires eight solenoid (injector) drivers in the controller, while bank-fire EFI uses only four drivers (on a V-8). Sequential does show a little better power production overall than the bank or batch systems, but not much. Usually, sequential EFI is used because it allows better control of the fuel and spark for better emissions and low-rpm driveability.

TUNING THE GEN III V-8 EFI

The Gen III V-8 might look like a simple engine design, but it is actually a very complex internal combustion engine designed to be operated precisely by electronic controls. The factory GM EFI controller reads input values from various sensors all over the vehicle, compares them to values on literally hundreds of lookup tables in the calibration, and selects the appropriate amount of fuel and timing advance to apply to each cylinder. This reading, comparing, and selecting of values happens multiple times a second, which is why the Gen III V-8 EFI system has such good manners, even with all of its power.

Cable Throttles vs. ETC

The LS6 engine in the Z06 Corvette and many of the truck 6.0-liter engines do not have a throttle cable running from the throttle pedal to the throttle blade. These engines are equipped with an electronic throttle control, or ETC. The ETC uses a small electric stepper motor to actuate a large throttle blade (sometimes as big as 85 mm) with impressive detail. The powertrain control module reads the throttle pedal position, wheel slippage, and other parameters to determine how far open the throttle blade should be for any specific instance. The ETC-equipped vehicles do not have an IAC because they don't need it. The engine controller can use the throttle blade stepper motor in the ETC to react quickly enough with the throttle blade to maintain the idle quality when the engine is cold or when the engine is at a higher RPM with the throttle blade shut. More and more GM vehicles are going to have ETC in the future.

Here are the Gen III V-8 Sensors

The block-mounted crank trigger is located at the rear, passenger side of the Gen III V-8 engine block (next to the starter). It sends a signal to the controller that it uses to decipher the RPM and crank angle (location).

The engine coolant temperature sensor is located on the driver-side cylinder head at the front near the exhaust manifold mounting flange.

Here is what the 24x crank wheel looks like on the stock crankshaft. The aftermarket crank manufacturers install this same crank wheel on their cranks. As a side-note, the Gen IV will have a "60 minus 2" wheel that is the global standard for crank-sensor wheels.

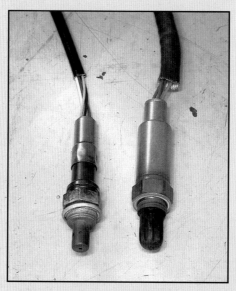

The Gen III V-8 uses four oxygen O2 sensors (like the one on the left), one before and one after each of the two catalytic converters (or "cats"). The PCM uses these sensors to compare the exhaust gases before and after the converters to make sure they are doing their job. For tuning expertise, a wide-band O2 sensor (on the right) will make the job go more quickly than a standard, narrow band O2 sensor (like the factory one on the left).

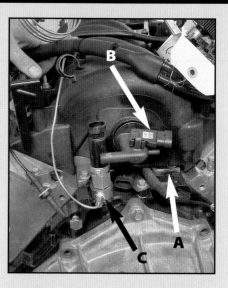

There are three sensors in this picture. The camshaft has a 2x wheel on it that the cam sensor (arrow A) reads to quickly determine where the crank is in regards to the firing order. This is important for the GM sequential fuel injection to be able to fire the engine in just a few seconds. At the back of the plastic factory intake manifold is the manifold air pressure (MAP) sensor (Arrow B). This sensor is the key that allows any EFI system to know how much fuel to apply at any given moment. The oil pressure sender for the PCM is also shown here (arrow C), with the gauge sender line tapped into the sender.

The Corvette is equipped with an oil temperature sender on the stock oil pan (arrow). All Gen III V-8 oil pans have an integral oil level sensor; you can see the float in the background to the left.

Here are the Gen III V-8 Sensors (continued)

The Gen III V-8 mass airflow (MAF) sensor had an integral air temperature sensor added to it on various platforms in the late 1990s.

Tip: You don't need an air temp sensor when you're starting to develop your calibration. We recommend that you zero out the air temp values to start without that input; this will simplify the process of creating a working calibration.

There are many various MAFs that came on Gen IIIs. The most desirable are the 85-mm units that came on Corvettes and Escalades.

On cable-actuated Gen III throttle bodies, the idle air control, or IAC valve (finger), and throttle blade position sensor (TPS) (behind finger) are located on the throttle body. On electronic throttle bodies (ETCs), there's no need for an IAC because the throttle blade can be stepped open slightly to give the engine enough air to idle.

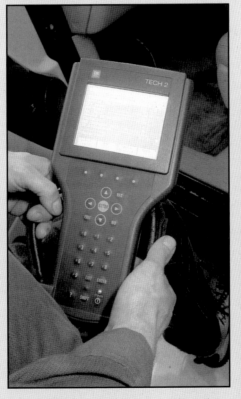

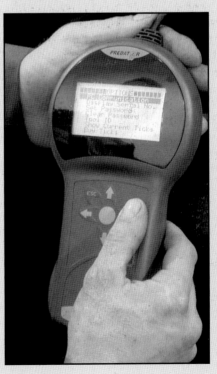

On the Gen III V-8, the valley cover plate houses two knock sensors. These are extremely sensitive to any performance-adding changes made to the engine combination and will usually need to be desensitized to keep the SES light from coming on.

Most GM dealers use the Tech II hand-held diagnostic tool to read the PCM's diagnostic codes. It costs a few thousand dollars and has great capability. As an option, there are other scan tools and software available that offer similar features at a much lower cost.

Another hand-held unit that has good capability is from DiabloSport. This pod makes it easy to alter the speed limiter on the full-size trucks.

GEN III V-8 ENGINE SENSOR INPUTS:

- Crank angle/Engine RPM
- Engine coolant temperature
- Oxygen sensors (in the exhaust)
- Oil temperature (on Corvette and some trucks)
- Air inlet temperature
- Throttle blade position
- Idle Air Control (IAC) location
- Manifold air pressure (MAP)
- Camshaft angle
- Knock sensors (to read detonation)

The factory GM EFI system and calibration have incredible capability, but this also makes tuning the controls for a modified engine combination a complex and often overwhelming task. Just to be clear, GM did not design the factory EFI system to be modified by consumers and does not offer any method for the public to do so. Various changes to the factory calibration can be made with equipment and software developed by automotive aftermarket companies. Some of these companies, like Hypertech, The Turbo Shop (TTS), JET, Diablo Sport, and LS1-Edit, have reverse engineered the GM code to allow automotive enthusiasts to access the electronic controls if they want more from their Gen III V-8.

The number of changes that can be made to the factory calibration varies depending on the aftermarket component being used. Most of the companies have simple, hand-held programmers that make changes based on menu-driven choices, but some of the more involved programming tools, like those available from Diablo Sport, TTS, and LS1-Edit, allow changes to just about any parameter you can imagine.

A lot of the aftermarket companies that sell products to alter the factory calibration, like Hypertech and DiabloSport, use handheld downloading pods. These handheld units are much more intuitive to operate than the full-blown calibration software programs. The pods use menu-driven questions with simple yes/no, true/false, or value-required questions that have value protections on them. This means you can't make the transmission downshift into

first when you go to WOT at 80 mph.

If you just want to make some finesse adjustments to your calibration, like gear ratio, tire size, and maybe add a little fuel here or there, these handhelds are a great solution.

DEEP CALIBRATING

Now, you might think the LS1-Edit-type systems are for you, but please exercise caution before reprogramming your vehicle's computer. To develop the original calibration, a team of GM engineers routinely spends at least 12 months or longer for each model of vehicle. Most calibrators have decades of experience doing what they do and have access to the finest diagnostic equipment on the planet. Each lookup table references many other tables as it makes minute decisions, multiple times per second. In other words, if you don't know what you're doing, get some guidance before making any changes!

There are many horror stories of enthusiasts scattering multiple engines, fragging control systems, and otherwise making a mess of a perfectly good car while attempting software changes without the proper knowledge. This isn't meant to scare anyone, but just to clarify the complexity and consequences of the task. The best way to start learning is to start actually doing calibration work, but here are some general tips:

Aftermarket OEM Controller Tuner Companies

Company	Phone	Website
DiabloSport	561-908-0040	www.diablosport.com
FastChip	918-446-3019	www.fastchip.com
Hypertech	901-382-8888	www.hypertech.com
LS1-Edit	n/a	www.carputing.com
Superchips	800-898-2447	www.superchips.com
TTS	310-669-8101	www.ttspowersystems.com

Input Signal Modification and Output Readers

While making dramatic changes to the calibration with software is exciting, there are some simple ways to alter the amount of fuel and spark being applied to the engine by the factory controller. One is the MAF Translator offered by Ramchargers.com. This unit plugs in between the factory mass airflow (MAF) meter and alters the signal being sent to the GM controller to get it to add more fuel. You just make changes with a simple interface and drive your car. Ramchargers also offers a way to see the results of your changes without needing a laptop computer. Their Scanmaster scan tool indicates fuel ratio and whether the engine is experiencing detonation, among other outputs, to allow for tuning the engine further. They can be contacted by calling 888-293-7267.

B&B Electronics is another company offering a well-regarded scan tool. Their Autotap software features real-time display and recording of all the vehicle's sensors. This means injector pulse width, spark advance/retard, the mass airflow, and diagnostic codes are all at your fingertips. As an added bonus, diagnostic codes can be reset once a repair has been made.

MODIFYING THE FACTORY CALIBRATION

The LS1-Edit software allows changes to a plethora of parameters on Gen III V-8 controls. Some of these changes include:

Engine Calibration
   Fuel
        Power enrichment tables
        Hardware values (like injector flow rate and volumetric efficiency)
        Maximum RPM values
        Idle speed values
   Spark
        Base spark tables
        Torque management values
        Knock sensor tables
        Spark advance vs. RPM and load
        Spark advance vs. engine temperature
Transmission
   Automatic
        WOT shift speed and RPM
        Part-throttle shift speed
        Line pressure
        Torque converter clutch lockup
   Manual
        Skip-shift operation
Cooling Fans
   Fan start temp (first and second fans)
   A/C engage parameters
Speedometer
   Gear/Tire
        Tire size value change
        Final gear ratio value change
   Speed limiter value change
Engine Diagnostics
   Diagnostic testing and correction
Transmission Diagnostics
   Component slipping

1. Save a few copies of the original calibration in a safe place.
2. Make small changes and test carefully, monitoring critical sensors to avoid damaging the powertrain.
3. When in doubt, stop, seek knowledge, and demand clarity before making further changes to the calibration.

Don't be the guy people talk about that confused transmission line pressure values with solenoid voltage, made a dramatic change to the calibration table, and blew the trans to smithereens on the next pass. Catastrophe is avoidable by simply stopping to ask for help.

The flip side of this discussion about avoiding damage is the rewarding experience of making hardware changes and being able to tune the calibration to take advantage of them. Simply put, the Gen III V-8 is one of the most impressive packages in how it positively reacts to power adding parts. As you saw early in this book, just bolting on a set of CNC-ported LS6 heads, an LS6 intake, and a performance cam boosted the power on a stock 345-hp LS1 (370 standard correction) to 450+ hp. That power increase wouldn't have come without making a calibration change.

The following information refers to mainly one calibration system, LS1-Edit, but there are other companies providing software to make changes. LS1-Edit seems to be the most accepted by late-model Gen III enthusiasts, and has a large number of features, which is why it was chosen here. While the software is called LS1-Edit, it works on all Gen III V-8 engines powering Corvettes, Camaros, Firebirds, and full-size GM trucks. Even some sample web locations are included for your reference in the future.

www.LS1.com
www.speartech.com

GETTING STARTED

The LS1-Edit software requires a laptop computer with the following capability:

- 200 Mhz Pentium or better
- 32 MB RAM
- Windows 98, NT, XP, or 2000
- A free serial communications port (RS-232)

To get started, load the software into a laptop with the LS1-Edit CD. Then, the first step is to install the cable between the laptop and vehicle diagnostic port so the laptop can read the factory calibration. It's best to read the factory software a few times to make sure the connection and system are robust enough for continuous communication. Having communication fail during software downloading could prove catastrophic for the calibration and controller.

Based on discussions with tuner shops and enthusiasts tuning GM Gen III V-8s, some of LS1-Edit's easiest calibration changes include changing the tire size, speed limiter, engine redline, gear ratio, and fan on/off temperature. Also, some of the simpler spark tables can be changed very easily.

The medium difficulty changes include the shifting speed, shift firmness, and torque converter lockup for automatic transmissions. The most difficult values to tune are in the fuel tables for the engine and the torque management for the transmission.

LS1-Edit

You can purchase LS1-Edit at their website, www.carputing.com. The LS1-Edit people prefer to handle tech questions via email. Loyal customers say this isn't inconvenient, since the answers come in a timely manner. To be honest, LS1-Edit has a different business model than most are used to, but their software does get the job done, so you decide if it's worth it or not.

We'd suggest you team up with a few other Gen III enthusiasts (car or truck) to buy the software together, as LS1-Edit has a package deal that makes the software much more affordable when you buy more than one single license.

There are two LS1-Edit software packages. The lower-cost system allows for complete changes to the calibration on one vehicle, as it attaches itself to the VIN. The high-priced system is usually purchased by tuner shops that want to tune multiple vehicles, as it doesn't latch on to a single VIN.

Be aware of one caveat: some other aftermarket tuners lock their calibrations, so LS1-Edit will often not work on a calibration that has been modified. LS1-Edit attaches to the original factory GM calibration and translates the GM code into something you and I can understand and manipulate.

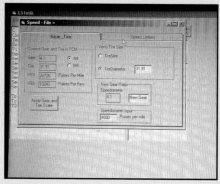

The LS1-Edit opening screen identifies the eight computer files that the factory PCM uses to run the Gen III powertrain. Each file is identified by an eight-digit GM part number. If the cal has been modified in any way by another program, LS1-Edit will probably not work on your PCM.

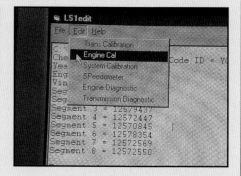

Here's the opening page showing the LS1-Edit drop-down boxes. As you can see, there are tables for working on the transmission cal, engine cal, system cal, speedometer settings, engine diagnostic codes, and transmission diagnostic codes.

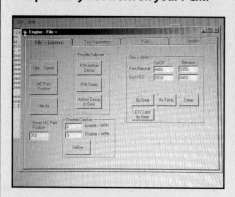

The LS1-Edit software allows you to adjust the RPM limit very easily. Obviously, having this type of control over the engine demands care, as moving the RPM limit too high will make it easier for you to damage your engine.

The hand-held calibrators and software-based systems, like LS1-Edit shown here, can easily make adjustments for the tire size, gear ratio, and speed limiter. This is helpful if you go to taller tires. We've been advised that more than a 2 percent variation from the assumed tire diameter in the calibration can cause powertrain damage.

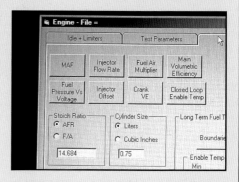

The fuel maps in LS1-Edit are probably one of its main draws. Practically any good hard-parts change can be tuned back to strength. A good example of this is fuel-injector selection — consult with the pros to get fuel injectors that are properly sized for your application.

LS1-Edit (continued)

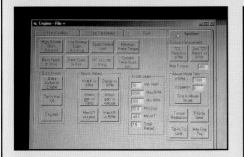

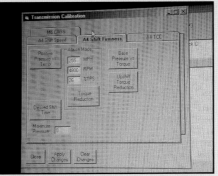

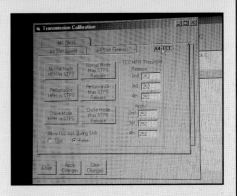

Many spark tables appear in the LS1-Edit software. They adjust the amount of spark advance and at what engine operation scenario the advance is applied — depending on many parameters like engine temperature, inlet air temp, RPM, manifold air pressure, and other values.

The 2001 and later full-size trucks need to have the controller removed from the vehicle to work on the cal due to the size of the calibration. Future versions of LS1-Edit won't require this, but current versions do.

Making more power with the Gen III V-8 engine is very simple, but knowing how to tune the transmission to handle the power is a little harder. Getting the trans line pressure and shifting points dialed in correctly will help the stock trans last with a lot of power, but if these aren't set properly — don't expect the trans to last long. Consult the pros before dipping into this side of the powertrain too heavily.

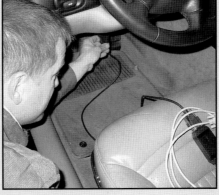

To insure that the powertrain survives practically any abuse, GM has built in torque management to pull timing and fuel out of the engine at strategic points. One classic example is the 1st-to-2nd-gear shift. GM retards the ignition and reduces the fuel going to the engine for a fraction of a second during this transition to minimize the chance of the transmission components being damaged. LS1-Edit allows these parameters to be changed, but be careful, because GM has done plenty of research to determine what abuse the drivetrain can withstand without failing.

The LS1-Edit software comes with the wiring to hook up to the LS1 engines and pre-'01 trucks. For the trucks where the controller needs to be removed, wiring is available from www.speartech.com.

AFTERMARKET CONTROLLERS

If you plan on using a Gen III V-8 in a past model vehicle that isn't emission controlled, like a street rod or muscle car, an aftermarket controller is often easier to hook up and tune for a specific application than the production controller and calibration. While there are some challenges getting up to speed on these stand-alone EFI systems, the rewards are simply amazing and com-

pletely worth the effort. What follows is an overview of the available systems, what it looks like to get an aftermarket controller system installed on a Gen III V-8, and some debugging tips and common pitfalls to avoid when creating a calibration.

The aftermarket controller business is still in its infancy, so there is really very little standardization (this is similar to the production vehicle controller business — as a tip, look for this busi-

ness to become much more standardized in years to come). This newness is good in that a lot of innovation and specialization exists, but bad in that each system has a relatively steep learning curve.

One of the first stand-alone systems on the scene was ACCEL's DFI EFI system. You can purchase everything you'll need from ACCEL, including fuel injectors, the controller, and the fuel pump, making ACCEL a rare find in the aftermarket EFI business. There have been many recent revisions to the ACCEL system, resulting in their latest Gen VII system and software. Navigating within Gen VII is very intuitive, as is creating a custom calibration. The intuitive nature of the Gen VII software and the completeness of the ACCEL package make it a true plug-and-play system.

The systems from F.A.S.T. (which stands for Fuel Air Spark Technologies) are more representative of the component-level systems in the aftermarket EFI business today. The controller they sell was originally developed for Fel Pro, then sold to Federal Mogul, and is now available directly from F.A.S.T.,

which is a division of Comp Cams. This unit has been the benchmark for racers and performance enthusiasts because of the balance between its capability and cost. The MoTeC and Electromotive units probably have more raw capability, but they are considered more complex and costly than the ACCEL and

F.A.S.T.

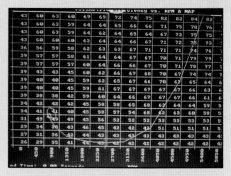

The F.A.S.T. controller software has been around for a few years, so there is a lot of streetwise knowledge about it. As you can tell by the opening screen, it can control many activities — including nitrous engagement and other performance systems.

The F.A.S.T. fuel table adjustment is very straightforward once the engine is up and running. You just place the cursor over the cell you want to adjust and move the fuel figure up or down as you desire.

The F.A.S.T. system has the capability to log a run, as shown in the line that traverses the fuel map, to help you determine what the engine is experiencing in fuel and spark, plus the outcome of the combustion, which is read by the O2 sensor(s).

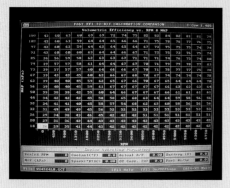

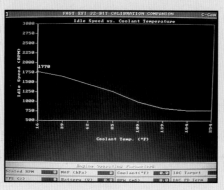

The IAC has the responsibility of keeping the engine running when it's cold and when the throttle is abruptly closed. This table adjusts one of the situations that the IAC impacts. The way to set this is to drive the vehicle and have another person adjust the IAC settings until the engine performs as expected.

The spark advance is adjusted in tables that look like this. The controller retards a mechanically advanced ignition to achieve the desired spark advance for the engine.

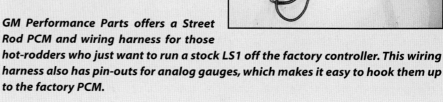

GM Performance Parts offers a Street Rod PCM and wiring harness for those hot-rodders who just want to run a stock LS1 off the factory controller. This wiring harness also has pin-outs for analog gauges, which makes it easy to hook them up to the factory PCM.

F.A.S.T systems. Understanding your needs in an EFI system will help to get you the best controller for your money.

What Aftermarket EFI You Need

Most aftermarket EFI systems are speed-density systems, and there are more than enough sensors on the Gen III V-8 for the controller to run the engine.

Probably one of the more interesting aspects of the Gen III V-8 is how the engine speed is provided to the controller. The Gen III V-8 does not have a traditional distributor or a keyed har-monic balancer on the crankshaft. Instead, it has a 24x crank trigger mounted on the block.

This sensor wheel is mounted on the crankshaft inside and near the back of the engine. The production controller reads the steps on the dual-track crank wheel using a block-mounted crank sensor and compares those values with the readings from a camshaft sensor to determine which cylinder is firing at what time. As this book is being created, there are only a few aftermarket controllers that can read the factory crank- and cam-sensor outputs, but almost all of them are developing either adapters or complete systems to take advantage of the Gen III's plug-and-play capability.

For those controllers that don't have the capability to use the factory crank trigger, you'll need to add a four-point trigger system. Aftermarket crank-trigger ignition systems, like those available from MSD, use trigger wheels with four small trigger magnets positioned at 90-degree increments on a wheel. A sensor reads the passing of each trigger magnet and the ignition controller uses this information to apply the correct spark to the engine. These aftermarket trigger wheels are usually installed on a Gen III V-8 either on the flywheel or in a wheel bolted to a har-monic balancer that is keyed to the crankshaft (usually by installing an aftermarket crank or having a keyway machined into the stock crank). But you probably won't have to worry about adding a four-point crank trigger for long, because the factory crank wheel is far superior, so the aftermarket should catch up soon.

Tuning Shops

If you don't want to learn how to do your own calibrations, there are plenty of local shops around the country that have a good working knowledge of how to tune with tools like LS1-Edit, the TTS software, and other systems. The only problem is determining if these shops really know what they are doing. Basically, if you know someone with a similar vehicle that has had a good calibration experience with a local shop, then that's about as much proof as you're going to get. If you talk to the shop about what performance parts you want to integrate into your vehicle and they reply, "Well, we'd be glad to take a shot at that," just walk away.

The calibration business is built on experience, and experience usually comes at the sacrifice of parts — finding the limits of components and systems. We'd suggest you not have somebody "take a shot" using your vehicle as a learning experience. Pay the money for an experienced calibrator that has broken their own parts or a more aggressive customer's parts.

Hooking Up an Aftermarket Controller to a Gen III V-8 Engine

Aftermarket EFI is easy to hook up to the Gen III V-8 because the engine is intended to be electronically controlled.

The following sensors are a plug-and-play program with many aftermarket controllers:

Sensor	Value
Manifold air pressure (MAP)	vacuum/pressure in manifold
Throttle position sensor (TPS)	throttle location
Engine coolant temperature	engine temp
Inlet air temperature	inlet temp
Crank trigger	revolutions per minute (RPM)
Exhaust gas oxygen sensor (O2)	air/fuel mixture

Aftermarket EFI Controllers

ACCEL (Mr. Gasket)
888-MR-GASKET
www.mrgasket.com

Electromotive
703-331-0100
www.electromotive.com

F.A.S.T.
810-225-2700
www.fuelairspark.com

Big Stuff 3
248-887-7072
www.bigstuff3.com

MoTeC
714-897-6804 (West Coast)
704-799-3800 (East Coast)
www.motec.com

Engine Performance Wants of Street Aftermarket EFI Customers

1. Start on the key

This is probably one of the coolest features of a hot-rod EFI engine. No matter how wild the cam or how much the supercharger or turbo is huffing, the EFI system can be tuned to compensate and get the engine to fire in a few revolutions.

Tip: When starting an EFI engine for the first time, if the engine doesn't start on the first cranking, refer to the "dashboard" on your laptop computer to see if there is a sensor reading incorrectly.

Example: If the air temp sensor is reading high, this often means there is no resistance — which is bad. This will usually set off some kind of alarm within the software.

2. Smooth Idle

Once the engine cranks and fires, the EFI system gets a chance to really show its capability. The portion of the calibration that runs the engine while it is coming up to temperature is different from the part that runs an engine at operating temperature. While everything is coming up to temperature, the EFI calibration keeps the idle a little higher by keeping the IAC open, adding more fuel, and keeping the spark advance at a minimum.

Tip: When improving an existing engine package with a performance component or system, it will probably require a change in the part-throttle and WOT calibration to fully take advantage of the new parts. But what you probably don't know is that it will also require a change in the idle parameters to keep everything smooth.

Example: Installing a performance air inlet tube and air cleaner changes the airspeed entering the engine. This changes all levels of flow. Conversely, if a tighter torque converter or different weight clutch is installed, expect the idle and off-idle calibration to require tuning, also.

3. Crisp Part Throttle

This is the other area in which an aftermarket EFI system on a hot-rod engine can really show itself. Properly calibrated, the EFI can keep the engine crisp in the middle of its powerband through many different ambient conditions, where a carburetor will often struggle. This is also one of the more challenging aspects to create in a calibration, but it's well worth the effort.

Creating the aftermarket controller calibration values for part throttle is a two-person job. Usually, one person drives the vehicle under normal conditions, while the other person makes adjustments on a laptop computer to the fuel, spark, acceleration enrichments, and deceleration MAP table values until the engine doesn't stall, stumble, die, blow black smoke, rattle (spark knock), or do other unpleasant activities.

4. Run Like Heck at Wide Open Throttle (WOT)

The carburetor and EFI system are very close in their capability at WOT. The one advantage the EFI system has is the O2 sensor in the exhaust system. It will tell the calibrator what the air-fuel ratio is, allowing quick adjustments for maximum power production.

Optimum Aftermarket O2 Installation

If you have 2-inch primary tubes (on a V-8), it's suggested that you put the O2 sensor about 8 inches back from the merge point in the collector. With 1-3/4-inch primaries, put the O2 sensor a little closer to the primaries. On a header with 2-1/4-inch primaries, put the O2 sensor a little farther down the collector.

Tip: Position the sensor as high as possible in the collector or pipe (between the nine- and three-o'clock position) to keep it away from condensation that gravity will bring to the bottom of the collector/pipe. Water causes the O2 sensors to deteriorate and will eventually cause them to fail.

Tuning in Closed-Loop Mode

Here's what to do once the engine is running in closed-loop mode on an engine dyno or in the vehicle on a chassis dyno.

1. Once the engine is up to temperature, drive the vehicle.

2. Make sure the O2 sensor is providing feedback to the controller.

3. Start calibrating at steady-state WOT under load.
Tip: This is where having the engine on a dyno comes in handy.
Take the engine to WOT and adjust the fuel/spark to get it close. If the engine is lean, take the engine off WOT immediately to avoid damaging engine components — you could be burning a piston, valve, or some other component.

4. Return engine to idle and adjust idle settings in fuel, spark, and IAC tables.

Some common advice from enthusiasts that have installed aftermarket controllers is to beg, borrow, or buy an initial calibration. If you don't get a calibration to start your engine with, the best way to begin is to just get the engine to run long enough to get it up to temp. All initial calibration tuning should be done only with everything up to temperature. So, if you have to run the engine at 2,000 rpm or higher to just get the temp in the package, then do it. Many aftermarket controller companies offer base calibrations or controllers that can create a calibration after the addition of your vehicle-specific information.

Basic Calibrating: After You Start it, Before You Drive it

1. Get everything up to temperature and set the idle to your desired level (below 900 rpm, above 450 rpm).

2. Get the fuel pressure to read 45 to 60 psi above idle pressure. If you have a vacuum-biased fuel-pressure regulator, the pressure will change constantly when the engine is at idle, but should change very little at WOT. There are simple reasons for this. First, more vacuum means lower fuel press (at idle, this lets the injector control the flow better because it can stay open longer for better resolution). And second, less vacuum means higher fuel pressure.

3. Check that the timing in the computer is in sync with the timing showing on the engine crankshaft. *Tip: The crank reference angle is usually set at 6 degrees BTDC. For EFI systems, put the timing light on the crank harmonic balancer and compare what you see at the crank with the ignition timing seen on the dashboard shown on the computer.*

4. Adjust the throttle blade location, the IAC positioning, and then the spark and fuel tables for hot-idle condition.

Top 9 Aftermarket EFI Calibration Problems

1. "My engine just will not run properly. I have not checked the timing in the computer or on the engine."

The mechanical timing on an EFI engine needs to be advanced so the computer can retard the ignition to the desired advance that the engine actually experiences.

Example: For the Gen III V-8, the F.A.S.T. system requests setting the ignition to fire at 50 degrees BTDC. Once the engine is running, the actual timing being applied to the engine is varied by retarding the ignition in the software of the computer. This is visible on the calibration software dashboard of the laptop computer and is adjustable in the spark advance tables.

2. "The engine idle goes up and down for no reason."

This is usually a combination of the timing being too far advanced, the IAC correction speed being too fast or slow, and the throttle blade being too far open when the computer thinks it's at rest. You can fix this by:

A. Setting the Timing

B. Setting the Fuel Pressure
   A good way to check this is by hooking up a mechanical gauge to the end of one of the fuel injector fuel rails. Pressure should be in the 40-psi range.

C. Setting the Throttle Blade Position
   A good way to tell whether the throttle blades are open far enough is to see whether the IAC is going out of its parameter when it moves the blade while attempting to get the engine to idle smoothly. "Going out of parameter," is calibrator-speak for the IAC piston hitting its seat and not being able to adjust anymore to correct the idle.

D. Resetting the IAC adjustment
   This is a simple electronic adjustment in the IAC calibration table.

E. Resetting the IAC Opening
   At idle with engine warmed up, the IAC needs to be somewhere between 15 to 25 percent open. That's so when the engine is cold, there's adjustment left for the IAC to open more to let more air in the engine. Set the throttle blade when the engine is fully warmed up so the IAC is in the right place.

3. "While driving, the engine hesitates or doesn't have good driveability."

The key to smoothing out an engine at part-throttle operation is to determine if it's running lean or rich. Usually in this situation, the engine is lean, and adjusting accelerator enrichments while driving the vehicle at various part-throttle roll-on situations will correct the issue.

This type of problem is often experienced after adding new hard parts without changing an existing calibration. Adding things like a more aggressive cam, a lower restriction air inlet, or even some extra displacement can throw things out of sync.

4. "The engine surges or won't run at wide open throttle."

Top 9 Aftermarket EFI
Calibration Problems (continued)

Surprisingly, the surging is often caused by too much fuel, and sometimes by too little timing. Both of these are adjusted in the calibration with the engine up to temperature and at WOT. If the engine won't run at WOT, it's usually because it doesn't have enough fuel. This can be adjusted in the base fuel calibration.

5. "The engine stalls during deceleration."

This is a common problem. The vehicle drives fine up the street, with good acceleration. But when you pull up to a stoplight, the engine dies. This situation is corrected by adjusting the IAC piston location and adjustment speed in regard to the throttle opening.

Solution: Leave the IAC slightly open during part-throttle stages. This way, when the throttle eventually closes, the IAC piston is in position to keep the engine running. Then, have the EFI calibration cycle the IAC piston closed, then opened, to prevent the idle from surging when the throttle is closed dramatically.

6. "The engine won't start on the first turn of the key."

There is a plethora of reasons for the engine not starting when it's first cranked. The first step is to revisit the hookup and startup procedure to make sure everything is installed properly.

7. "The engine starts, then stalls."

Check the enrichment in the after-start fuel tables and the decay of the enrichments fuel table after the engine starts up. The crank-to-run mode is a bridge for the moment between the engine not running and running. It's usually doing its thing from 200 to 800 rpm. The system is time delayed and has a decay factor on it so the base calibration can take over as the bridge stops adding fuel.

8. "The engine starts, then revs really high."

Often this is due to the throttle blade being open too much and/or the IAC piston being open too much during startup. The throttle setting is a mechanical issue; the IAC is a calibration table issue. The IAC has standardized info on where it should be programmed into the calibration.

9. "The engine idle surges randomly."

This issue involves up to seven different tables in the aftermarket calibration. They include the fuel, spark, IAC step, throttle follower (opening), speed of the IAC adjustment, coolant temperature, and more. Correcting this issue is what calibrating is all about.

The best way to go about it is to address the many engine scenarios separately, then in concert, with all the other scenarios. This is what makes calibrating a combination of art and science. So, for instance, do your best to settle the idle down while the engine has hot coolant, a cold intake, and cold oil. Then, go to an engine with hot coolant, cold intake, and hot oil with heat soaked engine. Just keep working each scenario, getting the engine to idle smoothly by working the multiple calibration values.

And that would be the end of this book.

Thanks for reading.

—Will